Police Vehicles and Firearms
Instruments of Deadly Force

Geoffrey P. Alpert
University of South Carolina

Lorie A. Fridell
Florida State University

WAVELAND
PRESS, INC.

Prospect Heights, Illinois

For information about this book, write or call:

Waveland Press, Inc.
P.O. Box 400
Prospect Heights, Illinois 60070
(708) 634-0081

Acknowledgements

A number of people deserve our thanks for their assistance with this project. Valuable reviewers include Kathryn Urbonya, James Fyfe, Mark Blumberg, William Geller, Bill Doerner, and Sam Walker. The input of these fine scholars greatly improved the final product. Chief Louie C. Caudell, Little Rock Police Department, gave us permission to reprint his excellent policies on Use of Force and Pursuit Driving. These policies were developed and written by Assistant Chief Randy Reed and Lieutenant Stuart Thomas.

The senior author is especially grateful to Roger Dunham, Dale Bowlin, John Chappelle, Steve Dillingham, William Smith, David LaBrec and Kevin Fagin for their assistance in different phases of the research and writing. Bené, Angie, Amanda and Ryan Alpert provided their love and companionship and can never be thanked adequately.

The second author is indebted to her mentor, Arnold Binder, who first introduced her to the fascinating topic of deadly force, has continued to provide support and encouragement during these early years of her academic career, and furnished feedback on several of the chapters of this book. Tony Pate made important suggestions on chapters, as well as provided emotional sustenance and arranged for needed breaks. "Bird," who sat on the second author's shoulder for many years providing support and companionship, died during the writing of Chapter 5. Prior to his passing, he had walked across several drafts, contributing the type of input which helps authors keep perspective. He is missed.

Contents

Foreword

This book opens an important new line of thinking about American policing. Alpert and Fridell have joined together two critical decisions by police officers: the decision to use firearms and the decision to undertake a high speed chase. The principal contribution their book makes lies in thinking about the common aspects of these two decisions. There is a large literature on the general subject of police discretion. There is a large and steadily growing literature on police use of deadly force. But as is so often the case in the academic world, specialists remained immersed in their particular subjects. Much is to be gained, however, by identifying the common elements in different subjects.

The common element here is the control of discretionary decisions that pose great risks to the community and to the police. This book appears at an important moment in the history of the police. We now have a body of information that permits us to make informed policy choices. The current body of literature includes data on the critical decisions themselves, the dynamics underlying those decisions, the consequences of those decisions—particularly in terms of the resulting harm—and the impact of policies designed to control those decisions.

The available literature is greatest with respect to police shootings. Challenges to police shooting practices emerged in the early 1960s as a consequence of the civil rights movement. Since then, the research on shooting incidents has become increasingly sophisticated. There has also been a virtual revolution in official policy as reflected in court decisions and internal police department rules. We also have some reliable data on the impact of the new restrictive shooting policies.

The literature is much less extensive on the subject of high speed pursuits. It is only comparatively recently that it has been defined as a social problem warranting research and new policy. Yet, many people will be surprised at the extent of the available literature. One of the major contributions of this book is to bring that material together in one place. While there has been substantial change in public policy on pursuits, we do not as yet have the same kind of information about the impact of those policies as we do with respect to shootings.

Bringing these two subjects together highlights the dominant trends in the development of police policy. In both instances, litigation has played a major role in stimulating change. While court decisions based on both constitutional law and tort law have framed the outer limits of policy, the specifics of policy are increasingly embodied in internal police department rules. These and other rules are collected in departmental policy and procedure manuals. The growth of these manuals has not received much attention from scholars. The larger question is not the role of procedure manuals per se but the viability of controlling police discretion through internal rules.

This book represents two case studies on this general question. The material here provides a new perspective on the evolution of police policy. It also serves to frame the questions that researchers and policy makers should be asking in the future.

Samuel Walker
Professor of Criminal Justice
University of Nebraska at Omaha

A Perspective and Understanding of Deadly Force

1

Police use of deadly force remains a critical issue for police and the public in the 1990s. Although the use of firearms by police has been a subject addressed by social scientists, reformers, criminal justice critics and progressive law enforcement professionals during the past two decades, it continues to be a topic of concern. For example, 14 fatal police shootings during the first five months of 1990 has shocked the New York City Police Department. In fact, the newly appointed Commissioner, Lee Brown, had to establish an outside committee to review the department's policy and practice, despite a restrictive policy and progressive training (Law Enforcement News XVI, May 31, 1990 p. 3).

Although the reform movement of the 1970s and 1980s resulted in a change of philosophy and practice concerning the use of firearms, it obviously has not eliminated the public's concern about abuse. Prior to 1985, many police officers were licensed to shoot any fleeing felon. The recent trend has been to limit that license to take a life to situations in which the officer is in danger of serious injury or death. Further, officers are being scrutinized for actions that could create situations calling for the use of deadly force. These changes were the consequence of both public concern and comprehensive research on the nature and extent of the use of deadly force by police in American society.

This monograph will include a brief review of that body of literature which traces the fleeing felon doctrine from its roots to the current standards established by the progressive law enforcement community and sanctioned by the United States Supreme Court. As there are numerous publications available concerning the police use of deadly force, our focus will move

1

beyond what is known and what is not known. We will analyze *why* as well as *how* this issue became an important cause.

Another type of force frequently used by the police which can also be deadly is police pursuit driving. It is important to note that no critical attention was given to pursuit either as a police tactic or as a threat to public safety until the 1980s. The research conducted on pursuit driving, although inadequate, will be examined as part of our discussion. Unlike the use of firearms, there has been relatively minor reform in the use of police pursuit and this voluntary change has been unsystematic. Why has there been such a dramatic difference in response to these two uses of deadly force? To date, only limited and unorganized public outcry concerning the use and abuse of pursuit driving has been heard.

While police use of firearms has constituted a genuine social problem, pursuit driving remains merely a contested tactic with a small but growing number of critics. Both the use of firearms and pursuit driving will be addressed comprehensively in later chapters. Before separating them, a singular approach to their study and understanding will be identified.

These two particular police practices, the use of firearms and pursuit driving, have developed over the years as part of police field operations. Until recently, each was a relatively protected tactic and therefore not scrutinized closely. Although the times have changed and many police administrators realize the necessity to amend policies, practices and custom, there exists a very strong current resisting reform among the officers in the street (Goldstein, 1990 and Van Maanen, 1974). That is, attempts to change the nature and extent of officers' use of firearms and authorization to continue a pursuit often run counter to the culture of the street officer.

One of the important considerations for policy makers and police administrators is the method used to inform the street officers about reform or changes in policy. Too often, there is insufficient involvement of the street officers in the modification of policy and the necessary training. When street-level officers are made part of the decision-making and implementation process, their commitment to the change can become internalized. Without the shared input and involvement, officers may view change as unwanted and unnecessary and abide by it only when reminded and required. In other words, it is the process of communication as well as the content of a policy that can ease the implementation of a controversial change (Manning, 1988).

Another factor related to officer compliance with policy is accountability to the administration. In other words, "[T]he speed of the boss is the speed of the crew" (Alpert, 1985: 29). As will be discussed in subsequent chapters, a written policy is effective to the extent that there is an administrative presence which demands compliance. Following the video-taped beating of Rodney King by members of the Los Angeles Police Department (LAPD) on March 3, 1991, Police Chief Daryl Gates came under great pressure to resign. The main argument made by his opponents was that his administrative posture was one which supported (by ignoring) police abuse of citizens. According to an article in the *Christian*

Science Monitor (March 25, 1991), "more than anything . . . experts say the key to curbing police misconduct lies in the tone set at the top—the central reason so much nationwide attention has focused on Los Angeles Police Chief Daryl Gates."

Although it is not clear what happened to King's passengers or what was the role of the California Highway Patrol Troopers, it is crystal clear that King was brutally beaten, kicked and shot with a Taser gun by at least three officers while more than twenty others watched. The Los Angeles Police Department prides itself as having some of the best training in the country, and there is no doubt that these officers were aware of the wrongfulness of their actions (or inactions) but intentionally chose to beat Mr. King.

The ordeal of Rodney King originated as a speeding violation and turned into a high-speed pursuit involving the members of the California Highway Patrol (CHP). Audio tapes of the CHP radio communications reported by the Los Angeles Times (March 23, 1991 A-1) demonstrate that King was driving no more than 65 miles per hour although members of the LAPD initially reported that he was driving 115 miles per hour. Apparently, King voluntarily stopped and exited his car. His actions outside the vehicle have been described as aggressive by the police and passive by civilian observers. There is no question what happened next, as a civilian witness, shocked by the police actions, videotaped their conduct. Obviously, the officers were unaware that their actions were being recorded. Similarly, the officers were unaware that their radio and computer messages— rife with racial slurs and laughter—were also being recorded.

The stress created by a suspect fighting with an officer or resisting arrest is immense; enormous stress is caused by a pursuit. As a fellow LAPD officer wrote in *Newsweek*, "Any officer pursuing King that night would have felt: how dare this person put innocent lives in jeopardy? What is he going to try when I catch him? When King's pursuers finally caught him, the adrenaline rush must have fueled the extremes of terror and anger. Police officers are human; those officers lost control and the beating resembled a feeding frenzy" (March 25, 1991: p. 34).

Mark Kroeker, Deputy Chief and Commanding Officer, Personnel and Training Bureau, Los Angeles Police Department and co-author Candace McCoy (1989: 109) noted that department policies are "designed to standardize the emotional event." They argue that improper actions are more likely in these highly emotional situations if a clear policy is not in place. And a well-written policy, as noted above, is only effective in an atmosphere demanding strict compliance. The ramifications for this violation of policy in Los Angeles are significant. The criminal charges against the officers may send them to prison. The civil suit will cost the insurance company and taxpayers an amount which includes two commas!

The type of incident involving the CHP and LAPD has occurred in other jurisdictions in previous years. For example, in Miami in 1980, Arthur McDuffie, a black insurance salesman was involved in a high-speed chase and was beaten to death by police officers. After a cover-up and acquittal of the officers by an all-white jury, the City of Miami experienced one of the worst riots in history (Porter and Dunn, 1984). Since that time, significant changes in police training have occurred in the region. Although the killing of Arthur McDuffie and subsequent riots made national news and invoked hearings by the United States Commission on Civil Rights, reform and improvement of the police did not reach beyond southeastern Florida. The improvements in the Metro-Dade Police Department whose officers were involved in the beating death in 1980 can be attributed to strong administrative leadership.

The King incident also included a chase and a beating but was captured on video and played on television for all to see. This one "lucky" difference has turned an incident which might have been lost into a catalyst for change. The United States Department of Justice and Congress have once again called for numerous studies and investigations, as the remedies and recommendations made in the 1970s and 1980s were not followed (see United States Commission on Civil Rights, 1982).

These outcomes are a direct result of the public's exposure to the horrible reality of this police misconduct in Los Angeles and reflect on the major theme of the present book: the importance of the citizenry in affecting the policies and practices of law enforcement. As part of our review of police use of firearms and vehicle pursuits, the emphasis is on the differential response of the public to these two dangerous police actions and the corresponding differential rate of reform.

Police officers in this country all have firearms and most drive vehicles. The elimination of either is beyond consideration, and any reform must first consider the safety of the police officer and the public. Obviously, police officers must be protected against attack and must be able to defend themselves and to protect the public. Similarly, citizens have a vested interest in the safe and prudent use of a tactic which can cause serious bodily harm or death. The public has a right to be protected from law violators who threaten their safety and police officers who are less than prudent in the attempt to make an arrest. The difficulty is in balancing effective law enforcement with officer and public safety. When the practices of the police overstep what is considered healthy or just by the public, protest will be forthcoming. How loud these protests become and whether or not they bring about or influence reform will be one recurring theme of this study. A compelling factor is the way deadly force is understood and interpreted by the public. In other words, the public's reaction is controlled by its understanding and interpretation of the police use of firearms and pursuit driving. This reaction can result in a few loud voices or it can materialize as a social movement.

Social Movements

Rather than attempt to place what we know about police use of deadly force into some grand theory, it is our approach to address the fundamental questions concerning what is involved in the analysis of a social movement. In an essay titled "The Meaning of the Social Movement," sociologist Albion Small set forth an interesting approach to the study of social change around the turn of the century. He noted "the social movement is today's form of the same vital facts which have always been the impulse of human advancement" (1897:345). The study of advancement or change from this perspective acknowledged the public's collective response as a powerful force. Applying Small's "vital facts" to our example of police use of deadly force places more importance on the perceptions and reactions of the public than on the actual use of deadly force.

Our decision to consider police use of deadly force in the context of a social movement requires an understanding of Durkheim's explanation of the collective conscience (1933) and what has been called the social construction of reality (Berger and Luckmann, 1967). Durkheim's famous quote underscores the importance of the collective response. "We must not say that an action shocks the common conscience because it is criminal, but rather that it is criminal because it shocks the common conscience. We do not reprove it because it is a crime, but it is a crime because we reprove it" (1933: 81). Durkheim asserted that behavior is defined as moral or immoral only by the collective responses of those affected.

W.I. Thomas stressed that whatever people believe to be real will be real in its consequences and that we learn to act on what we believe to be true. Certainly, Thomas found that to be true in his own life and career! Peter Burger and Thomas Luckmann (1967) carried these ideas out to their logical conclusion and informed us that no such thing as a single, objective definition of reality exists and that the same basic data are often interpreted in different ways, yielding different meanings to different groups. This concept becomes very important as police use of deadly force has disparate meanings and implications. In the case of firearms, the law enforcement community is often at odds with racial and ethnic groups, while the strategy of pursuit driving splits those who emphasize the need to apprehend suspects and those who underscore general safety on the roadways.

In other words, reality for one may be different from reality for another. The public reaction to police use of firearms has focused on the rights of suspects and has facilitated reform. Specifically, the changes have prevented the police from shooting any fleeing felon and have encouraged a defense of life standard. Most recently, a concern that police may create situations in which deadly force may be used as self-defense has been raised. Pursuit driving has received insufficient clamor or public outcry to require policies which reflect more concern for public safety than for the need to catch law violators. However, this very dangerous practice has earned its serious and vocal critics. Our analysis focuses on these examples of government action which have created or are creating a strong social response due to their public threat. One way to understand what has happened to the public response to the police use of deadly force is to understand another American dilemma, drunk driving.

A Critical Analogy:
The Social Movement Against Drunk Driving

Drunk driving has reached the level of an epidemic and has been identified as one of our most pressing social problems. Just as the analysis of police use of deadly force requires a balance of several law enforcement and public safety issues, drunk driving combines the interrelationships between two complex American institutions: drinking and driving. James Jacobs (1989) has written an exceptional monograph on drunk driving in which he explains that the history of drunk driving parallels the history of transportation. Jacobs provides his readers with a realistic and frightening account of the costs associated with drunk driving and the details of the social movement against it.

After recognizing the number of lives lost, other costs related to the problem of drunk driving and the ameliorative efforts, it is a discouraging fact that drunk driving remains a major social problem in the 1990s. The anti-drunk driving movement has catapulted beyond the informal and unorganized reform attempted in the 1950s and 1960s. During the 1970s, a remarkable grass-roots effort was directed at the eradication of drunk driving. Remove Intoxicated Drivers (RID), Mothers Against Drunk Drivers (MADD) and Students Against Drunk Driving (SADD) were all established and became part of an expansive network of federal, state, local and private agencies and organizations.

The National Highway Traffic Safety Administration (NHTSA) responded to the loud pleas for help and provided funding to assist governmental agencies and private organizations in working together to rid the roads of drunk drivers. The times (late 1970s and early 1980s) were favorable to confront drunk driving, as the public health campaign against alcohol had proven relatively successful. Further, the media were committed to the movement and provided significant time and space to anti-drunk driving information and vigorous coverage of spectacular events. In the 1980s, the national response against drunk driving continued to gain momentum and strength. In fact, Congress proclaimed a Drunk and Drugged Driving Awareness Week each December and put financial pressure on the states to strengthen drunk driving legislation (Jacobs, 1989: xvi-xvii). In 1982, President Reagan appointed a Presidential Committee on Drunk Driving which published its Final Report in 1983 and noted:

> In recent years, society has acted or reacted to the drunk driving problem in ways it has not in the past. A number of citizen groups have brought the problem of alcohol-related tragedies to the attention of the public and to officials at the local state and federal levels. The Presidential Commission is the culmination of a crescendo of voices—voices of victims and their families—who demand action. The demand for action is not new, but its intensity and extent have never been more dramatic (1983: 2).

In the 1990s, the movement against drunk drivers has continued. Although it started years ago as an unorganized effort without the benefit of leadership or recognized membership, the movement against drunk driving has become institutionalized. Jacobs (1989:40) provides a clear understanding of how and why drunk driving has earned the status of a social movement.

> . . . public opinion and public policy on drunk driving have been shaped more by perceptions and imagery than by facts. For example, the U.S. Department of Transportation's 1968 *Alcohol and Highway Safety* report's claim that 50% of all traffic fatalities — that is, twenty-five thousand deaths — are attributable to 'the use of alcohol by drivers and pedestrians' established drunk driving as a national problem, paved the way for the expenditure of public funds, and stimulated the anti-drunk driving movement. Even though traffic fatalities have decreased during the ensuing decades, these same statistics (or even larger numbers) have been recited again and again to prove the significance of drunk driving and to justify claims on resources and political attention. It seems a rule of American political life that a social problem has to be projected in large enough — even exaggerated — terms before it can command a place on the social problems agenda.

The successful fight against drunk drivers has been fueled by a frightened and concerned public which when threatened has reacted. It is a classic sociological example of how a problem is observed, defined and how reaction to it has been organized through a structure and membership into meaningful programs of education and enforcement (Spiegel, 1974 and Roberts and Kloss, 1974).

There are no reasonable arguments in favor of drunk driving! However, as Jacobs reminds us, we as a society are ambivalent to alcohol and we are a nation on wheels. Driving can be a hobby or even a sport, as can drinking. The combination can be deadly. Jacob's point regarding the social movement is the importance of image and perception.

Although the research is unable to pinpoint the exact effects of drinking and driving, the public has been made aware of its potential impact and has chosen to continue and to strengthen the movement to rid the road of drunk and drugged drivers. The police use of firearms as deadly force, also an American institution, has been limited to a standard which has been loosely defined as 'defense of life.' This occurred only after the image and perception of the use of firearms by police became threatening and resulted in a strong public protest. The strategy of police pursuit driving has only recently become the subject of organized concern and research. The line of inquiry concerning pursuit mirrors that of firearms but is a decade or two behind.

The analogy of drunk driving was introduced as an example of the elements necessary to challenge successfully a social problem. Further, the drunk driving example demonstrates how a social problem can be addressed by using the "vital facts" to organize against it, recruit a following and achieve some degree of success. But as Jacobs (1989:200) reminds us, "In dealing with drunk driving and other social problems, it is well to remember that total victory is not achievable." However, he continues that (1989:200), ". . . positive results require persistence, resources, and imagination. Success will not come in grand victories but in small achievements." The remainder of this book will investigate the small achievements and progress that have been made in the most common forms of deadly force by police: using firearms and vehicles. Our approach will include an analysis of the legal issues which shape the uses of deadly force, followed by chapters dedicated to firearms and pursuit driving which review the findings from research, look at trends in research and analyze how this knowledge influences policy and training. A final chapter will discuss the similarities and differences between society's reaction to the use of firearms and pursuit driving as police tactics.

The Use of Force and the Law

2

One of the fundamental characteristics of our legal system is its dynamic character. In other words, it is impossible to explain the law in 1991 and be confident that it will still be the same in 1992. The number of courts and legislative bodies in the United States further complicates the task of explaining the law, as it may differ among and between jurisdictions. In any situation, it is always necessary to seek advice of counsel to determine the most recent legislation, case law and interpretations. With that disclaimer, the following is offered as instructive background material rather than the authoritative basis for action.[1] Our aim in this chapter is to discuss the several types of law and legal proceedings which control and regulate police use of force. Our discussion concerning firearms will focus on the impact of the Civil Rights Act of 1871, § 1983.[2] Our introduction to the law of pursuit will emphasize the law of negligence. However, it is argued that pursuit is an attempted arrest or seizure and that the protection afforded citizens by the Fourth Amendment should apply.

The legal use of force refers to the amount of force lawfully available to local, state or federal law enforcement agents. Excessive force is that force which exceeds what is reasonable. Police officers are sworn to uphold the law and must attempt to apprehend law violators. Their duty is to protect the general citizenry, but their actions must be tempered by reasonableness (Note, 1981).

Laws, departmental policies and the courts specify the limits of force which are appropriate to the police, based on reasonableness. Recourse against the excessive use of force is available under state and federal law.[3] The legal theory of negligence can be employed in suits filed after an injury resulting from excessive force has occurred. In this type of lawsuit, the plaintiff

9

states that the police officer's unreasonable conduct has caused an injury. This injury can result from any unreasonable action or certain types of inaction. In many of these suits, a weapon of some type has been used by the police officer. Whether the officer injures a person with a PR-4, a baton, his fists, a vehicle or a weapon of opportunity (such as a brick or flashlight), it is the *reasonableness* of the act within the totality of circumstances that will be scrutinized. In recent years, this theory has been limited to actions filed in state court. The United States Supreme Court has held in two recent opinions that negligence does not rise to the constitutional level which is required for a substantive [3] 1983 action (*Davidson v. Cannon*, 1986 and *Daniels v. Williams*, 1986).[4] In other words, this type of litigation focuses upon the reasonable care used by an officer(s) during an apprehension or arrest or an attempt and is based on the following elements:

1. the officer owed the injured party a duty not to engage in certain conduct;
2. the officer's actions violated that duty;
3. the officer's negligent breach of that duty was the proximate cause of the injury; and
4. the injured party suffered actual and preventable damages.

Liability must be based on evidence that the police conduct in breaching a duty owed was the proximate cause of an injury. State court actions are suits against individuals, municipalities, counties or the state based on an alleged violation of state law.

When police officers or their departments are charged with brutality or excessive force, the defense, beyond qualified immunity[5] is that such force was *reasonable* under the circumstances. This defense of reasonableness is available either when an officer has been attacked or when the officer reasonably considers himself or another to be in imminent fear of bodily harm during an apprehension, attempted arrest or other activity (Silver, 1986). Defining what is reasonable is a complex task and will be explained below.

Federal Civil Rights Act: 4 U.S.C. § 1983[6]

When claims against the police include allegations of intentional injury or willful misconduct, it is likely that the case will be filed in federal court under the Civil Rights Act. Additionally, when a constitutional violation, such as an unreasonable seizure, is alleged, theories to demonstrate the government's deliberate indifference to the injured (see *City of Canton v. Harris*, 1989) can include the following:

1. Failure to train;
2. Failure to supervise;
3. Failure to have a departmental policy;
4. Negligent retention;

5. Negligent hiring;
6. Failure to discipline;
7. Failure to screen psychologically; and
8. Negligent entrustment.

Section 1983 of the Civil Rights Act has been the most effective device for making claims of liability against governmental entities and can be filed in both state and federal courts.

Originally passed in an effort to combat the Ku Klux Klan in the aftermath of the Civil War, § 1983 provides that any person acting under the color of state or local law who violates the federal constitutional or statutory rights of another shall be liable to the injured party. Rather than alleging a violation of substantive due process under the fourteenth amendment,[7] which prohibits egregious conduct (Urbonya, 1987), these complainants must allege that the force used by police during their arrests violates the Fourth Amendment, which prohibits unreasonable seizures (*Graham v. Connor*, 1989 and *Tennessee v. Garner*, 1985).[8] That is, since 1989 and the *Graham* decision, allegations of excessive force must be analyzed under the Fourth Amendment and its reasonableness standard.[9] The basic issue which controls the success of a § 1983 claim alleging excessive force is whether the police action or inaction deprives a citizen of his or her constitutional right against unreasonable seizures (*Tennessee v. Garner*, 1985 and *Graham v. Connor*, 1989).

Tennessee v. Garner[10]

At approximately 10:45 pm on the night of October 3, 1974, fifteen-year-old Edward Garner, unarmed and alone, broke a window and entered an unoccupied house in suburban Memphis with the intent to steal money and property. Two police officers, Elton Hymon and Leslie Wright responded to a call from a neighbor concerning a prowler. While Wright radioed dispatch, Hymon intercepted the youth as he ran from the back of the house to a six-foot cyclone fence. After shining a flashlight on the youth who was crouched by the fence, Hymon identified himself and yelled 'Halt.' He observed that the youth was unarmed. As the boy jumped to get over the fence, the officer fired his service revolver at the youth, as he was trained to do. Edward Garner was shot because the police officers were trained that under Tennessee law, it was proper to kill a fleeing felon rather than run the risk of allowing him to escape.

A divided Court held, in part, that apprehension by the use of deadly force is a seizure subject to the reasonableness requirement of the Fourth Amendment. The majority ruled that the facts did not justify the use of deadly force and that deadly force under these circumstances was unreasonable. To determine the constitutionality of a seizure, the Court detailed a balancing test:

The nature and quality of the intrusion on the individual's fourth amendment's interests (must be balanced) against the importance of the governmental interests alleged to justify the intrusion (*Tennessee v. Garner*, 1985:8, quoting U.S. V Place, 1983:703).

The Court held the Tennessee statute ". . . unconstitutional insofar as it authorizes the use of deadly force against . . . unarmed, nondangerous suspect[s]" (*Tennessee v. Garner*, 1985:11). The Court cited with approval the Model Penal Code:

The use of deadly force is not justifiable . . . unless (i) the arrest is for a felony; and (ii) the person effecting the arrest is authorized to act as a police officer . . .; and (iii) the actor believes that the force employed creates no substantial risk of injury to innocent persons; and (iv) the actor believes that (1) the crime for which the arrest is made involved conduct including the use or threatened use of deadly force; or (2) there is a substantial risk that a person to be arrested will cause death or serious bodily harm if his apprehension is delayed.[11]

In the final analysis, the Court ruled, "Where the suspect poses no immediate threat to the officer and no threat to others, the harm resulting from failing to apprehend him does not justify the use of deadly force to do so" (*Tennessee v. Garner*, 1985:11). And the nature of this threat is clear, "a significant threat of death or serious physical injury" (*Tennessee v. Garner*, 1985:11). It is significant that this pronouncement can be reduced to a moral judgment. This was made clear where the court noted, "It is not better that all felony suspects die than that they escape" (*Tennessee v. Garner*, 1985:11). This logic presents two concepts, deadly force and reasonableness, which need further clarification and interpretation.

Deadly Force and Reasonableness

Deadly force can best be defined as such force readily capable of, or likely to cause, death or serious bodily harm. While many states have specific statutory definitions, all do not. In any case, the use of deadly force neither requires nor dictates a specific outcome. Deadly force refers to a means, which when applied, is readily capable of causing serious bodily injury or death, and the outcome is only a chance happening. While it is clear that the *Garner* court established the principle that the use of unreasonable force by police violates the Fourth Amendment, it is unclear what was meant by reasonableness (*Tennessee v. Garner*, 1985: 7).[12]

In other words, ". . . reasonableness depends on not only when a seizure is made, but also how it is carried out" (*Tennessee v. Garner*, 1985:8). And the force must be considered within the totality of circumstances (*Tennessee v. Garner*, 1985: 9). The difficulty in defining deadly force is obviously mirrored by the difficulty in defining reasonableness.

The analysis of an incident involving police use of force which could be deadly or is readily capable of causing death, requires an evaluation of the process[13] as well as the outcome. This begets a very complicated task. If a death results from force being used by a police officer on a citizen, then a seizure will have taken place. For the seizure to be unreasonable depends on the totality of circumstances and a standard of objective reasonableness which considers whether a reasonable officer would have believed that the use of force was necessary (see *Johnson v. Glick*, 1973).[14] The *Garner* Court stated that (1985:11):

> . . . if the suspect threatens the officer with a weapon or there is probable cause to believe that he has committed a crime involving the infliction or threatened infliction of serious physical harm, deadly force may be used if necessary to prevent escape . . .

Although the *Garner* Court did not refer specifically to the factors cited in *Glick* as the blocks on which the constitutionality of a seizure is built, the Court created a standard utilizing three of those factors, including the need for the application of force, the relationship between the need and the amount of force that was used and the extent of injury inflicted. As previously noted, the Court "must balance the nature and quality of the intrusion on the individual's fourth amendment's interests alleged to justify the intrusion" (*Tennessee v. Garner*, 1985: 8).[15]

Kathryn Urbonya has summarized *Garner* as follows (1989:99-100 citations omitted):

> The *Garner* decision . . . suggests that the fourth amendment standard of liability does not question merely whether a police officer used unnecessary force; it also questions whether a reasonable police officer would have believed that the force was necessary. Police officers are not liable for 'every push and shove they make.' The standard affords them discretion to act decisively. In balancing the interests of the parties under the Fourth Amendment, courts recognize the need for such discretion when they consider the state's interest in law enforcement.

The *Garner* Court has established a normative standard, "whether a reasonable officer would have believed the force used was necessary" that could be tested empirically. However, in reality, the Court has provided no more than rhetoric and ambiguity which serve as guideposts for a post-hoc analysis. Even in *Graham v. Conner* (1986:9 citations omitted) the Court, quoting *Bell v. Wolfish* (1979:559) acknowledged that:

> 'the test of reasonableness under the Fourth Amendment is not capable of precise definition or mechanical application,' however, its proper application requires careful attention to the facts and circumstances of each particular case, including the severity of the crime at issue, whether the suspect poses an immediate threat to the safety of the officers or others, and whether he is actively resisting arrest or attempting to evade arrest by flight . . . The reasonableness of a particular use of force must be judged from the perspective of a reasonable officer on the scene, rather than with 20/20 vision of hindsight.

For a given fact situation, it is likely that the reasonableness of an officer's action will be addressed at several levels by analysts or experts who are asked to provide opinions. The ultimate fact finders will hear opinions tempered by the subjective interpretation of the events, hindsight, and the pre-determined attitudes and values of the actors (see Anderson and Winfree, 1988). We are left with a vague definition of deadly force which refers to a means, which when applied, is readily capable of causing serious bodily injury or death. The reasonableness of this force may be left to the battling experts, each with his or her own perspective and vision. The Court has left the constitutionality of behavior to an adversarial system which operates in a competitive marketplace (Alpert, 1988).

Firearms and Other Forms of Deadly Force Including Police Pursuit

The use of a weapon, whether it is a firearm, a knife, fists, a club or a vehicle, is capable of causing serious bodily harm or death. In other words, deadly force can be applied in a variety of ways and by a number of means. In two recent reports analyzing shooting incidents in the City of Miami and the Metro-Dade Police Departments in Dade County, Florida (Alpert, 1987b, 1989c) it was reported that more than 20% of the incidents when police officers fired their weapons, involved firing at a vehicle which, it was reported, had placed the officer in fear of his life.[16]

Jim Fyfe explains the consequences of firing a weapon (1988:166): "When police officers fire their guns, the immediate consequences of their decisions are realized at a rate of 750 feet per second and are beyond reversal by any level of official review." Most bullets fired do not hit their intended human targets and injuries due to stray bullets or accidental shootings are uncommon (Blumberg, 1989 and Alpert, 1989b). In fact, one court ruling on whether a fleeing suspect who ran onto a highway and was run over was seized, (*Cameron v. City of Pontiac*, 1985: 140)) cited Justice O'Connor's blistering dissent in *Garner* (1985:31)[17] and noted that "While officer Roberts fired his weapon as many as five times at the decedent, he did not seize him, since each time he used the weapon he either fired a warning shot or was errant in his aim." Such a luxury of error, however, may not be available when an officer employs a weapon other than a firearm. As Alpert and Anderson have previously noted, ". . . when a police officer engages in a high-speed chase in a high-powered police car, that vehicle becomes a potentially deadly weapon" (1986).

A Constitutional Analysis

The ultimate issue concerning pursuit may become whether the police "seize" a suspect by chasing him. This determination takes on critical proportions in the assessment of whether a fleeing vehicular suspect's fourth amendment rights have been violated. The Court has only flirted with the issue of seizures by vehicular deadly force (*Brower v. County of Inyo*, 1989 and *California v. Hodari D.*, 1991). It has yet to make the ultimate determination of whether the act of pursuit or the actions of an unreasonable pursuit, absent the fugitive's injury or death, is a "seizure" with corresponding fourth amendment implications.

A number of lower courts have interpreted *Brower's* statement that a seizure under the Fourth Amendment does not occur ". . . whenever there is a governmentally caused termination or governmentally desired termination of an individual's freedom of movement . . ., but only where there is a governmental termination of freedom of movement *through means intentionally applied*" (*Brower v. County of Inyo*, 1989: 1381, emphasis in original) to mean that the act of pursuit, per se, is not a seizure (*Roach v. City of Fredericktown, Missouri*, 1989 and *Britt v. Little Rock*, 1989).

What remains to be addressed, however, is the meaning of "means intentionally applied." Certainly, the deadman's roadblock involved in the *Brower* case could be seen as the inescapable destination of the fleeing felon. It is equally believable that a pursuing officer's reckless driving, in an effort to mount psychological pressure on a fleeing suspect, even absent physical contact or a preestablished blockade would have the same foreseeable outcome. That is, the reckless pursuit could be the moving force behind a collision in which the fleeing suspect may become involved. The question boils down to whether it is a matter of deliberate indifference to a fleeing suspect's right to be free from an unreasonable seizure that creates a situation for a foreseeable and predictable injurious or fatal outcome.

United States District Court Judge Lamberth, in *Wright v. District of Columbia* (1990:10),[18] relied upon the Supreme Court's decision in *Michigan v. Chesternut* (1988) and noted that "The reasonableness of a seizure is to be assessed by balancing the right of the individual to be free from unreasonable intrusions against the needs of the state to carry out its law enforcement function." The *Chesternut* Court (1988:575-576 note 9)[19] refused to detail the circumstances in which a pursuit would amount to a fourth amendment seizure but suggested that one element of a fourth amendment violation is that a pursuit "communicate to a reasonable person that he was not at liberty to ignore the police presence and go about his business" *Michigan v. Chesternut* (1988:569). It is important to examine the concurring opinions of Justices Kennedy and Scalia in *Chesternut* (1988:576-577) because they felt that "neither 'chase' nor 'investigative pursuit' need be included in the lexicon of the Fourth Amendment," but observed that hot pursuit might be an exception. Judge Lamberth found that exception in *Wright v. District of Columbia* (1990:9-10) and ruled "It is undisputed that the police engaged in a high speed vehicular pursuit of plaintiffs and intended to seize plaintiffs. Under these facts, the court finds that a seizure occurred, invoking the Fourth Amendment's requirements of reasonableness."

These inquiries have deep roots. The *Brower* (1989) Court recognized some of the similarities between the use of a firearm and a pursuit when it noted:

> Brower's independent decision to continue the chase can no more eliminate
> respondent's responsibility for the termination for his movement effected by
> the roadblock than Garner's independent decision to flee eliminated the
> Memphis police officer's responsibility for the termination of his movement
> effected by the bullet.

Obviously, the probability of a crash involving a concealed or 'deadman's'
roadblock which leaves little or no opportunity for escape is greater than the
probability of a crash involving a pursuit without a roadblock. However, it is
reasonable to expect that an accident will occur as the result of a pursuit which
takes place on a congested road in a reckless manner (Alpert and Dunham, 1990).[20]
And it is precisely this foreseeable consequence which creates problematic training
and policy issues for administrators.

A vehicle weighing close to two tons and travelling at relatively slow speeds
in a reckless manner is likely to do serious damage to property and person. The
more recklessly a vehicle is driven, the greater its likelihood of causing serious
bodily harm or death.[21] As we have noted, the law controlling police pursuit
is not nearly as defined as that regulating the use of other weapons such as fists
or firearms. Certainly, decision-making training and analysis of risk for use of
firearms far exceeds that which is required for pursuit driving.

While the Court has established that "[I]t is not better that all felony suspects
die than that they escape" (*Tennessee v. Garner*, 1985:11), it has not enforced
its advice. The Court has outlined in more detail its reasoning in *Graham v.
Conner* (1986:9) and focused on the reasonableness of deadly force by analyzing
"the severity of the crime at issue, whether the suspect poses an immediate threat
to the safety of the officers or others, and whether he is actively resisting arrest
or attempting to evade arrest by flight." Further, in *Garner* (1985:11), the Court
stated that, "[I]t is no doubt unfortunate when a suspect who is in sight escapes,
but the fact that the police arrive a little late or are a little slower afoot does
not always justify killing the suspect."

The Court in *Baker v. McCollan* (1979:144) informs us that the first inquiry
in any § 1983 suit is to isolate and identify the constitutional violation (see also
City of Oklahoma City v. Tuttle, 1985:84-85). In most cases, this will include
the Fourth Amendment's prohibition against unreasonable seizures (*Graham v.
Connor*, 1989:7). Pursuit driving has been identified as a seizure by one court
(*Wright v. District of Columbia*, 1990) which made a convincing constitutional
analysis. The mechanics of pursuit driving or the refusal by the suspect to give
up is similar to other attempted arrests and when unreasonable, lends itself to
an analysis as a seizure.

The Court in *Graham v. Conner* (1989:8) held "that *all* claims that law
enforcement officers have used excessive force—deadly or not—in the course
of arrest, investigatory stop, or other 'seizure' of a free citizen should be analyzed
under the Fourth Amendment and its 'reasonableness' standard." Coupled with
the Court's statement in *Terry v. Ohio* (1968:19, note 16) and *Brower v. County*

of Inyo (1989) that a seizure which establishes the Fourth Amendment's protections occurs only when the police have, "by means of physical force or show of authority . . . in some way restrained the liberty of a citizen," the opportunity exists for the Supreme Court to consider pursuit as a fourth amendment question. The language, "show of authority" (see *Terry v. Ohio*, 1968), establishes the possibility of police use of psychological force when they know or can reasonably predict the outcome of specific behavior.

The majority opinion in *Brower* (1989:3) noted that a seizure must be the result of a willful act and can not be applied to an unknowing act. The Court (1989:5) made reference to *Kibbe v. Springfield* (1987:80-803) and noted that "a roadblock is not just a significant show of authority to induce a voluntary stop, but is designed tb produce a stop by physical impact if voluntary compliance does not occur," in contrast to a police officer in the road signaling traffic to stop or a police car pursuing with flashing lights and a blaring siren. The minority opinion in *Brower* (1989) attacks the Court's condition that a seizure has to be an intentional act, and suggests that "There may be a case that someday comes before this Court in which the concept of intent is useful in applying the Fourth Amendment." An appropriate case for consideration is a reckless police pursuit.

On the one hand, the District of Columbia in *Wright v. District of Columbia* (1990) considers pursuit a seizure. On the other hand, the Sixth Circuit in *Galas v. McKee* (1986:04) remains unconvinced.

> Without question highspeed pursuit places the suspect, the officer, and the public in general at risk of death or serious bodily injury. In that respect highspeed pursuits are no different than the use of a firearm to apprehend fleeing suspects . . . We conclude that the minimal intrusion on a traffic offender's Fourth Amendment's right occasioned by the officer's participation in a highspeed pursuit does not outweigh a longstanding police practice which we consider 'essential to a coherent scheme of powers.' Accordingly, we hold that the use of high-speed pursuits to apprehend traffic violators is not unreasonable, and, thus, not violative of the Fourth Amendment.

Keeping with the Sixth Circuit's approach, the Supreme Court in *Michigan State Police v. Sitz* (1990), recently approved the use of temporary roadblocks for the initial questioning of motorists to check the driver's sobriety. The Court ruled that such an intrusion is minimal when compared to the duration and extent of the seizure and the effectiveness of the procedure. The Court relied on empirical data to demonstrate that approximately one percent of the motorists passing through the sobriety checkpoint was arrested. In other words, the Court ruled that it is reasonable to intrude upon 99% of the motorists who had done nothing wrong in an effort to curb drunk driving. The data we will present in later chapters will demonstrate the probability of a pursuit resulting in a successful outcome and the percent of accidents, injuries and deaths caused by pursuit driving. Hopefully, the Court will one day interpret the data on the effectiveness of pursuit more appropriately than they have interpreted the effectiveness of sobriety checkpoints (Alpert, 1991).

In a very confusing opinion, the Supreme Court decided the parameters of a fourth amendment seizure resulting from a foot chase. The Court relied upon the actions of a suspect to determine the essence of a governmental action, i.e. seizure (*California v. Hodari D.*, 1991). The implications for a fourth amendment analysis of vehicular pursuit are not fully defined but appear to leave the *Wright* decision intact. This result is due to the Court's recognition that a seizure may occur without physical force when there is an assertion of governmental authority and the suspect submits to arrest. What remains unclear, however, is to what extent the factual circumstances preceding the suspect's voluntary or involuntary submission may be considered.

For example, if an officer signals a motorist to stop, the motorist flees and crashes into a tree, may the officer's actions be considered as constituting a seizure or does the issue of proximate cause enter the equation? The *Hodari D.*, Court (1991: 5,7) reasons:

> An arrest requires *either* physical force *or*, where that is absent, *submission* to the assertion of authority . . . . We do not think it desirable, even as a policy matter, to stretch the Fourth Amendment beyond its words and beyond the meaning of arrest . . . . In sum, assuming that Pertoso's pursuit in the present case constituted a 'show of authority' enjoining Hodari to halt, since Hodari did not comply with the injunction he was not seized until he was tackled.

Police Pursuit Driving and the Law

Considering an unreasonable pursuit a seizure has not been a popular stance as most pursuits conducted today involve risk and end in arrest but do not result in accidents or injuries. However, most non-pursuit arrests, although seizures, are routine and do not result in injuries.[22] This comparison creates another thin line that is blurred by the protections guaranteed to citizens by the Fourth Amendment (Project, 1990).

Professor Kathryn Urbonya (1991) has written the most extensive and analytical treatise on the need to subject pursuit driving to constitutional scrutiny. She agrees that the question of responsibility for the harm that arises from a pursuit must be determined ultimately by the courts. She argues that this question is not only linked to constitutional doctrines associated with the Fourth and Fourteenth Amendments but also to complex social issues and policy. She applies an exceptional paradigm to the issue of pursuit which is grounded in Durkheim's sociology and updated and elaborated in Balkin's (1990) "The Rhetoric of Responsibility." Professor Urbonya's interpretation and analysis shed a bright light on the way courts must review this issue.

Basically, she notes the contrasting legal doctrines which influence decisions as "individualism" and "altruism." Although these terms retain meanings similar to those developed by Durkheim at the turn of the century, their application and influence to legal decision-making are unique. Urbonya's research indicates that, in the context of police pursuit, courts should adhere to a policy of altruism or communalism because any other course of action would grant pursuit an exception to constitutional scrutiny. She notes that a policy of altruism affords individuals more protection of their right to personal security than does that of individualism. The former recognizes that an injury to one person may implicate others in the harm. The latter emphasizes that each person needs to protect him or herself from harm associated with the presence of others. Because the approach of communalism/altruism may provide the injured individual with compensation for the harm, it may deter others not to conduct themselves in a similar fashion. Individualism, however, forces the harmed individual to incur a loss without any compensation and by definition, fails to deter the activity. She notes (1991: 218-219):

> When passengers, motorists, and pedestrians are injured, the central issue is who is responsible, the pursued driver or the police officers who pursued the driver. When police cruisers crash into one of these individuals, causation is not in issue because the police officer directly caused the harm. When the pursued's vehicle inflicts the harm, the causation question, however, is complex. The actions of the pursued driver cannot be subject to constitutional scrutiny because the driver is a private actor, not a state official. The actions of the police officers, do, however, signify the presence of state action, which can subject them to be causally implicated in the harm.

Resolving the legal causation issue depends upon how the facts are analyzed. The individualist perspective places the responsibility of harm to the driver while the communalist/altruist perspective permits courts to analyze how the police are implicated in the harm. This analysis implies that a psychological force can be used by the police and that they will be held responsible when that force is excessive or rises to a constitutional level. The precedent for this psychological force is the established "show of authority" as well as the psychological force used by police illegally to coerce confessions (Sasaki, 1988 and White, 1979). Certainly, the dynamics of a pursuit places a psychological force on those who flee the police and it is clear that these forces can intensify and escalate the problem of pursuit.

If courts follow the lead of social scientists and rely upon this type of analysis, it is clear that the potential harm created by a continued chase would be balanced against the state's interest in an immediate apprehension. In any case, the potential harm and risk of the pursuit is under the control of the police. By abandoning the chase, the psychological force applied by the police, which may be the force compelling the offender to continue, will cease.

Police officers, sworn to uphold the law, must attempt to apprehend law violators. They owe a duty to protect the general citizenry. As we previously noted, their actions must be tempered by reasonableness. When the actions of police during pursuit or the behavior of the pursued proximately caused by police raises the risks of motorists beyond a level of reasonableness, the pursuit should be considered an illegal seizure and the protections associated with the Fourth Amendment should attach (see *Wright v. District of Columbia*, 1990). In other words, a pursuit employs force which could be deadly and **could result in a seizure.** To determine the constitutionality of a pursuit, the Court should use the same logic it did in *Garner* to formulate a test balancing the need to apprehend immediately the suspect against the specific risks to the motoring public created by the pursuit (Alpert and Dunham, 1990).[23]

When a police officer engages in a pursuit, the officer is attempting to seize the offender. Too often, the risks created by the pursuit are unreasonable, and the officer and his or her supervisor and department should have known the factors which increase the risk. This information must be available in a departmental policy and its training.

The Supreme Court's view of policy in *City of Canton v. Harris* (1989) is one of deliberateness. That is, a policy which will be actionable under §1983 involves the deliberate choice of a conduct on the part of the government. Conduct which is deliberate is defined by Black's Law Dictionary (p. 384) to be "willful, rather than merely intentional." This language leaves the indication that an injury proximately caused by a government's unreasonable conduct which reflects willful or intentional behavior will be actionable as 'policy' under §1983.

The Supreme Court's only substantive indication of what it may consider deliberately indifferent appears in a footnote to the text and targets the issue of the need to train officers in the use of deadly force against fleeing felons in light of *Tennessee v. Garner* (*City of Canton v. Harris*, 1989: footnote 10). The clear statement from this note is that some training needs are "so obvious" that failure to train with respect to them shows deliberate indifference to constitutional rights. However, what the Court does not and could not delineate is which other areas are of most critical importance in law enforcement. Apparently, the Court leaves this effort to the trial courts and lower-level appellate courts.

One observer has commented that a law enforcement task analysis is useful in resolving this question. Empirical analyses might bring into recognition a small but critical mass of training required of all officers who enforce the laws.

> The Court's . . . method of demonstrating deliberate indifference links training
> needs to tasks the particular officer must perform. By creating such a link,
> the Court is requesting the determination of the extent and priority of police
> work. In other words, task analyses and empirical assessments of police duties
> may be used to establish training needs (Alpert, 1989a:470).

Until the Supreme Court acknowledges the severe danger of pursuit and its force which often causes injury and sometimes causes death, and the necessity of policy and training (as it has in the area of firearms), the law of pursuit will be that of negligence. The remainder of this chapter will focus on the concerns and issues discussed in the law which relate to the risk of pursuit driving.

Pursuit Driving and The Law of Negligence

Courts have been called upon to balance the importance of criminal apprehension (benefits) with the potential dangers related to pursuit driving (costs). The extent of this type of litigation has grown geometrically, and there now exists a substantial body of case law governing the operation of police vehicles in emergencies and especially in pursuits. As a result, "some of these suits have resulted in six or seven figure awards and several have nearly bankrupted some municipalities and townships" (Zevitz, 1987:37). Others have led to molding, shaping and restricting the policies of pursuit driving in numerous jurisdictions.

This discussion is limited to general principles and selected legal opinions which indicate an emerging judicial attitude concerning pursuit driving. Several publications are available which exhaust the arguments and to which reference must be made when discussing the legal issues related to pursuit driving (for example, see Urbonya, 1991, Schofield, 1988, Alpert, 1988, Zevitz, 1987, Silver, 1986, Smith, 1986 and Farber, 1985).

The legal theory underlying many law suits which are filed after a pursuit-related injury is negligence, which has been discussed earlier. One example comes from a recent Texas Supreme Court decision which reported that "The decision to initiate or continue pursuit may be negligent when the heightened risk of injury to third parties is unreasonable in relation to the interest in apprehending suspects" (*Travis v. City of Mesquite*, 1990). In a concurring opinion, Justice Doggott (1990) noted that the court did not prohibit pursuit driving, but ". . . it did require the use of judgment based upon the *risk* involved" (emphasis added). Further, it was noted, "Police officers must balance the risk to the public with their duty to enforce the law to choose an appropriate course of conduct. Public safety should not be thrown to the winds in the heat of the chase" (*Travis v. City of Mesquite*, 1990:7). We will follow the outline presented above and look at how reasonable care used by an officer(s) during a pursuit can be evaluated based on the duty the officer owed the injured party not to engage in certain conduct, whether or not the officer's actions violated that duty and whether the officer's negligent breach of that duty was the proximate cause of the injury.

Officers' Duty

Certain duties and obligations of police officers must be determined by local laws, policies, regulations and customs. It is accepted that a police officer can initiate the stop of an automobile for any articulable violation or suspected criminal offense (*Delaware v. Prouse*, 1979). If a motorist refuses to stop, an officer has no duty to refrain from pursuing, even where there is some risk of harm to the public (*Jackson v. Olsen*, 1985). Specifically, in *Smith v. City of West Point* (1985:818), the court noted that the police are under ". . . no duty to allow motorized suspects a leisurely escape." However, police must act with a duty of care and reasonableness when pursuing the offender. This duty of reasonableness is created from state statutes, case law and departmental policies and practices.

State statutes usually confer a special status upon police vehicles and other authorized emergency vehicles and exempt them from certain traffic regulations, including those related to speed, traffic signals, and the right of way. Often, the language from which this authorization is created is taken from The Uniform Vehicle Code and requires police officers to drive with due regard for the safety of others, but is without specificity. Farber (1985:87) explains the effect of this vagueness. "The exemptions granted emergency vehicles from certain traffic regulations do not necessarily relieve the drivers of emergency vehicles from the common law duty to exercise care, *commensurate with the circumstances*, for the safety of other travelers or persons." The language found in the Uniform Vehicle Code states that a driver of an emergency vehicle is not relieved "from the duty to drive with due regard for the safety of all persons using the highway, nor protect him from the consequences of an arbitrary exercise of the privileges granted under the exemption."[24] In other words, even when police officers are exempt from the laws regulating traffic flow (stop signs and traffic lights) and are authorized to drive faster than the speed limit, they must drive with *due regard* for the safety of all persons using the roads. This is analogous to the reasonableness standard discussed earlier and arguably places a special responsibility on the driver of an emergency vehicle who chooses to exercise this privilege. The driver of the emergency vehicle may be held to a higher standard than a citizen, as he is a professional, assumed to have the proper training and experience to warrant the special exemption.

One of the most cited decisions from a state court is *Thornton v. Shore* (1983), from the Kansas Supreme Court. This case has become essential for municipal defense attorneys because it uses only the actual driving of the officer as a measuring rod and relies upon deterrence theory which suggests that all violators will flee if they are not chased. In this case, the trial court issued a summary judgment for the Kansas University Police Department, which was sued pursuant to a chase that resulted in the death of two law abiding motorists. The plaintiffs in this law suit argued that the police officer should have terminated the pursuit based on the extreme reckless behavior of the individual being pursued and recognized the foreseeability of an accident and likelihood of injury. The defendant police officer argued that he was immune from liability pursuant to the state law permitting him to disregard certain traffic laws but not to disregard the duty to drive with due regard for the safety of all persons (*Thornton v. Shore*, 1983). The trial court ruled that the officer's driving was reasonable and granted summary judgment. On appeal, the Kansas Supreme Court affirmed the summary judgment for the officer and cited two statements which have become classic. The court noted in *Chambers v. Ideal Pure Milk Co.* (1952:590-591):

> Charged as they were with the obligation to enforce the law, the traffic laws included, they (the police) would have been derelict in their duty had they

not pursued him. The police were performing their duty when Shearer, in gross violation of his duty to obey the speed laws, crashed into the milk wagon. To argue that the officers' pursuit caused Shearer to speed may be factually true, but it does not follow that the officers are liable at law for the results of Shearer's negligent speed. Police, cannot be made insurers of the conduct of the culprits they chase.

The court also cited *West Virginia v. Fidelity Gas & Casualty Co. of N.Y.* (1967:90-91):

We are not prepared to hold an officer liable for damages inflicted by the driver of a stolen vehicle whom he was lawfully attempting to apprehend for the fortuitous reason only that the criminal drove through an urban area. To do so would open the door for every desperado to seek sanctuary in the congested confines of our municipalities, serene in the knowledge that an officer would not likely give chase for fear of being liable for the pursued recklessness. Such now is not the law nor should it be the law.

In the dissenting opinions of these cases lurks a more modern and likely scenario for the 1990s. Justice Herd dissenting in *Thornton* (1983:668) exemplifies a more contemporary view:

. . . Even with the [emergency] warnings, however, the driver must operate the [police] vehicle with due regard for the safety of all persons. The majority holds whenever a high speed chase results in a collision between the person pursued and a third party, the pursuing officer has, as a matter of law, met the 'due regard' standard . . . by merely turning on his warning signals . . . There are numerous scenarios where an accident is caused by one not a party to a collision. It is a question of causation.

In other words, the due regard criterion may not be limited to situations where police are directly involved in accidents. This notion of due regard may extend to the totality of the situation and the driving of the officer as well as the offender. Recent cases supporting each point of view demonstrate the confusion among the courts (see *Frohman v. City of Detroit*, 1989 and *Tomcsik v. United States*, 1989, *Smith v. City of West Point*, 1985 and *Oberkramer v. City of Ellisville*, 1983).

In the 1990s, the police will certainly be held to a standard judged by the informed reasonable man who is faced with the question: should this pursuit have taken place the way it did, with the risks it created and for the potential results it could have yielded? Unfortunately, the law has done no more than articulate vague standards and apply them on a case-by-case basis. In fact, terms such as "due regard" and "reasonable care" are relative terms, they can mean different things in different fact situations. While the "other circumstances" have been identified, they have not been systematically correlated to any specific outcome. In other words, each fact situation is argued on its own merits without the benefit of aggregated information or estimates of probabilities. The appropriate degree of reasonable care can vary from one situation to another, but the empirical analysis of pursuit outcomes can help determine which are the most important "circumstances." One factor which needs analysis to determine the duty owed is the departmental policy or custom under which the officer operates.

In most jurisdictions, the departmental pursuit policy, procedure, training, practice and proper supervision can all help determine the duty owed. When a claim of negligence is made, a court may admit into evidence the information which has guided the officer's actions. Specifically, the method by which officers determine the nature of the real or apparent emergency, the conduct during the pursuit and reason for not terminating the pursuit are all significant factors which must be weighed when determining the due regard for safety. Similarly, the action or inaction of the supervisors will also be scrutinized. One area which has received less attention than most is the action taken to end a pursuit. If, after disregarding several traffic signals, the pursued refuses to terminate voluntarily, what actions can the police take?

One of the most difficult issues involves the response of the police to a driver who is operating a vehicle in a manner likely to cause serious bodily injury or death. If a pursuit is initiated and the driver changes his behavior, either by driving more recklessly or slowing down, the change can be attributed to the police action. If the driver does not acknowledge the presence and influence of the police and does not modify his driving, the police actions can not be responsible for the driving of the law violator or the outcome of the pursuit.

Depending upon the jurisdiction, departmental records may serve as mere guidelines, or they may constitute a specific duty owed as their violation would be negligent (Silver, 1985). In addition to establishing a breach of the applicable duty of care, a successful cause of action must prove that damages were proximately caused by those actions. These policy issues will be discussed in Chapter 7.

Foreseeability and Proximate Cause

Liability must be determined on evidence that police conduct in breaching a duty owed was the proximate cause of a pursuit-related injury. On the one hand, if a police car speeds recklessly through a school zone at three in the afternoon when children are present, or could be present, such a determination can be made easily. On the other hand, the addition of an intervening influence, such as the involvement of other drivers, makes the determination of negligence increasingly difficult. Farber (1985:9) explains that

> [S]howing foreseeability and proximate cause is of vital importance particularly in those cases in which the intervening negligence of other persons has been raised as a defense, as where the fleeing motorist, and not the police, collides with a pedestrian or innocent motorist, causing injury or death.

The most frequent scenario is a pursuit which results in an injury rather than a police car striking a vehicle or pedestrian (Alpert, 1987). How to determine foreseeability and proximate cause is a difficult task but one which must be accomplished (Comment, 1986 and Zevitz, 1987). The Texas Supreme Court has defined foreseeability in the following manner (*Travis v City of Mesquite*, 1990: 6-7 footnotes omitted):

> 'Foreseeability' means that the actor, as a person of ordinary intelligence, should have anticipated the dangers that his negligent act created for others. Foreseeability does not require that a person anticipate the precise manner in which injury will occur once he has created a dangerous situation through his negligence. Although the criminal conduct of a third party may be a superceding cause which relieves the negligent actor from liability, the actor's negligence is not superseded and will not be excused when the criminal conduct is a foreseeable result of such negligence. There can be concurrent proximate causes of an accident. All persons whose negligent conduct contributes to the injury, proximately causing the injury, are liable. When the intervening illegal act is foreseeable, it does not negate the continuing proximate causation and consequent liability of the initial actor.

If the police know the identity of the fleeing law violator, liability may be justified if a collision occurs involving that individual and an innocent third party during a pursuit (Farber, 1985 and Silver, 1985). Similarly, police who are driving a vehicle which is clearly less powerful than that of the pursued and who are loosing ground are more likely to be held liable than if the police and offender's equipment are more equally matched and there is some likelihood that the law violator may terminate the pursuit. However, the police duty to warn other motorists is also an important consideration. In a Michigan case (*Frohman v City of Detroit*, 1989), a pursuit was initiated after an officer observed passengers in a van engaged in sexual intercourse. The pursuit escalated quickly to a high rate of speed. Another officer who had heard the chase on the radio was waiting in the center of three westbound lanes and observed in his rearview mirror the speeding van without its headlights illuminated. The van swerved around the police car which immediately joined the chase as the lead vehicle. As the van approached an intersection, the officer observed the light turn red. Not wanting to pursue the van into the intersection against the red light, the officer deactivated his siren and slowed down. The pursuit climaxed when the van proceeded part way through the intersection and struck a vehicle travelling lawfully with a green light. The trial court found the City of Detroit negligent and awarded $2,250,000. This decision and verdict were upheld by the Court of Appeals of Michigan.

After analyzing the current status of the law, Daniel Schofield (1988:5) concludes:

> When a pursuit related accident involves the fleeing motorist and not the police, most courts conclude that the proximate cause was not the manner in which the police conducted the pursuit but rather the manner in which the pursued driver negligently operated his vehicle.

There appears to be a trend to hold the person pursued responsible for his actions as long as the police officer demonstrates concern for public safety by his/her own actions. If this trend continues, an alleged offender who is chased by a police officer and who acts recklessly and crashes cannot blame the officer for being the moving force of the accident or injury, if the officer acted properly according to law and policy. Acting properly, however, requires that the officer not create or continue in a dangerous scenario or one in which an accident is foreseeable. If this trend is modified, it is likely that the police will be held accountable for the psychological pressure put on the pursued to escape and that one's recklessness will be related to the other's recklessness (*Wright v. District of Columbia*, 1990 and Alpert and Smith, 1991).

Immunity

The issue of who is immune from civil actions and under what conditions has been partially determined by a combination of state legislation and judicial decisions. Statutes in many states provide limited sovereign immunity to discretionary rather than ministerial decisions. The State of California has aggressively attempted to protect its police by enacting a statute which provides immunity from liability for civil damages for property damage, personal injury, or death resulting from a collision involving a pursued driver, if the law enforcement agency adopts and adheres to an appropriate written pursuit policy. California Vehicle Code, Chapter 105, § 17004.7 states, in part:

> A public agency employing peace officers which adopts a written policy on vehicular pursuits complying with subdivision (C) is immune from liability . . .
>
> (C) If the public entity has adopted a policy for the safe conduct of vehicular pursuits by peace officers, it shall meet all of the following minimum standards:
>
> (1) It provides that, if available, there be supervisory control of the pursuit.
>
> (2) It provides procedures for designating the primary pursuit vehicle and for determining the total number of vehicles to be permitted to participate at one time in the pursuit.
>
> (3) It provides procedures for coordinating operations with other jurisdictions.
>
> (4) It provides guidelines for determining when the interests of public safety and effective law enforcement justify a vehicular pursuit and when a vehicular pursuit should not be initiated or should be terminated.

If interpreted to protect the motoring public and the police, this statute represents a large step in the right direction. That is, to control the discretion and judgment of individual police officers and to provide immunity for the municipality when proper rules are established and followed. However, if interpreted as a license to continue an unreasonable or dangerous pursuit, without exposure, this legislation could encourage the police to raise the risks to the motoring public.

In most states, the decision to pursue is discretionary, but the actions employed during the pursuit may be ministerial. In other words, there may be general immunity for initiating a pursuit, but not for the manner of the pursuit (Comment, 1986). In *Rhodes v. Lamar* (1986), the court held that the decision to pursue was discretionary, and carried sovereign immunity, but liability was not precluded if the pursuit was conducted in a manner which violated a reasonable duty of care. Determining immunity during pursuits requires a careful analysis of state laws and relevant court decisions, and is far beyond the limited scope of this chapter (see Urbonya, 1989 and Silver, 1986).

Criminal Prosecutions

Fleeing from a police officer, or not stopping for an officer who has properly warned a motor vehicle operator, is a misdemeanor or felony in all states (see *State v. Malone*, [1986], in which eluding a police officer is made a class C felony). Additionally, charges stemming from injuries related to a pursuit, including the death of another, can be brought against the pursued or the police officer, if either acts maliciously with reckless disregard for the safety of others. While many offenders are prosecuted for their criminal actions, the penalties and punishments do not often reach the level of harm caused by the crime.

In many states and in Canada, there has been a drive to increase the penalties for eluding police (Solicitor General, 1985). More attention must be paid to criminal prosecutions of offenders who evade police officers. For example, a drunk driver, in some states, will lose nothing by not stopping for the officer who signals him or her to pull over. The penalties for drunk driving are comparatively severe so that fleeing a police officer or the violation of a similar law will add nothing to a drunk driving conviction, yet the risk and potential harm of a pursuit involving a drunk driver are extreme. The next section of this chapter will review the factors affecting the reasonableness of pursuit driving.

Factors Affecting Reasonableness and Liability

William Farber has accumulated an extensive list of factors which can affect the reasonableness and liability of pursuits and notes that (1986:93):

> There are a number of factors which are used in almost every police-chase case to determine whether the conduct of the police during the chase violated the duty of care applicable in the jurisdiction in question. These factors include evidence of excessive speed, the use of warning signals, such as the police siren or flashing lights, police disobedience of traffic signals, such as the running of red lights, and various combinations thereof with or without other evidence that may vary from case to case, including such considerations as driving conditions and the purpose of the pursuit.

Schofield (1988: 6) has assembled a similar list and suggests that the factors are "nothing more than common sense considerations of whether and how to pursue. Each pursuit situation is different and requires a particularized assessment."

The above discussion has demonstrated the importance of the factors which the courts rely upon to determine the reasonableness of behavior during pursuits. They are the ones which ultimately affect liability. Fortunately, social science research can determine the statistical importance of each of these factors in explaining the variance in the outcome of pursuits (see Chapter 6).

Perhaps the issue has best been summarized in a recent Florida District Court of Appeals ruling (*Brown v. City of Pinnellas Park*, 1990:475-476 citations omitted):

> This case involves two societal values which conflict: (1) that of encouraging motor vehicle pursuits of lawbreakers by law enforcement officers, thereby encouraging apprehensions of lawbreakers, and (2) that of discouraging injury or death to innocent bystanders resulting from motor vehicle pursuits of lawbreakers by law enforcement officers. Our decision to reverse in effect assigns to the value reflected in (2) more weight than to that in (1) under the alleged circumstances of this case. Our reversal therefore is to the effect that the protection of innocent bystanders from what may be considered under the alleged circumstances as being likely, or at least foreseeable and readily avoidable, injury or death outweighs the importance of the pursuit and possible apprehension of the lawbreaker in this case who had run a red light. This result is consistent with what has been called 'the modern tendency . . . against the rule of nonliabilty of governmental units for the acts of their policemen . . .'

The specific facts, figures and results from our empirical investigations are presented in subsequent chapters but the following discussion addresses those issues which have most interested the courts (Schofield, 1988 and Farber, 1986).

Purpose of Pursuit

Why a pursuit has been initiated is a significant factor in determining the risks that a police officer is justified in taking during a pursuit. The courts are asking whether the purpose of the pursuit warrants the risks involved. Conventional wisdom is that a pursuit for a traffic offense does not license an officer to involve the degree of risk which may be acceptable when chasing a violent felony suspect. Apparently the courts agree that the police should not pursue the traffic violator aggressively but can pursue at greater risk the suspected felon (*West v. United States*, 1985, *Baratier v. State*, 1983, *Mobell v. Denver*, 1983, *Tetro v. Town of Stratford*, 1983 and *Fiser v. City of Ann Arbor*, 1983).

One of the obvious indicators to help police determine the necessity for a pursuit is the fact that the suspect does not stop when signaled. If, after observing a minor traffic infraction, the officer signals the offender to pull over and the driver elects to flee, it is common for the police officer to believe or suspect that the driver or passenger is involved in more than a mere traffic violation. That is, the act of not stopping for an emergency vehicle triggers suspicion that the offender is involved in serious criminal conduct and must be prevented from escaping. Although this issue will be discussed as a policy consideration in Chapter 7, it warrants mention of a few applicable cases. A good rule to follow is that officers should limit their actions to what is known about the law violator rather than what is suspected or inferred. This limits the officers' general conduct and any corresponding risk created by the pursuit to the seriousness of what is known about the offense (Project, 1990:699-705 and *U.S. v. Trullo*, 1987). Several related cases may prove important as pursuit driving continues to be shaped, managed and controlled by the courts. For example, in *Ybarra v. Illinois* (1979:9-93) the Court noted that general suspicion with no direct link to a specific suspect will not justify an individual's detention. In *Reid v. Georgia* (1980:441), the Court ruled that an officer may not base reasonable suspicion merely on innocent activities. At this time, it is difficult to predict how these cases will impact pursuit, but there appears to be a trend that permits police to act only on what is known or on a strong basis of suspicion rather than on what they think might have occurred.

If a motorist has been identified by the police or is driving in a manner likely to place someone in a life-threatening situation, what level of risk can the police take? Knowing the purpose of the pursuit helps us interpret the importance of the other factors.

Driving Conditions

Driving conditions pertain to the type and condition of equipment, weather, road and traffic conditions, and the experience and abilities of the drivers. The performance characteristics of police cars have declined in recent years and their abilities must be considered when an officer becomes involved in a pursuit. Except for the Mustang or other high-performance vehicles, police cars are no match for the reborn "muscle cars," and would have no real chance of catching them. In a pursuit situation in which a car is pulling away from a police vehicle on a freeway, the police operator must consider and weigh the low probability of capture against the high-risk and potential costs of high-speed reckless driving. The equation must differ in pursuits which take place in residential areas or commercial districts and inner-cities or freeways (Alpert, 1987 and California Highway Patrol, 1983). Other environmental factors, including weather conditions and road congestion, may not only affect the maneuverability of the vehicles but also the ability to see or hear emergency equipment.

Use of Warning Signals

As we have noted, emergency vehicles are often granted special privileges on the roads. It is prudent to expect that the operators of these emergency vehicles will use all available methods to warn other motorists and pedestrians of their approach and to yield the right-of-way. Unfortunately, it is unreliable to assume that all drivers will pay attention to and obey flashing lights and sirens. First, many drivers do not pay sufficient attention and drive with windows closed, stereos blasting and air-conditioners set on high. Second, it is not predictable what a motorist will do upon hearing a siren.

It is also important to consider the message that these warning devices suggest to the pursued. As long as the police are chasing with activated emergency equipment, the pursued and the public can assume that the police believe the current risks do not outweigh the potential benefits of the chase. In other words, once a decision has been made that the risks of the pursuit outweigh the benefits, all emergency warning equipment must be deactivated to give the pursued the message that there is no longer a chase. Hopefully, the law violator will slow down and proceed more safely (see Note, 1981).

Excessive Speed

Farber (1986:93) warns us that "Excessive speed is one of the most important factors considered by the courts in determining whether or not a police officer was negligent while pursuing another motorist." Although most jurisdictions have implemented a version of the Uniform Vehicle Code and permit police vehicles to violate the rules of the road (such exemptions remove any prima facia inference of negligence for speeding and other violations), no rules exist which relieve the police officer from the duty of exercising due care.

Pursuits can involve low and high speeds. In the lower speed pursuits, police negligence may be based upon their failure to slow sufficiently when approaching an intersection or curve in the road. Also, highly dense roadways do not permit high speeds. In pursuits which involve higher speeds, other indicators of negligence including failure to use emergency warning lights, crowded roadways, likelihood of traffic, or the use of an unmarked patrol car are usually necessary in addition to high speeds to make that driving unreasonable and unnecessary.

Balancing the Factors Affecting Liability

The factors discussed above are viewed by the courts as the most important determinants of reasonableness and liability. In addition, disobeying traffic signals, such as the running of red lights, passing in a "no passing zone," and going the wrong way on a one way street are all dangerous and must be considered within the totality of the circumstances. Various combinations of these and other factors can theoretically increase or decrease the level of risk involved in a pursuit. One final consideration is noted by Schofield (1988:8), who concludes, "If it is reasonable to conclude that the fleeing motorist will not voluntarily stop and that there is no realistic way to stop him without recklessly endangering others, the pursuit should be terminated because the risks are greater than the government's interest in pursuing." Unfortunately, there is no magic formula to determine when the risk becomes greater than the potential benefit to the police. Further, some fleeing motorists voluntarily end their flight which increases the government's interest in pursuing.

One method commonly used to balance the liability factors and to judge the appropriateness of a pursuit is to compare the police pursuit training, policies, procedures and practices to the manner in which the chase is conducted, as a violation, per se, may constitute negligence. Training, when available, traditionally has focused on defensive driving tactics and skid-pad exercises. While this is necessary it is not sufficient. Accidents resulting from pursuit driving involve police vehicles infrequently. Once defensive driving skills are learned, officers who may become involved in pursuits must be trained in the likely consequences of chasing law violators and the factors related to negative outcomes. Failure to train officers in the consequences of their actions, including the increased risk to citizens created even when *the officers* drive safely, should be considered as deliberate indifference on the part of the government (see *City of Canton v. Harris*, 1989). Most departmental policies incorporate some mention of the importance of this risk and include some generic phrase warning officers not to engage in a pursuit which includes unnecessary risk or to terminate a pursuit when the risk becomes greater than the government's interest in the immediate apprehension of the suspect. Unfortunately, few specific rules are offered. In fact, the vague language used in most policies permits multiple interpretations (International Association of Chiefs of Police, 1989). Balancing the various factors and discussing foreseeability is a complex task which should rely upon empirical research for guidance, but too often is performed by the former police officer who acts as an expert witness (Alpert and Anderson, 1986, Fyfe, 1987b and Koonz and Regan, 1985).

The empirical research on police pursuits is expanding and improving quickly, as police departments (and one state, Minnesota) are conducting their own studies and requesting that outside researchers assess their records. In subsequent chapters, the prior research on the use of firearms and pursuit driving is reviewed. It is obvious that social scientists are developing a unique opportunity to evaluate empirical data to assist legal arguments and to take a leadership role in guiding law enforcement policies and training. Obviously, not all answers can be found in empirical studies on police pursuits. However, risk and benefit factors and ratios can be computed for specific factors or types of pursuits.

The remainder of the monograph will discuss in detail the findings and conclusions from empirical research, representing the first step which must be taken to assess risk factors. Research findings can analyze the results of pursuits and discriminate statistically between those factors which affect the negative outcomes of pursuits. Without the benefit of research, the courts are left to the opinions and testimony of the expert witnesses who are often former police officers relying solely upon personal experiences (see *Tomcsik v. United States*, 1989).

In an opinion which commented on the qualifications of experts to testify in a pursuit-related death case, the court in *Pincock v. Dupnik*, 1985:145) agreed with the common sense approach set forth by Schofield, and ruled:

> We believe that it is within the knowledge of the average juror that a high-
> speed chase poses more danger to both the participants and innocent
> bystanders when traffic is heavy, when weather conditions are poor, when
> it is night, when there is a great deal of pedestrian traffic, when the driver
> is unfamiliar with the area . . . We also believe that is within the knowledge
> and expertise of the jurors that engaging a bank robber in a high-speed pursuit
> may be more reasonable than chasing, at high speeds, a person who has failed
> to come to a complete stop at a stop sign. In short, we do not believe that
> the opinions of Drs. Territo and Kirkham as to whether or not Officer Baired
> acted reasonably would be of any assistance to the trier of fact since no special
> knowledge is required.

This is a bold decision which discounts the opinions of the expert witnesses. The court noted (*Pincock v. Dupnik*, 1985:14) that one of the witnesses "had been involved in over 100 cases that centered on questions of vehicle pursuit." If this witness were influenced by the factors which contributed to the negative outcomes of those 100 cases, his opinions would be biased, as it is safe to assume that he was not involved in many pursuit-related law suits which ended without accident, injury or death. In other words, this is a good example of sampling error, in which only pursuits with negative outcomes are used rather than a sample or population of pursuits in which some end negatively and some end without negative outcomes. Results from empirical research are far more persuasive than the opinions of experts who may be honest individuals offering opinions based upon experience, or who may be "charlatans, people with skeletons in their closets, and individuals, who for a fee, will swear to anything" (Fyfe, 1987:106). This is not to condemn all expert witnesses, but to warn of the inherent biases which can be brought by them into the courtroom (Ingraham, 1987) and to emphasize the important role empirical research can play in analyzing the testimony of an expert and balancing the factors which determine the appropriateness of a pursuit.

Summing Up

This chapter has discussed some of the legal issues concerning the use of deadly force and focused on firearms and pursuit driving. Many questions which are addressed by the courts can be answered by results from social science research. The reasonable use of firearms and pursuit is not easily determined, and there are no clear-cut answers for policy makers or the judiciary. As the courts have been called upon to distinguish among reasonable and unreasonable use of force, both physical and psychological, they have had to balance the importance of criminal apprehension with the potential dangers related to the use of all weapons. The remainder of the monograph will examine the available data and will make policy suggestions for law enforcement agencies.

Notes

[1] The majority of legal cases reported here are from the federal circuits. This emphasis is predicated on the notion that the precedents established in federal cases are more likely to become the bases of future decisions.

[2] Civil Rights Act of 1871, 42 U.S.C. § 1983.

[3] For the purposes of this discussion, a claim in state court will refer to a violation of state law and a claim in federal court will refer to a violation alleging a deprivation of constitutional rights.

[4] In state court actions, the cases alleging negligence continue to occur but have been impeded by limits placed on liability by passage of Tort Claims Acts which limits the liability of the governmental entity and its employees.

[5] Urbonya summarizes the issues succinctly (1989:114-115):

> When alleging that officers used excessive force during an arrest, plaintiffs have asserted violations of both the fourteenth amendment, which prohibits conduct that shocks the conscience, and the Fourth Amendment, which prohibits unreasonable conduct. Courts have agreed that officers who violate the fourteenth amendment may not assert the affirmative defense of qualified immunity, which shields officers from liability if their conduct was objectively reasonable. Courts have disagreed, however, as to whether officers who use unreasonable force during an arrest may properly assert the defense of qualified immunity. The disagreement has arisen because the Supreme Court has adopted two standards of reasonableness for fourth amendment claims. It has stated that conduct 'unreasonable' within the meaning of the Fourth Amendment may nevertheless be 'objectively reasonable' for the purposes of qualified immunity.

She argues that in a fourth amendment claim challenging excessive use of force, qualified immunity is an unnecessary defense because the standard for liability is identical to the standard for qualified immunity. Each questions whether a reasonable police officer would have believed that the force was necessary (Urbonya, 1989:67 and *Tennessee v. Garner*, 1985:11-12).

In *Graham*, the Court expressed no view concerning the proper application of qualified immunity in excessive force cases (1989):12, note 12).

[6] Civil Rights Act of 1871, 42 U.S.C. § 1983.

[7] U.S. Constitution, Amendment XIV, § 1. The Fourteenth Amendment prohibits state officials from depriving a person "of life [or] liberty without due process of law. The Fifth Amendment to the U.S. Constitution similarly prohibits federal officials.

[8] Prior to 1985 and the *Garner* decision, few courts would determine if force used by police violated the Fourth Amendment (see Urbonya, 1987).

[9] The Court has not resolved the question of how the Fourth Amendment protects individuals against the deliberate use of excessive force beyond an arrest and pretrial detention (*Graham v. Connor*, U.S., note 10 (1986). However, *Bell v. Wolfish*, 441 U.S. 520, 535-539 (1979) protects a detainee from the amount of excessive force that amounts to punishment and *Whitely v. Albers*, 475 U.S. 312, 327 (1986) protects the incarcerated under the Eighth Amendment where deliberate force is excessive and unjustified.

[10] 471 U.S. 1 (1985).

[11] Model Penal Code § 3.07(2)(b) (1962), cited in *Garner*, at 6-7, note 7.

[12] The Court in *Graham v. Connor*, U.S. (1989: 8, 10) reasoned:

> Today we make explicit what was implicit in *Garner's* analysis, and hold that *all* claims that law enforcement officers have used excessive force — deadly or not — in the course of an arrest, investigatory stop, or other 'seizure' of a free citizen should be analyzed under the Fourth Amendment and its reasonableness standard. As in other Fourth Amendment contexts, however, the 'reasonableness' inquiry in an excessive force case is an objective one: the questions whether the officers' actions are 'objectively reasonable' in light of the facts and circumstances confronting them, without regard to their underlying intent or motivation.

[13] The analysis of the split-second syndrome, backing up from the final frame and de-escalation of violence will be discussed thoroughly in Chapter 4. In *Gilmere v. City of Atlanta*, 774 F.2d 1495, 1502 (11th Cir. 1985), *cert. denied*, 476 U.S. 115 (1986), the court entered into the balancing act, "the scope of the particular intrusion, the manner in which it is conducted, the justification for initiating it, and the place in which it is conducted" quoting *Bell v. Wolfish*, 441 U.S. 520, 559 (1979).

[14] Judge Friendly's decision for the Second Circuit in *Johnson v. Glick*, 481 F.2d 1028, 1033 (2d Cir.), *cert. denied*, 414 U.S. 1033 (1973) articulated the following factors as essential in determining when conduct is egregious under substantive due process claims:

    1. the need for the application of force;

    2. the relationship between the need and the amount of force that was used;

    3. the extent of injury inflicted; and

    4. whether force was applied in a good faith effort to maintain or restore discipline or maliciously and sadistically for the very purpose of causing harm.

[15] Quoting from *United States v. Place*, 462 U.S. 696, 703 (1983).

[16] These Reports were compiled by Geoffrey Alpert and were used as a basis of his testimony in *State of Florida v. Officer William Lozano* (Case No. 89-2972). Miami City police officer William Lozano shot the driver of a motorcycle who was fleeing police in a high-speed pursuit. Officer Lozano stepped into the street and testified that the motorcycle was being driven towards him, that he was in fear of his life and shot to protect himself. Officer Lozano was convicted of manslaughter in December, 1989. This conviction was overturned on appeal.

[17] Justice O'Connor's dissent in *Garner* (1985:31) reads, in part, "Although it is unclear from the language of the opinion, I conclude that the majority intends to use the word 'use' to include only those circumstances in which the suspect is actually apprehended. Absent apprehension of the suspect, there is no seizure for Fourth Amendment purposes."

[18] The court's logic is found in *Wright v. District of Columbia*, 1990:8 (citations omitted):

The first step this court must take is to determine whether there has been a seizure in this case to which the Fourth Amendment applies. The Supreme Court has rejected the notion that *any* "investigatory pursuit" of a person undertaken by the police necessarily constitutes a seizure under the Fourth Amendment. The Court has likewise rejected the notion that the Fourth Amendment is *never* implicated during a chase, no matter how coercive the police conduct until an individual stops in response to the officer's show of authority. However, the Court has explicitly refused to decide the circumstances in which police pursuit would amount to a fourth amendment seizure. This court has, however, suggested that when the police operate the chasing vehicle in an aggressive manner to block a fleeing vehicle or to otherwise control its speed or direction, their actions might communicate to a reasonable person an attempt to capture or otherwise intrude upon the person's freedom of movement and thus be a seizure.

[19] In *Michigan v. Chesternut* (1988), the Court questioned whether or not a pursuit took place. The officer in question was not intending to stop the suspect, but rather follow the suspect to see where he was going. There was no evidence that anything occurred to communicate to the defendant that he was not at liberty to ignore the police presence and go about his business.

[20] The statistical information concerning pursuit driving will be presented in Chapter 6.

[21] The National Highway Traffic Safety Administration reports more than 47,000 deaths in more than 42,000 fatal accidents (1989:1).

[22] Ibid.

[23] The prior research on pursuit driving is scant but suggests factors which increase risk during pursuit. This research is reviewed in Chapters 6 and 7.

[24] Uniform Vehicle Code 11-106.

An Examination of
Research on Deadly
Force with Firearms

3

Discussing the progress in deadly force research, Fyfe (1988:166) notes, "20 years ago, those who had studied deadly force could have been driven to dinner in the back seat of a compact car." Since that time, however, a number of researchers have focused on the important topic of deadly force, and during the last two decades there has been a dramatic increase in our knowledge about this police power. A vast majority of the empirical studies on "deadly force" has focused on shootings, as opposed to other police actions, such as pursuit driving, which are also likely to cause death or serious bodily harm. This chapter will summarize the prior research in the area of police use of deadly force with firearms. The following chapter will chronicle how methodology in the study of this topic has improved and will describe the "state of the art" of research. It is important for the reader to keep in mind that the research reviewed in this chapter covers a span of time in which major changes occurred in the area of deadly force both in terms of law and technology. Some studies were conducted prior to *Tennessee v. Garner* (which, as covered in Chapter 2, ruled that laws allowing for the shooting of any fleeing felon were unconstitutional) and thus may refer to categories of shootings that presently violate that standard. Similarly, the increased sophistication of weaponry allows us to question whether the results of earlier studies regarding, for instance, the extent to which shots fired resulted in deaths, woundings, and misses, holds true in the 1990s.

The chapter begins with coverage of the frequency of police firearms use at present and in recent history, and coverage of the proportions of shootings which result in deaths, woundings, and misses. Subsequent sections address the situational, community, officer, and opponent characteristics associated with shooting events. Particular attention is paid to the research addressing the controversy surrounding the fact that blacks have been the victims of police shootings in numbers disproportionate to their representation in the population. This issue is critical to our discussion of the differential public response to police shootings and police pursuit driving.

Frequency, Trends, and Shooting Outcomes

Police authority to use deadly force against citizens represents one of the most dramatic, most ominous powers of government. Despite the importance of this police response, there are no reliable, national data regarding the frequency of its occurrence. There have been several calls for national data (e.g., Sherman and Langworthy, 1979; Sherman, et al., 1986; Fridell, 1989) including one from Blumberg (1985a:341) in which he noted: "It is difficult to believe that a society which keeps careful records on all types of less significant events would not be concerned enough to begin collecting accurate information on the number of citizens shot by law enforcement officers."

The Federal Bureau of Investigation (FBI) has requested data from individual law enforcement agencies on their use of deadly force for the Uniform Crime Report forms. The data received have not been published, however, "because of the FBI's reservations about the quality of those data" (Sherman and Langworthy, 1979:547). The concerns emanate in large part from the fact that these FBI data forms are supplementary and voluntary.

The Center for Health Statistics publishes *Vital Statistics* which provides data on police killings based on death certificates filed with state health departments by coroners or designated medical examiners. Unfortunately, this source of data is inadequate for providing valid information regarding deaths by police intervention. Sherman and Langworthy (1979) compared these figures with data generated by individual police departments and found 51 percent fewer shootings reported by *Vital Statistics* for the years they examined (1970-1976). The 1970-76 average yearly police killings of citizens was calculated at 735 per police-generated reports and 360 per *Vital Statistics*. Sherman and Langworthy (1979:560) pointed out that "while the police may have the most to gain by undercounting the number of citizens they kill it is the police that have provided the largest figures on the numbers of citizens killed."

Indeed, most research on police use of deadly force has relied on the superior quality data provided directly by individual law enforcement agencies. Not surprisingly, most researchers have studied large U.S. cities where a vast majority of deadly force incidents occur (New York State Commission on Criminal Justice and the Use of Force, 1987; cited hereafter as New York State Commission). Sherman, et al., (1986) presented information regarding police killings of citizens in "Big Cities" (U.S. cities with populations over 250,000) between 1970 and 1984. They used (unpublished) FBI/UCR data for the years 1970-1974, data collected from individual police departments (supplemented, as necessary by FBI data) by the International Association of Chiefs of Police (Matulia, 1982, 1985) for 1975-1979, and direct reports from police departments for 1980-1984. They reported a large decrease in shootings within the police departments studied between 1971 and 1984. Specifically, within those cities, police killed 353 citizens in 1971, compared to 172 in 1984. Acknowledging the questionable accuracy (specifically underreporting) of FBI/UCR data used for the years 1970-1974, they noted that (1986:20):

> there has been an even greater decline in the number of citizens killed by police in these cities than these flawed numbers suggest, since there were probably even more citizens killed in the 1970s than we report.

This decline was *not* accompanied by a decrease in either homicide rates or violent crime rates during this period, but there was a 65 percent reduction (from 38 to 13) in the number of police officers killed in the line of duty in these 50 cities (excluding auto accidents) during this period.

The authors also provided some interesting figures in their report which reflect two important points regarding the frequency of police use of deadly force: first, that there are vast differences across cities in the rates of police killings of citizens; second, that even in the cities with high rates, most officers will never kill a citizen. Specifically, Sherman, et al., reported (1986:I):

> Police in all cities kill rarely, but at widely varying rates. The average Jacksonville police officer would have to work 139 years before killing anyone. In New York City, the wait would be 694 years. It would be 1,299 in Milwaukee and 7,692 years in Honolulu, all based on 1980-84 rates of killing.

Relative to the city-to-city variation in rates of police killings of citizens is the variation in actual "police use of deadly force" by firearms, which, as noted above, refers to force readily capable of causing or likely to cause death or serious bodily harm. "Deadly force" by firearms, then, encompasses *deaths* as a result of police shootings by firearms as well as shots fired by police which result in *woundings* and *misses*. In fact, several authors have criticized research which purports to examine "deadly force" but focuses merely on police-caused homicides. (This criticism is discussed more thoroughly in the next chapter on research trends.)

Researchers have reported information from cities studied regarding the percentage of shots fired which hit a citizen and then the percentage of those hits resulting in deaths versus woundings. Geller and Karales (1981) reported that 18 percent of the shots fired in Chicago during the period 1974-1978 hit a citizen; of those hit, 25 percent were killed. Fyfe (1978) reported a higher percentage of hits (31 percent) in New York City, as well as a higher percentage (33 percent) of hits resulting in death. Horvath (1987) collected statewide data from Michigan and reported that 32 percent of the shots fired hit a citizen and 35 percent of those incidents resulted in a fatality. (This latter figure excludes incidents involving multiple opponents with both kill and wound outcomes.)

Blumberg (1983) compared hits and harmless discharges within two cities: Kansas City, Missouri and Atlanta, Georgia to determine whether these two categories of shootings differed across various factors. He found no differences between hits and harmless discharges with regard to the time of day of the incident, the event which precipitated the shooting (e.g., robbery, burglary), whether police mobilization was proactive or reactive, and whether the officer or opponent fired first. Blumberg also compared incidents involving hits and incidents involving misses in terms of whether the incident took place indoors or outdoors. In Kansas City, he found that a significantly greater proportion of incidents which resulted in hits, compared to harmless discharges, took place indoors. (In Atlanta, as well, a greater proportion of incidents resulting in hits took place indoors, but the difference between the two groups was not statistically significant.) Blumberg hypothesized that this relationship might be due to the shorter distance between officer and opponent indoors and confirmed this relationship with data from New York City. Not surprisingly, Blumberg also found that significantly more shots were fired in hit incidents (4.1 per hit) than miss incidents (2.2 per miss). Similarly, hit incidents were more likely to involve more than one officer shooter.

This information is helpful in outlining the possible explanations for why cities vary in terms of the percent of discharges which result in hits. An intuitive explanation would be that cities with a relatively large proportion of shots hitting the targets have more skillful officers, perhaps as a result of superior marksmanship training. But, as Blumberg's results indicate, other factors may be at work. Some cities may have more indoor encounters or perhaps more two-person patrol cars which result in a greater number of officers on the scene of a potentially violent encounter.

Restrictiveness of policy is also a factor relevant to city-to-city variations in percentage of discharges which result in hits. For instance, a department which (prior to *Garner*) had a policy which allowed for the shooting of any fleeing felon would likely have a larger percentage of missed shots or non-fatal hits than a department with a strict defense of life policy, due to the nature of the shootings in which persons within each of the departments would become involved. As Fyfe (1988:188) noted, "It is far easier to hit someone who is standing eight or ten feet away with a shotgun in his hands than someone who is running away in the dark."

It is important to note that reporting differences are a probable factor in the variation, as well. More departments are collecting detailed information regarding officer firearms discharges. This usually takes the form of a mandatory report following each incident. However, there may be variation in officer compliance even within cities with similar reporting rules. Blumberg referred to this in his discussion of possible explanations for the finding that 58 percent of the shots in Atlanta compared to 40 percent of the shots in Kansas City, resulted in hits. He wrote in 1983 (169-170):

> It is conceivable that the above disparity may result from officer reporting
> differences between the two departments. The possibility that Atlanta officers

are less likely than Kansas City officers to report a "harmless discharge" to their superiors cannot be ruled out. Intuitively, one would think that the opposite would be true. Because Kansas City includes many miles of incorporated rural territory north of the river, the opportunity for a firearms discharge to go unnoticed would seem to be greater. However, this may be offset by other factors. Kansas City officers have been required to make full reports on *all* discharges since the early 1970s. This has only been the case in Atlanta since 1976. Thus, Kansas City appears to have more of a tradition with regard to the reporting and recording of "harmless discharges." Whether this accounts for the disparity between the cities or not is something about which we can only speculate.

Jurisdictions may also vary with regard to how "discharge" is officially defined for report purposes. The data for some cities, but not others, might include shots to summon help, shots to disable autos, shots to kill wounded animals, suicide attempts, shooting lights out (e.g., by swat teams), and so forth.

The information regarding death, wounding, and miss outcomes above can be used to extrapolate from the data provided by Sherman, et al., (1986) on justifiable homicides by police to estimate the number of shots fired in the 50 largest U.S. cities in 1984, as well as the number of hits and misses. Based on the previous research in various cities it is not unreasonable to estimate, as Binder and Fridell (1984) did, that approximately 48 percent of all police shooting incidents result in hits (that is, where civilians are struck by gunfire) and 52 percent ended in misses. Further, they estimated that of the shooting incidents that result in suspect hits 30 percent of the opponents are killed and 70 percent wounded. Applying these figures to the number of justifiable homicides for the 50 largest U.S. cities reported by Sherman, et al., (1986) for 1984 leads one to conclude that there were approximately 1,229 deadly force incidents resulting in 418 woundings and the 172 deaths, as seen in Table 3.1.

Situational Characteristics of Shooting Incidents

Research on police use of deadly force by firearms has greatly improved since the early 1960s when Robin's (1963) study of justifiable homicides by police in Philadelphia between 1950 and 1960 received national attention. More recent research has gone beyond mere descriptions of the extent and trends of the phenomenon to analyze the characteristics of the encounters between citizens and law enforcement officers which result in the police use of deadly force (and, more recently, the characteristics of potentially violent encounters which do not result in police use of deadly force).

After reviewing the studies on the subject (which are discussed below), Geller (1984:204) reported that:

the most common type of incident in which police and civilians shoot one another in urban America involves an on-duty, uniformed, white, male officer and an armed, black, male civilian between the ages of 17 and 30 and occurs at night, in a "public" location within a "high-crime" precinct, in connection with a suspected armed robbery or a "man with gun" call.

Precipitating Events

One aspect of police shootings which has received attention by researchers is the event which precipitated the shooting. Fyfe (1978) looked at this characteristic in his comprehensive study of firearms discharges by the New York City Police Department for the period 1971-1975. He found that 37 percent of the shootings by police at citizens occurred in conjunction with robberies. The next largest categories were traffic pursuits/car stops and "investigating suspicious persons" (both at 12 percent), and the fourth was response to disturbances (11 percent). Related to Fyfe's findings regarding traffic pursuits, is Alpert's (1987b) finding that a full 20 percent of discharge incidents by the Miami Police Department between 1980 and 1986 were in conjunction with vehicle chases. The most frequent precipitating events reported by Geller and Karales (1981) were robbery (24 percent), use of a gun (21 percent), and burglary (14 percent). Blumberg (1982), compiling information on shots fired in eight cities, found robbery (23 percent); possession of, threat with, or use of a deadly weapon (22 percent); and burglary (17 percent) to be the most common precipitating events of deadly force encounters. The study of deadly force in the Metro-Dade, Florida Police

Table 3.1

Shooting Incidents: Deaths, Woundings, and Misses

	Percentage Estimates*	Shooting Incidents in the 50 Largest U.S. Cities in 1984: Extrapolations**
Shooting Incidents: Hits and Misses		
Hits	48%	590
Misses	52%	639
Hits: Deaths and Woundings		
Deaths	30%	172
Woundings	70%	418
Deaths, Woundings, and Misses		
Deaths	14%	172
Woundings	34%	418
Misses	52%	639

*Based on a review of the literature (Binder and Fridell, 1984)
**Applies the percentage estimates for deaths, woundings, and misses by Binder and Fridell (1984) to the 172 justifiable homicides by police reported by Sherman, et al., (1986).

Department (Alpert, 1989c) incorporated both purposeful and accidental shootings and did not restrict the data to shootings at persons, as did most other studies. Alpert reports that 28.9 percent of the shots fired by police were "animal related" and 26.4 percent of the shots were accidental. The next most frequently occurring shooting circumstances were felony stops (11.5 percent), felony in progress calls (10.6 percent), and traffic stops (8.1 percent).

The findings above that traffic stops and responses to disturbances (e.g., domestic disturbances) comprise 12 percent and 11 percent of precipitating events for shootings in New York City, respectively (Fyfe, 1978), lead to claims (though certainly not by Fyfe) that these types of calls are particularly dangerous for police (as discussed in Margarita, 1980). Scharf and Binder (1983) pointed out, however, that percentages such as those provided above can be misleading because information regarding the frequency of each type of call is not considered. They noted (pp. 66-67):

> Simply knowing the relative proportion of incidents that result in a fatality or a wounding by a police officer will not be very helpful. Knowing the proportion of hits or fatalities associated with a particular incident tells us little about the relative hazard of such incidents. For example, knowing that 25 percent of all New York City shots fired evolved from "disturbance" calls . . . does not yield any useful information about the relative danger of such calls. Such information is similar in kind to knowing that in a certain city, 25 percent of all deaths were related to influenza, whereas only 1 percent were related to the always fatal myasthenia gravis (or Lou Gehrig's disease). From such information one might, wrongly, conclude that influenza was more hazardous than is myasthenia gravis. In reality, myasthenia gravis is infinitely more hazardous; however, it is also far rarer. The lower proportion of deaths from myasthenia gravis is attributable to its rareness, not its benignity; similarly, influenza causes many deaths because it is an extremely common, if only occasionally fatal, disease.

Similarly, the large number of shootings during traffic stops and domestic disturbances is due primarily to the overall frequency of those types of calls (see e.g., Webster, 1970). Robbery calls are less frequent, but more dangerous.

Another way to classify precipitating circumstances is to determine the "potential lethality" of the opponent immediately preceding the firing of the officer's gun by examining the weapon of the opponent, or more appropriately, the behavior of the opponent in conjunction with whether or not he is armed. For, as Blumberg (1985b:2) pointed out, "In many cases, deadly force is required not because of the original character of the situation that prompted the police intervention (e.g., personal dispute between two citizens), but because of the response of the parties to this intervention (e.g., pointing a pistol at the officer)." Focusing on opponent weapon, Meyer (1980) reported that one-fourth of the shooting opponents in Los Angeles were found to be unarmed, 51 percent had guns, and the remaining 24 percent had some other type of weapon (e.g., knife, blunt instrument, or auto). Donahue (1983) found that 60 percent of the shooting opponents in a "large midwestern city" were armed. Of these, 50 percent had handguns, 20 percent had long guns, and 15 percent had knives. Thirteen percent of the opponents used a vehicle as a weapon. Alpert (1987c, 1989c) reported that 15 percent and 28 percent of the shooting opponents of officers in the Dallas and Metro-Dade police departments, respectively, used a vehicle as a weapon.

Fyfe (1988:186) developed the following typology to categorize police shootings in terms of both opponent weapon and behavior:

Gun assault: Citizen(s) armed with gun uses or attempts to use it against police.

Knife or other assault: Citizen(s) armed with cutting instrument or other weapon (e.g., bat, chain, club, hammer, vehicle) uses or attempts to use it against police.

Physical assault: Citizen(s) attacks or attempts to attack police with fists, feet, or other purely physical means.

Unarmed, no assault: Unarmed citizen(s) makes no threat and attempts no attack on police or on any other person.

Table 3.2 provides Fyfe's application of this typology to shootings in New York City during 1971-1975, Philadelphia during 1971-1975, and Chicago during 1974-1978. He noted significant differences in the percentages of shooting incidents within the types of circumstances across cities. Approximately 80 percent of the shootings in New York City and Chicago were precipitated by an attack on the officer with a gun or other weapon. In contrast, only 58.6 percent of Philadelphia's shootings fell into these more lethal categories. Instead, a full 41.4 percent of the shooting incidents in Philadelphia occurred as a result of a

Table 3.2
Shooting Incident Types in New York City, Philadelphia, and Chicago*

	City		
Shooting Type	New York 1971-1975	Philadelphia 1971-1975	Chicago 1974-1978
Gun Assault	53.0%	39.0%	62.1%
Knife/Other Assault	34.0%	19.6%	15.3%
Physical Assault	4.5%	16.5%	1.7%
Unarmed, No Assault	8.5%	24.9%	20.9%
Totals	100.0%	100.0%	100.0%

*From Fyfe (1988), p. 187.

"physical assault" (as defined above) or involved an unarmed citizen who was not attacking the police officer or any other person. Fyfe attributed these differences, in part, to the different policies in place in the cities during the period studied. Similarly, Blumberg (1985b) reported variations across cities in the potential lethality of opponent actions and concluded (p. 3), "clearly, the impact of policy on the type of police shootings that occur in a particular city is substantial."

Officer Status and Assignment

Other situational aspects of police shootings include whether the officer is on-duty or off-duty at the time of the incident and, if on-duty, the nature of the officer's assignment. A 1981 survey of cities with populations over 50,000 found one-fourth of these police departments required officers to carry guns while off-duty (Police Executive Research Forum and the Police Foundation, 1981). Departmental policy regarding whether off-duty guns are required or permitted could account, in part, for the wide variation in off-duty shootings rates across cities. Binder, Scharf and Galvin (1982) found that 28 percent of the shootings of citizens by police in Newark, New Jersey occurred while the officers were off-duty, compared to 11, 10, and 8 percent, respectively in Oakland, Birmingham, and Miami. Blumberg (1983) also found a wide variation in off-duty shooting percentages in eight cities studied, ranging from zero in Portland (where only 10 shooting incidents occurred during the period of study) to 23 in Detroit.

Fyfe (1978, 1980a) found that off-duty shootings were more likely to violate policy or law. Consistent with this is a report by Hart (1979, described in Fyfe, 1988) submitted to the Detroit Board of Police Commissioners regarding the use of firearms by officers during a four and one-half year period in the late 1970s. Twenty of the 92 incidents (22 percent) involved off-duty officers; and only four of these off-duty incidents involved shooting felons engaged in or fleeing from their crimes. The largest number of victims of these officers were spouses, ex-spouses, or girlfriends, followed by opponents in street and barroom "altercations." One officer shot his kids and several committed suicide. Further indication that off duty shootings can be problematic is Alpert's (1987b) finding that 21 percent of the 69 accidental discharges in Miami between 1980 and 1986 were by off-duty officers. It is possible that some of these reportedly "accidental discharges" were, in fact, unjustified intentional shootings which officers were trying to cover up.

Most police shootings of citizens are by on-duty officers, and the majority of these shootings are by officers assigned to patrol. For instance, 81 percent of the shootings in New York City (Fyfe, 1978), 53 percent of the shootings in Chicago (Geller and Karales, 1981), and 68 percent of the shootings in Kansas City (Blumberg, 1983) were by patrol officers. This frequency is explained by the relatively large numbers of officers on patrol. Indeed, the *rate* of shootings for patrol officers (per officer) was exceeded by the narcotics/anticrime unit in New York City (Fyfe, 1978); by the Special Operations, tactical, and robbery units in Chicago (Geller and Karales, 1981); and by tactical and vice units in Kansas City (Blumberg, 1983).

Location of Shootings

The location of shootings, for instance, whether they occur in residences, commercial establishments, on the street, or elsewhere, is also of interest to researchers. The New York State Commission on Criminal Justice and the Use of Force (New York State Commission, 1987) gathered statewide information regarding all of the citizen deaths resulting from police use of deadly force. Table 3.3 provides information regarding the locations of those fatal shooting incidents. Almost one-half (46 percent) of the incidents took place on a roadway (street, highway, or alley). A relatively large percentage took place in or around residences; that is within or around a multifamily dwelling (18 percent), or within or around a single family dwelling (9 percent). Because the New York State data provide information only on those police shooting incidents which resulted in a fatality, one must of course be careful not to assume that they are representative of all deadly force encounters. Indeed, as noted above, Blumberg (1983) found that a greater proportion of incidents where a subject was hit occurred indoors, apparently due to the shorter distance between officer and opponent.

Binder, et al. (1982) looked not only at fatal shootings or encounters between citizens and police where police resorted to their firearms but at both shooting incidents and potentially violent encounters where the police officers could have resorted to deadly force, but did not. In contrast to the New York State Commission, they found that over 80 percent (81.3 percent) of these encounters took place outdoors. Of the encounters that occurred inside, about one-third (36.6 percent) took place in apartments, about one-fifth (19.5 percent) in houses, and 16 percent took place in retail stores.

Community Characteristics

At a higher level of analysis for assessing the "location" of police shootings, researchers have focused on neighborhood and/or community characteristics. For instance, the particular area of a city an officer is assigned to can affect the likelihood of involvement in a shooting incident. Fyfe (1978; 1980b) compared various zones (groups of three to five neighboring precincts) in New York City and found significantly different rates of police use of deadly force which, not surprisingly, correlated with the levels of violence within those areas. Specifically, he found a strong relationship between arrest rates for violent crime and police shootings, and between reported murders and non-negligent manslaughters and police shootings.

Similar findings are reported by Kania and Mackey (1977) who tested the relationship between violent crime and police killings of citizens for larger

Table 3.3

Locations Where Fatal Shootings Occurred
New York State 1981-1985*

Location Number	Number	%
Street, Highway, Alley	103	46
Residence—Multifamily Dwelling	23	10
Lobbies, Stairwells, Elevators, etc.—Multifamily Dwelling	17	8
Public Transit Property (bus, subway train or platform)	16	7
Eating and Drinking Establishment	15	7
Property Surrounding Residence (front or back yard)	14	6
Other Outdoor Locations	9	4
Parking Areas	7	3
Single Family Dwelling	6	3
Retail Establishments	3	1
Other Public Buildings	3	1
Other Structures (e.g., Factory, Warehouse etc.)	2	1
Parks and School Yards	2	1
Police Facility	2	1
Other Residential	1	**
Total	223	100%***

*From the New York State Commission on Criminal Justice and the Use of Force, Volume I, 1987.
**Less than 1 percent.
***May not total 100 percent due to rounding.

geographic units: states. They found strong correlations between justifiable homicides by police and both public homicide rate and police exposure to violent crime.

Both Fyfe (1980b) and Kania and Mackey (1977) attribute the relationship between violent crime and police shootings to perceived danger on the part of police. That is, they believe the high rate of violence in a particular geographic area leads police to perceive the environment as dangerous and thus makes them more inclined to use deadly force. In adopting this explanation, these researchers reject two alternative hypotheses to explain the relationship between violent crime and police shootings. One of these, the brutalization hypothesis, suggests that police shootings lead to increased community violence because ". . . the population, when assaulted by the state, will be less restrained in using violence against each other" (Langworthy, 1986:378-379).

A second alternative hypotheses was supported by secondary analyses of Fyfe's New York data by Langworthy (1986). This research used time series analysis to examine the temporal relationship between criminal homicide and police use of deadly force. The finding of no temporal relationship between the two variables led Langworthy to conclude that there is no direct cause and effect relationship between police shootings and criminal homicide. Rather, a third unknown variable (or set of variables) affects the rates of both.

Some of the more recent studies have downplayed the strength of the relationship between community violence and deadly force. Sherman, et al. (1986), for instance, found that great variations in rates of justifiable homicide among large U.S. cities remain after public homicide rate is controlled for. Similarly, Fyfe (1988) found that public homicide rates account for only 13 percent of the variation in police homicide rates.

Officer Characteristics

In addition to providing data on the immediate situational characteristics (e.g., precipitating events and officer assignments) and the broader community characteristics (e.g., level of violence), studies on this topic have generated information on the individuals (both officers and opponents) involved in shooting incidents. Several researchers have sought to determine whether or not there are individual characteristics which differentiate officers who shoot and officers who don't shoot. Blumberg (1983) compared 235 officers in Kansas City, Missouri, who shot at citizens between 1972 and 1978 and an equal number of randomly selected officers who had not been involved in shooting incidents. He tested the differences between these officer groups across various demographic characteristics and job performance indicators, while controlling for exposure to violence by assignments. Variables which did not differentiate between the two groups included: race, height, prior military experience, marital status at hiring, socioeconomic status, firearms experience prior to hiring, and pre-service arrests (that is, the prior criminal record of the officer). However, Blumberg found shooters were significantly younger, and relatedly, had fewer years of service as police officers, than non-shooters. Aadland (1981), too, found an inverse relationship between shooting and both age and law enforcement experience.

Blumberg was not able to test adequately the difference between males and females on shooting behavior because of the small number of females in the sample. The limited analysis he was able to conduct, however, indicated that female officers were less likely than male officers to become involved in deadly force incidents.

Blumberg used a reduced sample to assess the relationship between job performance indicators and shooting behavior. There were no significant differences between "shoot" and "non-shoot" officers with regard to the number of citizen complaints, days lost due to departmental suspension, and three measures of aggressiveness (on-duty vehicular accidents, arrest activity, and injuries).

Binder, et al., (1982) also found no differences between shooters and non-shooters with regard to overall aggressiveness, except that they found non-shooters had significantly more arrest activity. (In contrast, Blumberg hypothesized non-shooters would have less arrest activity and found no difference.) Further, the findings of Binder, et al., indicate non-shooters are superior to their shooter counterparts in that they have more education, experience, and citizen and departmental commendations; fewer disciplinary findings; and higher marksmanship scores.

Officer Race

Geller and Karales (1981) and Fyfe (1981a) looked at the rates of shootings across officers of different races, and reported that black officers have the highest rate. Geller and Karales attributed this finding to an overrepresentation of black officers in off-duty shootings due to their residences being located in higher-crime areas. Fyfe (1978, 1981a) looked at on-duty assignment in an attempt to explain the higher shooting rates of on-duty minority officers and found (1978:188): "the disproportionate assignment of Black and Hispanic officers to high crime areas is . . . the major reason for their disproportionate involvement in on-duty shootings." This is consistent with Blumberg's (1983) finding, reported above, that showed no significant difference in shooting behavior of white and black officers when exposure to violence is controlled.

Opponent Race and Police Shootings

Most of the research on the racial aspects of police shootings has focused, not on the officer's race, but on the opponent's race. And, indeed, it is clear that blacks are disproportionately the opponents in police shootings relative to their representation in the population. As seen in Table 3.4, Kobler (1975) reported national statistics for the years of 1952-1969 showing that blacks accounted for almost 50 percent of all homicides resulting from police shootings while they represented only 12 to 14 percent of the nation's population. Similarly, Milton, Halleck, Lardner, and Abrecht (1977) found that blacks, representing 39 percent of the population in seven U.S. cities, were the victims of police shootings in 79 percent of the incidents. More recently, black population representation compared to shooting victimization in percentages were 20 and 60 in New York City (Fyfe, 1978; 1981b), 18 and 55 in Los Angeles (Meyer, 1980), 56 and 79 in Birmingham, 25 and 51 in Miami, 58 and 78 in Newark, and 47 and 79 in Oakland (Binder, et al., 1982).

Table 3.4

**Police Use of Deadly Force Against Blacks
Compared with Black Representation in the Population**

	Percent Black Victims* of PUDF	Percent Blacks in Population
Kobler (1975)	50	12-14
Milton, et al. (1977)	79	39
Fyfe (1978, 1981b)	60	20
Meyer (1980)	55	18
Binder, et al. (1982)		
Birmingham	79	56
Miami	51	25
Newark	78	58
Oakland	79	47

* Studies vary with regard to whether "police use of deadly force" encompasses deaths, hits, or shots fires

Conflicting explanations are offered to account for these data. The major debate centers on whether the disproportionate number of black shootings is due to selective law enforcement based on racial bias or on the higher degree of black criminality. That is, are police using proportionately more deadly force against blacks than whites as a result of racial prejudice (e.g., in the form of overt racism or the more subtle exaggerated fears based on bias), or are officers involved in proportionately more dangerous situations involving black opponents as a result of the disproportionately higher involvement of blacks in violent crime?

The study by Milton, et al. (1977) examined deadly force victimization rates and arrest rates for the two ethnic groups for seven cities to determine whether black involvement as opponents in shooting incidents corresponded to their involvement in violent crime. The data revealed that blacks, involved in 79 percent of the shooting incidents, accounted for 73 percent of the arrests for Index Crimes (murder, robbery, forcible rape, aggravated assault, burglary, larceny and auto theft). (See Table 3.5.) Other investigators had similar findings: Harding and Fahey (1973) found that blacks, representing 75 percent of the police deadly force victimizations, account for 73 percent of the violent or potentially violent crime arrests. Burnham (1973) discovered that arrest figures for violent felonies showed that 62 percent of the suspects were black, with members of this racial group accounting for 59 percent of the deadly force victimizations. Fyfe (1978) and Meyer (1980) reported that 60 percent and 55 percent of the deadly force incidents in New York City and Los Angeles, respectively, involved black opponents, with corresponding black arrest percentages of 62 and 46. The New York State Commission (1987) reported that blacks comprised only 39 percent of the fatal shooting incidents, though they comprised 56 percent of the arrestees for violent Part I crimes.

Table 3.5

Police Use of Deadly Force Against Blacks
Compared with Black Arrests

	Percent Black Victims* of PUDF	Percent Black Arrests
Harding and Fahey (1973)	75	73 (Violent Crimes)
Burnham (1973)	59	62 (Violent Felonies)
Milton, et al. (1977)	79	73 (Index Crimes)
Meyer (1980)	55	46 (Index Crimes)
Fyfe (1978, 1981b)	60	62 (Felonies)
NY State Commission (1987)	39	56 (Violent Part 1)

*Studies vary with regard to whether "police use of deadly force" encompases deaths, hits, or shots fired.

Goldkamp (1976:177) posed the critical follow-up question to these findings: are the disproportionate arrest rates of blacks relative to their representation in the population "manufactured by some mechanism of control which is differentially directed at minorities, or are they reasonable reflections of disproportionate participation by minorities in crimes of violence?" That is, he pointed out that showing a correspondence between black involvement as opponents in deadly force incidents and arrests of blacks for violent crime is not convincing evidence of a lack of bias in police shootings. For indeed, there are those who argue that the arrest data may be indicative of differential arrest activity by police based on racial bias (Forsland, 1972; Sutherland and Cressey, 1970). In essence, they assert that the arrest statistics are not valid reflections of the criminal activity of blacks, maintaining, perhaps that the "police have one trigger finger for blacks and another for whites" (see Takagi, 1974:32 and also Hinds, 1979).

On the one hand, proponents of the argument that the disproportionate arrest rates of blacks are the result of racial prejudice point to research examining arrests controlling for seriousness of offense and prior records that indicates that police are more inclined to arrest a black or minority youth (Ferdinand and Luchterhand, 1979; Goldman, 1963; Thornberry, 1973). Additionally, they cite research showing that police officers use preconceived stereotypes (e.g., race) as the bases for their responses to citizens (Piliavin and Briar, 1964; Pope, 1979). On the other hand, there are those who argue that arrest data adequately reflect differential rates of violent criminal behavior, and thus it is reasonable to conclude that the rates of police shootings at the various racial groups reflect differences in exposure of the police to danger posed by the racial groups (e.g., Blumberg, 1981; Fyfe, 1981b; Geller and Karales, 1981). In support of this latter argument, Fyfe (1978) reported that a greater proportion of black than white opponents in the New York City shooting incidents he studied were armed. Sixty-one percent of the black opponents in deadly force incidents carried firearms compared to 36 percent of the whites.

Others have used a similar model to assess whether bias or exposure of police to danger accounts for the large proportion of blacks among opponents of deadly force. The methodology involves analyzing characteristics of shooting incidents to determine whether blacks are shot under circumstances involving less danger to the police or others than whites. As Blumberg (1986:237) notes: "The assumption underlining this approach is that if race discrimination is present, we should find that blacks are shot and/or killed under circumstances that present less justification."

Meyer (1980) used this methodology to examine the use of deadly force in Los Angeles over a four year period. The shooting incidents in Los Angeles which occurred between January 1974 and December 1978 were examined to assess the differences among incidents involving black, Hispanic, and Anglo (non-Hispanic white) suspects with regard to the circumstances surrounding the incidents. Meyer found that the circumstances surrounding the black shootings differed from those of Hispanic and Anglo incidents. On examining the suspects' actions prior to the shootings, he found (as shown in Table 3.6) a significantly larger percentage of black shootings (15%) than Hispanic (9%) or Anglo (9%) were preceded by the suspect disobeying the officers' orders to halt. He also found that a larger percentage of black shootings (12%) than Hispanic shootings (6%) or Anglo shootings (9%) followed suspects appearing to reach for weapons. In contrast, the Anglo and Hispanic shootings were more likely to involve the more clearly dangerous situations where the suspect threatens to use, or actually uses, a weapon. Moreover, 28 percent of the black suspects were ultimately found to be unarmed, compared to the figures of 22 percent for Hispanics and 20 percent for Anglos.

Table 3.6

Comparison of the Situational Aspects of Deadly Force Encounters with Black, White, and Hispanic Opponents (Meyer, 1980)

	Percent of Black Opponents	Percent of White Opponents	Percent of Hispanic Opponents
Using Weapon	22	28	23
Threatening Use of Weapon	39	43	45
Displaying Weapon	5	5	6
Assaulting Officer or Civilian	5	6	9
Appearing to Reach for Weapon	12	9	6
Disobeying Command to Halt	15	9	9
Other Precipitating Action	1	1	3
	99	101	101

Research using this methodology, comparing the situational characteristics of police shootings involving black and white opponents, has been conducted by Blumberg (1981) in Atlanta and Kansas City, by Geller and Karales (1981) in Chicago, by Fyfe in New York City (1981b) and Memphis (1982), and by Binder, et al., (1982) in Birmingham, Newark, Miami, and Oakland.

Fyfe (1982) made the point that research on an individual city looking at police shooting behavior in relationship to opponent race is not necessarily generalizable to other cities due to "the wide range of restrictiveness of police shooting policies and other internal organizational variables across jurisdictions" (p. 710). He classified deadly force incidents according to the rationale for the shooting (e.g., defend life, apprehend fleeing suspect) to compare the shootings in Memphis during 1969 to 1974 and New York City during 1971 to 1975. He found that Memphis had a much higher annual shooting rate per 1,000 officers (33.5 versus 19.6) and, relatedly, that Memphis had a large number of shootings involving fleeing property crime suspects, instead of, for instance, shootings due to defense of life situations. Fyfe went further to explore, as best he could with limited data, the race of the opponents in the shootings involving persons fleeing from property crime. He reported that proportionately more black than white property crime suspects were shot. Similarly, he reported that the rate of police shootings at "unarmed and nonassaultive" blacks was 18 times higher than the corresponding rate for whites. These data, Fyfe noted (1982:72), "strongly support the assertion that police (in Memphis) did differentiate racially with their trigger fingers, by shooting blacks in circumstances less threatening than those in which they shot whites." In contrast, Fyfe did not find evidence of racial bias associated with shootings in New York, nor did Blumberg find such evidence in either Kansas City or Atlanta. Similarly, research described in the next chapter (Fridell and Binder, 1989) found no evidence of racial bias associated with police shootings in Miami, Birmingham, Oakland, and Newark.

Other Characteristics of Opponents

Other personal characteristics of opponents about which information has been collected include gender, age, and criminal history. Female opponents in police use of deadly force incidents are fairly rare. Ninety-eight percent of the victims of fatal encounters in the seven cities studied by the Police Foundation were males (Milton, et al., 1977). In New York City (Fyfe, 1978), New York State (New York State Commission, 1987), Chicago (Geller and Karales, 1981), Atlanta, Detroit, Kansas City, and Washington, D.C. (see Blumberg, 1983) over 96 percent of the opponents were male.

Generally, the opponents are between the ages of 18 and 30. The average age of opponents killed by police firearms in New York State was 30 with 45 percent between the ages of 20 and 29, and 27 percent between ages 30 and 39. Fyfe (1978) reported that 70 percent of the opponents in New York City were between the ages of 17 and 30, and 89 percent of the opponents across eight cities were between 18 and 39 (Blumberg, 1983).

Both Blumberg (1983) and the New York State Commission (1987) collected information on shooting opponents' criminal histories. Blumberg, however, had a large amount of missing data for his combined Atlanta and Kansas City opponent sample and presented his data with doubts about its validity. The New York State data showed that 84 percent of the persons killed by police gunfire had "some prior arrest history" (p. 180). Of those with arrest histories, 70 percent had one to five prior arrests, 18 percent had six to ten, and 12 percent had 11 or more.

Conclusion

It is clear that the back seat of a compact car would no longer be sufficient to transport those who conduct research on police use of deadly force. A number of individuals have contributed substantially to what we know about police shootings. Research has expanded beyond a mere reporting of frequencies to address individual, situational, and community factors as they relate to police use of deadly force with firearms. As this book goes to press, so does a volume authored by Geller and Scott (1991) which contains the most comprehensive and current compilation of city-by-city and national data on use of deadly force by police (as well as against police). Their book contains previously unpublished data through 1990. It includes coverage of the circumstances surrounding and reasons provided by police for the shootings, as well as information on control strategies. The length of the volume — 400 pages — indicates the relative wealth of information we have about shootings today, compared to even ten years ago.

As discussed in the final chapter, attention received by this area of study over the last three decades is due in large part to public outcry, particularly by the minority community, regarding the perceived misuse of this police power. A massive study (actually multiple studies) completed and published in 1987 by the New York State Commission on Criminal Justice and the Use of Force was the result of controversial shooting deaths of five black citizens at the hands of police. The experience in New York attests to the fact that this concern is not merely a historical note and that research addressing police use of deadly force with firearms continues.

The current direction of the ongoing research on this topic is discussed in the following chapter.

Trends in Research on Deadly Force with Firearms

4

As noted in the previous chapter, most research on deadly force has been conducted since 1963, when Robin's findings with regard to justifiable homicide by police in Philadelphia between 1950 and 1960 were published. As one might expect, the methodology in this area has increased in its sophistication over the years. Specifically, advances include existence of and access to superior data, more valid measures of "deadly force," attention to incidents of officer restraint, and a broader conceptualization of police-citizen violent encounters. In this chapter we discuss these research trends as they relate to police use of deadly force by firearms. These issues, however, are also relevant to the developing research in police pursuits, as well as other aspects of policing.

Data Sources

The dismal state of affairs with regard to nationwide data on police shootings has already been discussed. As a result of this deficiency, most of the significant studies addressing this topic have been based upon data provided by individual departments. It is impressive that police departments have been so cooperative in light of the potential risks involved in making information regarding this volatile aspect of policing available to researchers, and thus the general public. Regarding the progress within police research resulting from agency cooperation, researcher Lawrence Sherman commented in a recent interview (*Law Enforcement News*, 1990:11) that:

The 20-year difference in the willingness of police agencies to cooperate with research is astounding. It is a record to be very proud of and it is an embarrassment to the prosecutors and the judges in this country who still have their heads in the sand with respect to the need for experimentation to evaluate what they're doing. The police are right out front with the medical community in doing the best possible kinds of research to evaluate what they're doing.

Earlier, Blumberg (1983) had pointed out, however, that the police departments which have made their deadly force data available to researchers may not be representative of all departments. He noted (p. 299), "Police agencies which allow researchers access to their files are probably more progressive and more committed to eliminating abuses in this area. In addition, they probably have less to hide from the public." Another problem with using police department data (see e.g., Blumberg, 1983) is that some of the police sources of information may not provide accurate data. Particularly problematic is the use of agency accounts of specific deadly force incidents which may be colored by the retrospective interpretation of an officer who needs to justify his use of force to himself, to the department, and possibly to other members of the criminal justice system (e.g., the prosecutor and grand jurors). Possible, too, is that an officer would intentionally lie in his report to cover up an out-of-policy shooting.

One seemingly attractive data collection strategy would involve putting observers in all patrol and special unit cars to document the circumstances of all deadly force incidents. This, however, is clearly impractical for deadly force research because of the infrequency of the behavior. Recall, Sherman, et al., (1986) estimated that, on the average, a New York City police officer would kill a citizen once every 694 years. Even if the observer in the patrol car were to focus on all deadly force incidents—including those where shots resulted in woundings or misses—we would wait an average of 97 years for a single data entry for a particular New York City officer.

Because reliance on departmental records of deadly force incidents can be problematic and because gathering information on deadly force incidents as they occur is impractical, some researchers have conducted "laboratory" studies. One of these methods involves using officer responses to stimuli in the form of hypothetical situations. Brown (1984), for instance, administered a survey containing hypothetical deadly force situations to assess officer attitudes toward police use of deadly force. The 12 scenarios were based on actual situations in which firearms were used. Officers rated each scenario in terms of whether the deadly force was, in fact, appropriate. The researcher tested hypotheses related to training and victim race as they influence police use of deadly force.

Hayden (1981:103) undertook a study to determine "what situational factors police take into account in circumstances that may involve the use of force." To do this, officers were presented descriptions of potentially-violent encounters with minimal information and then the officers were to choose, in order of priority, what additional information they would use to make decisions regarding whether deadly force was required. The officer could get additional information on the suspect (e.g., age, sex, race, demeanor), the physical environment (e.g., visibility, availability of cover, presence of bystanders), and so forth. The actual information requested and the sequence (priority) of its selection presumably provided insight into factors affecting use of deadly force decisions. Using a similar methodology, Holzworth and Pipping (1985) varied situational conditions within hypothetical police-citizen potentially violent encounters to determine the extent to which the various "cues" affected police officers' decisions to use their firearms.

Research using hypothetical situations, while capable of generating large samples and controlling for important factors, suffers from some serious drawbacks. Doerner and Ho (n.d.) point out that such an approach provides a measure of what police *say* they *would* do, and not necessarily what they actually would do. Clearly, responding to hypothetical situations in a paper and pencil test does not provide the high stress, split-second-decision reality of the field.

Somewhat more realism is achieved in simulation studies. The simulations are provided via computerized training programs which place the officer in various potentially violent encounters in which he must decide whether to shoot or not to shoot. The scenario plays itself out visually in life-size form in front of the officer in a training room. Doerner and Ho (n.d.:p. 8) outline the advantages of this data source for analyzing deadly force decisions:

> First, since many agencies use these modules as part of mandatory firearms qualification, officers take these exercises seriously. Second, the scenarios are so realistic that officers feel they are participating in an actual high-risk encounter. Third, this laboratory-like approach means that researchers can gather data on a huge number of high-risk incidents in a controlled setting.

Doerner and Ho (n.d.) used computerized training simulations to analyze individual and situational variables related to shooting decisions. Similarly, Aadland (1981) used "shoot, don't shoot" training (discussed more thoroughly below) to test hypotheses related to officer characteristics and police use of deadly force.

Results from research using hypothetical scenarios and simulation research can be useful, but clearly these types of studies cannot achieve the reality of actual encounters. However, there are problems, as noted above, with field studies, as well. In sum, though there has been an increase in the number and quality of sources of data for researching police use of firearms over the years, all types of data have certain drawbacks. The tradeoffs associated with the various sources must be kept in mind when evaluating individual studies.

Measures of "Deadly Force"

Another way in which research methodology in this area has improved is through the increased refinement in measures of "deadly force." Early research used only *fatal* shootings by police as the dependent, or outcome, measure in deadly force research (e.g., Robin, 1963; Harding, 1970; Harding and Fahey, 1973; Jenkins and Faison, 1974; Kobler, 1975). But several researchers (e.g., Fyfe, 1978, 1981c; Blumberg, 1983; Geller, 1982; Scharf and Binder, 1983) criticized the use of this measure as the unit of analysis in deadly force research. For instance, Fyfe (1978:31), denounced the use of fatal shootings as the dependent variable, stating:

> Although these reports provide valuable information upon the loss of life resulting from police firearms discharges, research which focuses solely upon incidents in which police bullets actually struck and killed individuals for whom they were intended cannot be described as having comprehensively examined either police firearms discharges or the consequences of arming the police with the means for employing deadly force.

In later years police departments collected and made available to scholars data regarding police shootings which resulted in either a death or wounding (e.g., Milton, et al., 1977; Geller and Karales, 1981; Blumberg, 1983; Waegel, 1984). These data on all police shootings resulting in a "hit" were more representative of "deadly force" than data comprised only of those shots which resulted in a citizen death. But even this more advanced measure was less than ideal.

If a study purports to examine "police use of deadly force by firearms," which is that force likely to cause death, the researchers must examine all decisions to shoot, regardless of whether the outcome is a death, wounding, or miss. Binder (1983) noted that one cannot presume that misses are a representative subset of decisions to use deadly force. That is, the circumstances under which misses occur may be different from shots which are on target. He explained (1983:182):

> It is clear, for example, that the distance between a shooting officer and a fleeing felon tends to be substantially greater than the distance between opponents in a strict defense-of-life shooting, and since accuracy is related to shooting distance, there are obvious implications for selection on the basis of a hit having occurred.

And as covered in the previous chapter, Blumberg (1983) compared incidents that resulted in hits and incidents of "harmless discharges" in two cities across various aspects of armed confrontations, and reported significant and "meaningful" differences between hits and misses.

In a recent study, Fridell (1989) compared rates of police discharges with rates of police shootings which resulted in deaths across 35 major U.S. cities using data which were originally collected by Matulia on behalf of the International Association of Chiefs of Police (IACP) (Matulia 1982, 1985). Matulia and his colleagues sent questionnaires to police agencies serving cities with populations of 250,000 or more to gather information on, among other things, the number of incidents in which police firearms were discharged for the years 1975-1979. Using the information regarding the number of shooting incidents that resulted in opponent death (verified by FBI crime data), the research team computed six separate rates of justifiable homicide by police for each of the responding agencies. One rate was obtained by dividing the number of police justifiable homicides in a city by the number of reported violent crimes. Other rates were based on the number of robberies, city population, the size of the police force, and so forth. Sacramento had the lowest rate of justifiable homicide by police for all the cities studied, regardless of how the rate was calculated. Matulia equated this homicide rate with "police use of deadly force" and implied that a low justifiable homicide rate reflected commendable restraint in the area of police shootings. Justifiable homicide rates for the cities were used by the IACP to test 40 hypotheses regarding the relationship between departmental variables (e.g., management conditions, methods of control, training methods, types of weapons used) and the police use of deadly force.

Fridell questioned whether justifiable homicide rates were adequate reflections of police decisions to shoot and looked to the discharge data for these 35 cities which were made available in the Appendices of the IACP publication. She reported that Sacramento, though ranked lowest in terms of justifiable homicide rates, ranked fourteenth among the 35 cities in rate of discharges. Remarkably, just two percent of the discharges by officers in the Sacramento Police Department were lethal. She found that 80 percent of the discharges in Sacramento missed their target, compared to 66 percent for the other cities, and only 10 percent of the hits resulted in a civilian death, compared to an average percent killed of 31 for all 35 cities. Fridell (1989:160-1) commented:

> Thus, the dependent measure for this city—used in the IACP research to rank it relative to the other cities and to test all of the hypotheses—did not reflect the use of deadly force by the Sacramento Police Department, but rather reflected a relatively high percentage of off target shots and a relatively low percentage of hits resulting in deaths.

An increasing number of departments are collecting information on all discharges, instead of just collecting information on hits and/or deaths. As a result, researchers are able to utilize this superior measure in their studies. Discharge data have been used in several well-known studies (e.g., Fyfe, 1978; Meyer, 1980) as well as several recent dissertations (e.g., Domm, 1981; Donahue, 1983).

The Potentially Violent Encounter

Binder, et al. (1982) and Scharf and Binder (1983) argue that even research on police discharges is too limited in focus. Instead, they maintain that research should use as a unit of analysis a police-citizen encounter in which a police shooting could reasonably be expected, whether or not it occurs. This broader conceptualization encompasses decisions to shoot and decisions *not* to shoot. Indeed, leading researchers (e.g., Meyer, 1980; Reiss, 1980; Geller and Karales, 1981; Blumberg,

1983; Geller, 1985) have commented on the need to study averted shootings, as well as decisions to shoot. The incorporation of averted shootings, that is, incidents of officer restraint, is what Geller (1985:153) referred to as the "next frontier in police shooting research." He referred to the "high-risk encounter" as the preferred unit of analysis and defined it as "police-civilian contacts in which the officer reasonably believes he would be legally justified in using deadly force regardless of whether he uses such force or averts its use" (1985:154).

This expanded focus has two major and related advantages: first, the circumstances surrounding (e.g., the precipitating event) and factors related to (e.g., officer experience, race of opponent) the deadly force decision can be understood more fully. Second, officer behavior which leads to the resolution of potentially violent encounters without resorting to deadly force can be determined (Geller, 1985).

The various methodologies described above have been utilized to gather "shoot, non-shoot" data. Hypothetical scenarios have been used by Uelman (1973) and Scharf, et al. (1978) to assess the relationship between officer characteristics and shooting behavior. Simulation studies, too, have allowed for shoot, non-shoot comparisons. The challenge, however, has been to incorporate the shoot, non-shoot focus into field research. This was attempted by Inn (1976) who used police files to identify incidents where two or more officers responded simultaneously to a scene and made different decisions regarding the use of deadly force. This method was used to examine the relationship between officer characteristics and shooting behavior. The problem with this selection process, however, as Blumberg (1986) noted, is that even on the same scene, officers could be facing very different stimuli. For instance, one officer could be facing an armed assailant on the front steps while his partner is in the back yard facing only a barking dog. As such, one cannot draw conclusions about how individual characteristics might explain differing behavior. Another problem is that this process excludes situations with a single officer on the scene and situations with two or more officers who make the same deadly force decision.

The Four-City Study: Shoot and Non-Shoot Decisions

Geller (1985) reported that he had research in progress looking at officer restraint in the Chicago Police Department. The only other field data for shoot, non-shoot samples of which we are aware were collected by Binder, Scharf, and Galvin (1982) with a grant from the National Institute of Justice. The data came from four U.S. cities: Birmingham, Alabama; Miami, Florida; Newark, New Jersey; and Oakland, California. For each city, information was collected regarding police shootings which occurred between January 1977 and June 1980. Additionally, information was collected regarding police-citizen confrontations occurring during the same period in which a police shooting could reasonably have been expected but did not occur.

A critical aspect of this study was the selection of non-shoot groups in each city. To do this, the researchers first asked both officers and non-sworn officials associated with the department to identify incidents where officers could have used deadly force but in fact did not. Documentation from department files for all cases that emerged from this stage of selection were given to local teams of judges to determine the appropriateness of each incident for inclusion in the study. It was to be included if judged to be a genuinely violent encounter where the use of deadly force was a reasonable option. (Indeed, the two groups were compared across various risk measures of the confrontation—e.g., precipitating event, opponent weapon—and found to be equivalent.)

Data were collected on the officers, opponents, and situational aspects of all the shoot and non-shoot incidents from departmental files and from interviews with involved officers.

This shoot, non-shoot data set was used to analyze various aspects of deadly force. The previous chapter reported the Binder, et al. (1982) results regarding differences between officers involved in shooting incidents and officers involved in incidents of restraint. Further, these researchers found no significant differences between shoot and non-shoot incidents with regard to situational factors such as location, weather, lighting, time of day, and time of year, and no significant differences with regard to the personal characteristics of suspects. There were significant differences between the two groups with regard to the availability to the officer of hard cover and use of protective clothing (e.g., a bullet-resistant vest). More non-shooters had hard cover available during the encounter, but more shooters wore protective clothing.

Some of the findings from secondary analyses of the four-city data led Fridell and Binder (1988) to speculate that encounters characterized by ambiguity or surprise are more likely to result in the use of deadly force. Specifically, Fridell and Binder (1988) found that significantly more of the non-shooters than shooters knew their opponents. Also, significantly more non-shooters reported being able to determine the emotional state of their opponents. In contrast, many shooters reported being uncertain about the opponents' emotional states. Further, they found that significantly more non-shooters perceived at an early stage in the encounter that this was "probably" or "certainly" a situation which would require use of deadly force; many shooters had not formed that expectation.

The Four-City Data: Racial Aspects

The value of the shoot, non-shoot data can be seen from the analysis of the racial aspects of police use of deadly force using the four-city data. In Chapter 3 we presented various studies which attempted to determine whether racial bias is a part of police decisions to shoot. Blumberg (1986) discussed the several methodologies which have been used in this area. The first methodology involves the comparison of the rates of blacks as opponents in incidents of deadly force and rates of black involvement in various types of crime (Geller and Karales,

1981; Fyfe, 1978; Milton, et al., 1977; Burnham, 1973). One weakness of this methodology is the lack of clarity regarding which arrest statistics (e.g. arrests for all felonies, for violent felonies, or for Part 1 felonies) are appropriate for the comparison (Blumberg, 1981). Also, this methodology does not control for the possibility that arrest statistics are affected by racial bias.

The second methodology discussed by Blumberg (1986) involves analyzing characteristics of shooting incidents to determine whether blacks are shot under circumstances involving less danger to the police or others than whites. Recall that Meyer (1980) used this methodology to compare the circumstances surrounding the shootings of suspects of various racial/ethnic backgrounds in Los Angeles. This methodology has facilitated our understanding of variations in shooting rates across subpopulations. Its weakness, however, is that it does not incorporate baseline information regarding black encounters with the police and white encounters with the police.

As Blumberg (1986:238) noted, this second methodology "is not able to determine whether the police are more likely to shoot blacks than whites under the same circumstances." To do this, one would need to know the proportion of incidents (with various characteristics) involving black or white suspects that resulted in a shooting. That is, we would need to know the percentage of incidents involving knife-wielding black suspects and the percentage of incidents involving knife-wielding white suspects which resulted in a shooting. If we found that police used deadly force in 50 percent of all knife-wielding confrontations involving black suspects and only 20 percent of all knife-wielding confrontations involving white suspects, we might legitimately conclude that police officers had different trigger fingers for blacks and whites.

A more elaborate hypothetical presentation may further clarify the distinction between methodologies. Table 4.1 contains fictional data (unrealistic in several ways) for a city that had 600 shootings of armed subjects during a 10-year period, 300 involving black opponents and 300 involving white opponents. Opponents are categorized according to whether their weapons were firearms or other less lethal types of weapons. Using Meyer's method of evaluating racial bias, we would note in Part A that a larger percentage (50 percent) of black-opponent shootings than white-opponent shootings (17 percent) involved a generally less serious situation, that is, where the suspect has a weapon other than a firearm (e.g., a knife or blunt object). This information might be interpreted as indicating racial bias because it appears blacks are shot under circumstances involving less danger to the police or others than are whites. Part B has available as a denominator, not *all shootings* as in Part A, but rather all *armed confrontations*, including those where a decision *not* to shoot was made. Here, we can see how frequently officers shot black opponents who were armed with weapons other than guns in *all* situations. In this hypothetical, we see that of all the times police faced armed black opponents with the less-lethal types of weapons, the officers fired in 30 percent of the incidents. In contrast, these data indicate that when the opponent with a less-lethal type of weapon was white, police shot 50 percent

Table 4.1

Two Methods for Comparing Shootings of White and Black Opponents Using Hypothetical Data

	A Percentage of Shootings Within Categories of Race, Involving a Gun or Other Weapon		B Percentage of Armed Confrontations Which Resulted in a Shooting Within Categories of Race, Involving a Gun or Other Weapon	
	Black	**White**	**Black**	**White**
Armed with gun	150 (50%)	250 (83%)	150/200 (75%)	250/350 (71%)
Other weapon	150 (50%)	50 (17%)	150/500 (30%)	50/100 (50%)
Total	300 (100%)	300 (100%)	300/700 (43%)	300/450 (67%)

of the time. A completely opposite conclusion follows from use of the percentages in Part B: police appear biased against whites!!

For a study to determine police bias accurately, it would require the data suggested in Part B. These data provide the necessary information for evaluating hypotheses regarding deadly force and race; it is the type of information which Binder, et al. (1982) provide with the shoot, non-shoot data. To evaluate the racial hypothesis, officers involved in either shoot or non-shoot incidents were asked in the interviews to describe the circumstances which required police attention (i.e., shooting, robbery, burglary, and other) and what actions the subject took immediately prior to the officer's decision to shoot or not shoot (e.g., held a firearm, ran away). Additionally, shooters were asked what their justification was for using deadly force (e.g., defense of life) and non-shooters were asked what their justification would have been if they had used deadly force.

With this information, Fridell and Binder (1989) were able to compare incidents involving black opponents and incidents involving white opponents with regard to the percent of decisions to shoot within various categories of police-citizen violent encounters. (The relatively high percentages of shoot, as opposed to non-shoot outcomes reflect their disproportionate representation in the data set.) For example, data in Table 4.2 provide the results for various precipitating circumstances. Of the confrontations with Caucasians precipitated by a citizen-citizen shooting, 66.7 percent resulted in the officer firing at the opponent. A similar percentage, 62.5 percent, is obtained for these situations involving black opponents. Chi square statistics indicate that the difference between these percentages is not significant. Additional analyses indicate the different percentages for black and white incidents precipitated by robberies or "other" circumstances are also not significant. Similar results were obtained when shootings were categorized by opponent action and then by officer justification. No differences between shootings of black and white suspects were found.

As the authors noted, this research is limited in that it combines information regarding shootings in four cities into one data base. This was necessary because the numbers within cities were not large enough to conduct independent statistical analyses. This pooling of data might mask results of racial bias within individual

Table 4.2

Percent of Black and White Opponents Shot at Within Various Types of Armed Confrontations

	White (46)	Black (221)	Overall (267)	Chi Square (df = 1)	Significance (p = .05)
All Incidents (267)	85.9 (73/85)	81.3 (148/182)	82.8	0.85	n.s.
Precipitating Circumstance					
Shooting (84)	66.7 (8/12)	62.5 (45/72)	63.1	0.08*	n.s.
Robbery (49)	75.0 (6/8)	82.9 (34/41)	81.6	0.28*	n.s.
Burglary (30)	100.0 (7/7)	87.0 (20/23)	90.0	**	
Other (71)	68.8 (11/16)	61.8 (34/55)	63.4	0.26	n.s.
Missing (33)					
Opponent Action (Multiple responses possible)					
Ran Away (92)	69.2 (9/13)	83.5 (66/79)	81.5	1.52*	n.s.
Attack with Bare Hands (18)	100.0 (5/5)	92.3 (12/13)	94.4	**	
Attack with Blunt Object (5)	100.0 (2/2)	100.0 (3/3)	100.0	**	
Attack with Sharp Object (8)	100.0 (2/2)	66.7 (4/6)	75.0	**	
Held Firearm (77)	55.6 (5/9)	63.2 (43/68)	62.3	0.20*	n.s.
Pointed Firearm (96)	81.8 (9/11)	70.6 (60/85)	71.9	0.61*	n.s.
Fired Firearm (46)	75.0 (3/4)	81.0 (34/42)	80.4	**	
Other (66)	73.7 (14/19)	53.2 (25/47)	59.1	2.35	n.s.
Missing (4)					
Justification (Multiple responses possible)					
Apprehend Fleeing Felon (54)	77.8 (7/9)	80.0 (36/45)	79.6	0.02*	n.s.
Stop Dangerous Felon (67)	60.0 (6/10)	82.5 (47/57)	79.1	2.60*	n.s.
Protect Own Life (196)	76.7 (23/30)	65.7 (109/166)	67.3	1.40	n.s.
Protect Citizen (48)	70.0 (7/10)	65.8 (25/38)	66.7	0.06*	n.s.
Prevent Crime (13)	50.0 (1/2)	54.5 (6/11)	53.8	**	
Protect Other Officer (92)	63.2 (12/19)	56.2 (41/73)	57.6	0.30	n.s.
Other (2)					
Missing (7)					

* Yates' Correction Used (if the expected frequency in one cell was less than five)
** Statistics were not computed because of empty rows or because cells with expected frequencies of less than five exceeded one.

cities. However, this study highlights the importance of including non-shoot incidents in research on deadly force.

Phases of Deadly Force Encounters

As stated earlier, one of the advantages of including non-shoot information is that it allows us to assess whether or not there are factors that differentiate shoot and non-shoot incidents. If we can identify the differentiating factors which involve police behavior, training which addresses these factors might reduce shooting outcomes and increase non-shooting outcomes. But, as Scharf and Binder (1983) pointed out, training should not focus so heavily on the final decision in a potentially-violent situation to shoot or not shoot, but rather, give attention to decisions made early in such an encounter which may increase or decrease the likelihood of a shooting response. This involves conceptualizing potentially violent encounters, not merely as "split-second decisions" made by officers, but as incidents involving multiple decisions made by both opponents and officers where early decisions in an encounter affect the options available at a later point. Or as Binder and Scarf (1980:111) explained, "the violent police-citizen encounter . . . is . . . a developmental process in which successive decisions and behaviors by either police officer or citizen, or both, make the violent outcome more or less likely."

This broader conceptualization allows for a second way to evaluate outcomes (i.e., evaluate decisions to shoot and decisions not to shoot) of armed confrontations. Traditionally and legally, decisions to shoot have been examined in terms of the opponent's actions immediately prior to the officer's use of deadly force. The decision is considered "justifiable" or "unjustifiable" depending on these circumstances. Thus, a shooting of an opponent who is aiming a gun at an officer (or innocent bystander) would be justifiable. It could be, however, that though legally "justifiable," the shooting of an armed opponent was *avoidable*. That is, it could be that if the officer had acted differently at some point during the course of the entire encounter, he would not have been facing that pointed gun at the end, or "final frame."

Scharf and Binder (1983) provided a good example of a shooting—determined to be legally justifiable—which many experts believe was avoidable, had the officers made better decisions earlier in the encounter. They reported that on January 3, 1979 in Los Angeles an employee of the gas company arrived at Mrs. Eulia Love's residence to turn off the gas because Mrs. Love was $80 in arrears. The very angry woman yelled at the gas employee and struck him on the arm with a shovel. That afternoon another gas company employee arranged to have the police meet him at the Love residence. This gas man arrived first and was told by Mrs. Love in the front yard that she would not pay the full amount. (Evidence indicated that she intended to pay part of the overdue bill.) She went into the house and came out with a knife with which she hacked at the branches of some trees in her front yard. Officers Hopson and O'Callaghan pulled up soon thereafter.

Mrs. Love yelled at the officers who approached with drawn guns. The officers directed her to drop the knife. Mrs. Love moved away from the officers down the walkway. Officer O'Callaghan followed her at a distance of about six feet. He had his firearm in his right (strong) hand pointed toward the ground and his baton in his left hand. Officer Hopson moved to a position about 15 feet from the angry woman; his drawn weapon was pointed downward, as well.

The reports indicate Mrs. Love thrust the knife toward O'Callaghan several times. The officers continued to request that Love drop the weapon, assuring her they would not harm her. She refused. She moved further backward toward her house with O'Callaghan (baton in one hand and gun in the other) approximately five feet away and Hopson (with gun out stretched) approximately 10 feet away. Love was still thrusting at the officers with her knife.

Several witnesses thought that Mrs. Love started to relax at this point: lowering her knife and moving toward the house. But, as Scharf and Binder (1983:105) wrote: "Instead of her returning to the house, perhaps unharmed, the following seconds would see a series of decisions that altered the careers of the two officers, killed Mrs. Love, and threw the city of Los Angeles into year long political turmoil."

There are some differences in the accounts of witnesses and participants, but it seems O'Callaghan knocked the knife out of Mrs. Love's hand and both he and Mrs. Love reached for it. Mrs. Love retrieved the knife and held it as if to throw it overhand. Returning to Scharf and Binder's account (1983:106):

> O'Callaghan then dropped his baton and shifted simultaneously into a two-handed gun position, less than eight feet from Mrs. Love. Hopson froze in his two-handed, semicrouched position. Mrs. Love then took a step backward and raised the knife with her right hand about her head. No one will ever know for certain what her intentions were in raising her right hand in this manner. Almost instantaneously, both officers fired six rounds each in a rapid-fire sequence; eight of the twelve bullets entered the body. Eulia Love was dead.

This controversial shooting resulted in hundreds of newspaper articles, several commission reports, and a congressional subcommittee hearing (Uchida, 1982; Scharf and Binder, 1983). The focus of critics in analyzing the incident was not on the ultimate decision to shoot—which, in light of the immediate circumstances, could be considered understandable—but rather, on the decisions made earlier in the encounter which led to those "immediate circumstances." Actions on the part of the officers which were questioned include:

—failing to plan their intervention prior to confrontation,

—unholstering the guns upon arrival,

—advancing toward Mrs. Love as she backed away,

—Officer O'Callaghan holding a gun in one hand and baton in the other,

—positioning the white officer, rather than the black officer, closer to the black woman, and

—failing to call for back-up.

Many felt that the officers could have avoided the shooting by making wiser decisions during the encounter.

Scharf and Binder (1983) contrasted this incident with another involving a police officer and an angry knife-wielding woman who had just stabbed someone to death. In this case, the skilled and patient officer was able to get the woman to forfeit her weapon without further trouble.

To facilitate the analysis of potentially violent armed confrontations between citizens and police from beginning to end, Binder and Scharf (1980) and Scharf and Binder (1983) developed a four-phase model. The four phases of the confrontations are Anticipation, Entry and Initial Contact, Information Exchange, and Final Phase. Within each of the phases, various alternative behaviors of officers, actions of opponents, and situational factors are analyzed which may affect whether the encounter moves toward a violent or nonviolent resolution.

The Anticipation phase begins when the officer is initially made aware of the situation or event, for instance, through the officer's own observation, via dispatch, or through some other means. During the first stage, the officer will acquire information (again, through observation, dispatch, etc.) which may affect his early conceptions of the event, and subsequently his early decisions. The information will determine whether or not he makes a plan for approaching the situation and the content of that plan.

The next phase, Entry and Initial Contact, encompasses the entry of the officer onto the scene and the initial contact with the opponent. The officer will get more information at this time which may confirm or contradict earlier information and which will affect decisions. Some decisions which might be made at this stage include taking cover, unholstering a weapon, and calling for backup. In accordance with the Binder/Scharf conceptualization of potentially violent encounters, the decisions made during the early stages are likely to affect options available to both the officer and opponent in later stages.

Many, but certainly not all, potentially violent encounters have an Information Exchange stage. Binder, et al. (1982:22) explain:

> An officer might tell a citizen to "freeze" or "drop his gun" or possibly order him to stop. A police officer might similarly say something to distract or intimidate the citizen. Some "information exchanges" with opponents, as with opponents holding hostages, might proceed for hours or even days. Often the information exchange phase in armed confrontations ends with only short epithets.

It is possible that non-verbal, as well as verbal, communication may affect the interaction between the offender and opponent.

The Final Phase encompasses the moments immediately prior to the actual shooting or the decision not to shoot. Important aspects of this final phase include the opponent's action (e.g., drawing and pointing a weapon) and the availability of cover to the officer.

The traditional conceptualization encompasses only the final phase, whereas the Binder/Scharf model incorporates early phases of the event, maintaining that the decisions made in the final frame to shoot or not shoot are dependent upon the interaction among earlier decisions, earlier actions, and situational features. Decisions made and actions taken may increase or decrease the likelihood of a shooting (versus non-shooting) outcome.

Fridell and Binder (1988) have reported some preliminary findings from the four-city data with regard to the circumstances of early phases of potentially violent encounters as they relate to the incident outcome as either a decision to shoot or not shoot. One finding was that the third phase, information exchange, appeared to be critical in terms of whether the encounter ended with a shooting or not. A larger percentage of shooters (44 percent) than non-shooters (28 percent) reported that the verbal communication made the opponents angrier. Conversely, a larger percentage of non-shooters than shooters (20 percent versus 6 percent) reported that the communication made the opponent calmer. Further, more of the non-shoot opponents complied with the commands of the officer.

Thus, this information exchange stage appears pivotal. Significantly more of the shoot encounters have communication phases that result in an angrier opponent, who does not comply with officer commands. The communication of non-shoot encounters leads to a calming of the subjects and compliance. It is important to note that we cannot conclude based on these preliminary results that the nature of the shoot and non-shoot officers' communications affected the probabilities of a compliant versus angry response from the opponent. That is, we cannot conclude that the actions of the shoot officers increased the probability of a negative outcome or that the actions of the non-shoot officers decreased the probability of a negative outcome. It may be, instead, that shoot incidents are characterized by opponents who are more prone to anger and less likely to comply with officer commands and that the converse is true for non-shoot incidents. It will take additional research to determine if specific officer behaviors and communications during this phase can affect the probabilities of alternative outcomes.

If research can determine how officer behavior affects outcome, departments can intervene with officer training to reduce avoidable shootings. A training intervention based on the phase conceptualization of police-citizen violence in Dade County, Florida is discussed in the next chapter. Other policy and training issues emanating from the phase analysis are covered in the next chapter, as well.

Concerns Regarding the Shoot, Non-Shoot Methodology

As noted above, deadly force researchers have called for the inclusion of non-shooting incidents in deadly force studies, and Binder, et al. were the first to do so using actual (as opposed to hypothetical or simulated) incidents. None of the advocates of this form of research, however, has implied that this is an easy methodological task. Geller (1985:155) noted:

> (One) reason . . . that police high-risk encounters have resisted analysis is that police departments keep no systematic records of averted shooting incidents, as such. In part, this is because in prevailing police norms averted shootings are nonevents—that is, "nothing happened." The arrests are recorded, of course, but typically there is no ready way to pick out the incidents in which the officers would have been justified in shooting from among the mass of arrests where shooting would not have been acceptable.

Similarly, Fyfe (1985) pointed out that to identify restraint incidents requires relying on police anecdotes, "which is hardly a reliable means of data collection" (p. 1).

Related to the above problem is the issue of defining what constitutes a "non-shoot" incident. As Geller (1985:159) pointed out, "a critical part of the needed methodological work will be to define the parameters of the term 'high-risk encounters' clearly enough that we can identify these incidents with an acceptable degree of consistency." This definitional problem is especially problematic when collecting information across multiple jurisdictions because "there is a lot of variation among jurisdictions in the definition of encounters where shooting could reasonably be expected" (Fyfe, 1985:1).

The four-city data base of Binder, et al. (1982) has been criticized because of the problems outlined above, and because a major source of the information regarding both the shoot and non-shoot incidents was interviews with officers. As a result of using officer reports of the incidents, some of these data may reflect faulty or self-serving memories. Nonetheless, this data base represents the first attempt to cross into "the next frontier of police shooting research" (Geller, 1985:153) and will serve as a model for future similar endeavors.

Future Research

Future research shall continue to focus on the early, as well as the later, stages of deadly force encounters and continue to study incidents of police restraint as well as incidents where deadly force was used. Questions regarding high-risk situations that Scharf and Binder (1983:66) proposed be addressed include:

1. Which types of confrontation present the greatest risk?
2. What are the most common types of opponents faced by police officers in armed confrontations?
3. Of the total number of types of armed confrontation, which particular types most frequently result in a shot being fired by a police officer?
4. What types of training are most appropriate to particular types of confrontation?

5. Is it possible to develop special training methods to avert particular types of shootings?

6. Are there interactions among types of incidents (for example, an apparently insane opponent in an off-duty confrontation) that make a particular type of confrontation inordinately risky?

Many of these inquiries are also applicable to police pursuit studies which might attempt to determine, for instance, whether there are actions on the part of an officer early in an encounter which might prevent a motorist from driving away from police, or actions later in the encounter which might effect an earlier resolution.

Studies in both of these areas will reflect the major methodological advances in police use of deadly force research over the last 25 to 30 years. The number and sophistication of studies were made possible by three related factors: the interest of criminal justice scholars, the concern on the part of the law enforcement community, and the availability of research funds. This interest, concern, and financial support were stimulated in large part, by the public outcry regarding the perceived excessive use of deadly force against racial minority persons. The attention to deadly force included a focus on departmental policies and training, which are covered in the next chapter.

Policy and Training for the Use of Firearms

5

The impact of *Tennessee v. Garner* on deadly force policy was more symbolic than real. Minority community pressures (in conjunction with other factors) had already effected substantial changes in shooting guidelines prior to this 1985 U.S. Supreme Court decision. This chapter begins with a discussion of the general considerations of deadly force law and the types of situations covered by this law. The four major types or models of deadly force policy which have been used over the years and the various sources of these guidelines, in addition to the U.S. Supreme Court, are outlined. This chapter also addresses the specific components of firearms policies, the research on policies, and the advances which have been made in training officers to act in accordance with these guidelines. In the final chapter of the book, we return to discuss the social forces which caused the changes in policy and training.

General Considerations of Policy and Law

Rules regarding police procedures (including those addressing deadly force during arrests and police pursuits) reflect an attempt to balance the competing goals of crime control and individual liberty. On the one hand, we need effective law enforcement to control crime; that is, we need officers who have sufficient powers to intervene in citizens' lives to stop crime and/or bring offenders to justice. On the other hand, we value freedom and dignity; we want citizens to be relatively free from governmental intrusion into their lives and homes. In fact, this has been a critical concern historically. A major impetus to the colonies separating from England was anger regarding the abuses of citizens' liberty by government in the name of enforcing the law. These two goals reflect the scales of the "balancing test" used by courts to determine the extent to which police can deprive citizens of liberty to achieve the governmental goal of effective crime control. As was discussed previously, the courts balance the extent of the police intrusion against the need for it. Each increase in police power results in a decrease in citizens' freedom. Conversely, increases in individual freedoms can reduce the power of law enforcement to control crime.

69

There are two types of situations related to officer use of deadly force which are addressed by law: shooting in self-defense and shooting to make an arrest. There has been little or no controversy regarding the former. As permitted by law, citizens and officers can use deadly force to defend themselves or others against the immediate threat of death or seriously bodily harm. Thus, if an officer is being fired upon, or a hostage is being held at gunpoint, the officer may shoot the offender in self defense (or defense of others). This power is reflected in all deadly force laws. In terms of the balancing test, it reflects the greater value placed on an innocent rather than a criminal life.

The controversy, instead, concerns the circumstances under which an officer should be allowed to use deadly force to effect the arrest of a fleeing suspect. In terms of the balancing test, the specific governmental goal is to take into custody a person the officer has probable cause to believe has committed a crime and the intrusion into individual freedom is "unmatched" (*Garner v. Tennessee*: 9); "there being no greater way of preventing the freedom of movement of an individual" than killing him (IACP, 1986:138). This aspect of deadly force parameters, shooting to make an arrest, is the focus of our coverage of law and policy.

Four Policy Models

The four models which have served as guidelines for police use of deadly force in various jurisdictions across the United States reflect differential emphasis on the need to catch suspected criminals and the sanctity of human life.

The Any-Fleeing-Felon Rule

The any-fleeing-felon rule, which was the rule at Common Law when all felonies were punishable by death, provides the most latitude to officers. Law enforcement officers could use deadly force if it were necessary to capture or to overcome the resistance of any felon. When English law was incorporated into American law, statutes dealing with deadly force reflected this common law rule and this is the standard which was challenged in *Tennessee v. Garner*. As covered in Chapter 2, the U.S. Supreme Court held that this rule does not reflect an appropriate balance between effective law enforcement and individual liberty. Specifically, the Court held that loss of life was too high a price to pay in terms of individual liberty for arresting a non-violent fleeing felon. As such, the *Garner* case limited use of deadly force to the arrest of dangerous fleeing felony suspects.

The Model Penal Code

Specifically, the *Garner* holding reflects another deadly force guideline outlined in the Model Penal Code. The Model Penal Code, developed by the American Law Institute (ALI), provides model statutes for states to consider for adoption. The ALI advocates that police use of deadly force be limited to situations in which the officer believes (1) "the crime for which the arrest is made involved conduct including the use or threatened use of deadly force," or (2) "there is a substantial risk that the person to be arrested will cause death or serious bodily harm if his apprehension is delayed"[Section 3.08(2)(b)(i), (iv), Proposed Official Draft, 1962].

The Forcible Felony Rule

The Model Penal Code Standard is not very different from the third type of deadly force law which has been incorporated into some statutes and policies over the years: the Forcible Felony Rule. Under this rule, officers could use deadly force to effect the arrest of persons suspected of certain specified felonies which pose a risk of great bodily harm or death. Thus, a state law or departmental policy might restrict use of deadly force to the arrest of persons suspected of committing a "dangerous or atrocious" felony. These felonies usually include murder, arson, mayhem, burglary, aggravated assault, rape, kidnapping, extortion, or robbery (Matulia, 1985).

The Defense of Life Standard

The most restrictive policy type is the Defense of Life standard under which an officer cannot use deadly force "unless someone's life is in direct jeopardy even if the suspect has allegedly committed a heinous crime and was believed to be dangerous" (Griswold, 1985:103). The Federal Bureau of Investigation has this policy in place at the time of this writing, but is contemplating the adoption of a broader policy reflecting the *Garner* standard.

Sources of Control

Sources of procedural guidelines for police — including those for use of firearms and pursuits — are constitutions, case law, statutory law, and police departmental policy. Thus, several governmental entities are involved; these include the U.S. Supreme Court, other federal courts, state legislatures, state courts, and individual police departments. The U.S. Supreme Court, in its role of ensuring that police procedures are consistent with the Federal Constitution, can set minimum standards nationwide. A U.S. Supreme Court decision regarding citizens' constitutional rights vis-à-vis the police must not be abridged by any other source of guidelines, except that another source may set a different standard if it *expands* citizens' rights (and thus reduces law enforcement power), but not vice-versa. Until *Tennessee v. Garner* (1985), there was no U.S. Supreme Court case specifically addressing the parameters on police use of deadly force. Now, laws and policies must reflect either the *Garner* rule or the more restrictive defense-of-life guideline.

A standard regarding this police power set by a lower level federal court via case law must be abided by within that court's jurisdiction. For several years (until *Garner* was decided), there was disparity between case law on deadly force in the Sixth Circuit Court of Appeals and the Eighth Circuit Court of Appeals. Specifically, the Sixth Circuit said that the Common Law any-fleeing-felon rule was constitutional (in *Wiley v. Memphis Police Department*, 1977), while the Eighth Circuit said it was not (*Mattis v. Schnarr*, 1976).

Most states have a statute regarding police use of deadly force. This statute must not violate the U.S. Constitution (as interpreted by the courts) or the state constitution. With regard to the latter, a state statute might be modified or interpreted by a state court in light of a provision within the state constitution. For instance, in California the statute, as written, reflects the common law any-fleeing-felon rule. However, several case decisions interpreted "felonies" to mean those of a "violent variety," that is, "a forcible and atrocious one which threatens death or serious bodily harm, or there are other circumstances which reasonably create a fear of death or serious bodily harm to the officer or to another" (*Kortum v. Alkire*, 1977:333). This case law changed the California law on police use of deadly force into one resembling the Model Penal Code.

At the lowest level, police department policies on firearms use must be at least as restrictive on police power as the higher levels of control (e.g., statutes and case law) and usually provide more detailed guidelines than the higher levels (as discussed more thoroughly below).

These various sources of control can cause confusion when trying to determine the deadly force law in various jurisdictions. For instance, states were frequently classified (prior to *Garner*) as Common law, Model Penal Code, or Forcible Felony states according to their *statutes*, in disregard of the federal or state case law which had modified the written statutory law. So, for instance, Matulia (1982) focused on statutory law to classify states and reported that 23 states had Common Law statutes, 12 had Forcible Felony statutes, seven had Model Penal Code statutes, and 8 had no statutes addressing police use of deadly force. In contrast, Geller and Karales (1981) incorporated case law into their classification and provide numbers of states with Common Law, Model Penal Code, and Forcible Felony laws as 29, 12, and 9, respectively. Matulia (1982) compounded his misrepresentation of the law by classifying cities as being within Common Law, Model Penal Code, or Forcible Felony states by relying on state statutes, and then drawing conclusions regarding the effect of guidelines on deadly force rates using city-level data! The inappropriate use of this classification system is made apparent by the fact that over 40 percent of the cities in Matulia's Common Law category were in states where case law had, in fact, changed the state law into either a Model Penal Code or Forcible Felony form. Further, it is quite possible, even likely, that the remaining cities had policies more restrictive than the state statute.

The confusion regarding laws in various jurisdictions has been lessened by the *Garner* decision, setting forth a minimum Model Penal Code standard.

Components of Firearms Policies

As noted above, the *broad* guidelines for use of deadly force are set forth by the courts and legislatures. The *specific* guidelines are contained in police department policy. Many, but not all, departments have deadly force policies. The larger the city, the more likely it is that a written deadly force policy has been developed and implemented. As early as 1964, 42 of 45 cities with populations over 250,000 had deadly force policies (President's Commission on Law Enforcement and Administration of Justice, 1967). Similarly, Matulia (1982), in his survey of the nation's largest police departments, found that 53 of 54 cities responding had deadly force policies in place. Nielsen (1983) surveyed smaller departments, as well as large ones; specifically, he surveyed all county sheriffs' departments and all police departments in jurisdictions serving 20,000 persons or more in five states regarding their deadly force policies. He found that 37.4 percent of the responding agencies had no written policy. Over half of the responding agencies in the states of North Dakota and Mississippi reported they had no written policies.

A 1988 survey of state law enforcement agencies in South Carolina indicated that the smaller the agency, the less likely it is to have a firearms policy. Unfortunately, the results from that study are biased as the non-response for the smallest agencies was extremely high. In fact, approximately 50% of the agencies with one to nine officers did not respond and approximately 25% of the agencies with ten to twenty-four officers did not respond. The reported data reveal that only 68% of the agencies with one to nine officers were operating with a firearm policy. Similarly, 84% of the agencies with ten to twenty-four officers were operating with a firearm policy, 85% of the agencies with twenty-five to forty-nine officers were operating with a firearm policy, while 94% of the agencies with fifty to ninety-nine officers were operating with a firearm policy and fully 100% of the agencies with one hundred or more officers were operating with a firearm policy (Office of Agency Research and Service, 1990: 50).

The trend, however, is toward implementing specific policies regarding firearms use at the departmental level. The International Association of Chiefs of Police publication, *A Balance of Forces: Model Deadly Force Policy and Procedure* (Matulia, 1985:63) addressed the importance of this:

> Critical deadly force policy decisions are not easily made, nor is the ultimate on-street decision to shoot an easy one for the police officer. The consequences of either decision are far-reaching. It is, however, far better that most of the decision considerations be critically analyzed from within the calm, rational atmosphere of the administrator's office, rather than from the more explosive, often irrational, and unpredictable "office" (the street) of the police officer.

The IACP publication (Matulia, 1985) recommended specific guidelines for firearms policies. This organization suggested that a policy begin with both a definition of deadly force and a statement regarding the value of human life.

Regarding the latter, the IACP recommended the following statement which reflects the mission of police (Matulia, 1985:68):

> The value of human life is immeasurable in our society. Police officers have been delegated the awesome responsibility to protect life and property and apprehend criminal offenders. The apprehension of criminal offenders and protection must at all times be subservient to the protection of life. The officer's responsibility for protecting life must include his own.

A major component of a comprehensive policy would, of course, be the general parameters on using deadly force. This would include reference to the officer's legal authority to shoot in defense of self or others in a situation where death or serious bodily harm was immediate. Additional provisions would reference the officer's authority to shoot dangerous fleeing felony suspects, as outlined in *Garner*.

The IACP also suggested that:

- no distinction be made with regard to use of deadly force against juveniles versus adults,
- warning shots be prohibited,
- deadly force be prohibited in situations where an innocent person is likely to be injured,
- there be strict restrictions regarding shots at or from moving vehicles,
- the killing of animals be allowed in specified situations,
- the department control the types of weapons and ammunition used by officers,
- there be restrictions on the carrying of secondary (back-up) weapons,
- officers be "encouraged, but not mandated" to carry an off-duty weapon,
- soft body armor be mandated,
- officers involved in shootings should be placed on "administrative leave" following the incidents, and
- psychological counseling be required for officers involved in shootings.

The manual also suggested that components of firearms training, criteria for firearms certification, and the departmental investigative process following a shooting be outlined in the policy. Further, the IACP recommended the inclusion of a legal disclaimer which would provide a statement to the effect that departmental guidelines should not be used as the standard for criminal or civil liability. Instead, criminal action or lawsuits against officers for alleged excessive force should be based on the state law.

Protection of Life Policy

The Little Rock Police Department Deadly Force policy (a copy of which is provided at the end of this section) contains many of the policy components outlined above. Additionally, it contains a provision which reflects the goal of *avoiding* deadly force situations. Specifically, this "Protection of Life" policy includes a provision that "officers will plan ahead and consider alternatives which will reduce the possibility of needing to use Deadly Force" (Section IV, D-2). Many departments nationwide are incorporating this provision into their policies which reflects the Binder/Scharf notion that decisions made early in police/citizen encounters increase or decrease the likelihood of a shooting outcome.

A "Protection of Life" policy in Dallas, Texas provided the basis for the disciplining of an officer who precipitated a justifiable, but avoidable, shooting. Because the provision was a part of policy, not law, the officer was not prosecuted for his actions. In the legal area, the "final frame" has thus far been the focus of analysis. That is, the legal question for civil and/or criminal proceedings is whether the opponent's actions immediately preceding the officer's firing justified the use of deadly force. Thus, in the case of Eulia Love, the legal focus was on Love's raising of her arm with a knife in a threatening manner during those final seconds.

A *Michigan Law Review* Note discussed the possibility of making officers legally accountable for decisions that lead to an otherwise avoidable shooting. The author noted that police liability could take the form of either criminal or civil liability for "creat(ing) the need to use deadly force in self-defense" (1988:1983). This Note looked at the legal principles which would apply in a legal analysis of this sort. The focus of the criminal or civil claim would be that the officer was negligent in his duties in that he deviated from normal police procedure. The author argued that a standard of "mere negligence" would be too harsh. He claimed (1988:1994):

> It would be bad policy—and unfair—to hold an officer accountable for ordinary acts of inadvertence since such acts are all the more likely to occur in the often dangerous and unpredictable environment in which police officers must operate.

Instead, the author argued for a standard of gross negligence and the use of civil, not criminal remedies. This issue will undoubtedly receive more attention in the years to come.

LITTLE ROCK POLICE DEPARTMENT
GENERAL ORDER

TITLE:

USE OF FORCE

DATE:	DISTRIBUTION:	REPLACES:	NUMBER:
12/01/90	DEPARTMENTAL	EXISTING	G. O. 13

I.   **Purpose**

    A.   The policies of the Little Rock Police Department regarding the use of physical force, non-lethal weapons, deadly force and discharging weapons are set forth in this General Order.

II.   **Use of Physical Force and Non-Lethal Weapons**

    A.   This section establishes the type and degree of force which may be used to overcome resistance, control persons who are in custody and prevent escape. The type and degree of force will only be that which is reasonable and necessary based on the circumstances.

    B.   Police Baton - A police baton may be used when considerable force is necessary. The baton will permit an officer to defend himself or others in situations where the use of firearms may not be necessary or justified.

        1.   Straight Baton - Officers may carry straight batons at their discretion. When carried, the only authorized baton will be the Departmentally issued straight baton.

            a)   When the use of the baton is warranted, officers will attempt to strike the suspect's arms or legs. Officers should not attempt to strike suspects on the head, neck, groin or kidneys.

            b)   Jabs to the body with the baton should be used under circumstances that preclude the officer from striking the suspect in the arms or legs [crowded areas, other officers in the area, etc.].

    C.   Side Handle Baton - The side handle baton is the baton currently issued to recruits and officers who have received certified training in its use.

        1.   Officers who have not completed the certified training are not authorized to carry the side handle baton.

*2.   Officers should not attempt to strike the head, neck, sternum, spine, groin and kidneys.

D.   Flashlights - In the event it becomes necessary to use a flashlight as a defensive weapon, officers will use it in the same manner as the baton. Suspects should not be struck in the head, neck, groin area or kidneys.

    1.   Departmentally approved flashlights must meet the following requirements:

        a)   A.B.S. plastic construction;

        b)   Overall length of 12 7/16 inches;

        c)   Light head no larger than 2 5/8 inches in diameter;

        d)   Total weight, with batteries inserted, of 24 ounces;

        e)   Flashlights will be of the 3 cell type or less.

        f)   Aircraft aluminum or metal flashlights are prohibited.

    2.   Officers may purchase, at their own expense, any rechargeable flashlight which is constructed of A.B.S. plastic and meets the guidelines set forth in the preceeding Section.

    3.   MiniMag flashlights are authorized under this Order.

E.   Police Vehicles - Officers will not attempt to deliberately collide with other vehicles or to use police vehicles to force any vehicle off the roadway.

F.   Weaponless Defense/Arrest Tactics - Officers may use defense tactics in which Departmental training has been given to control or arrest uncooperative suspects.

G.   Taser Weapons -Taser devices are authorized for use by personnel who are trained and qualified with the weapon.

**H.   Canines - The use of a police canine to search for or apprehend suspects will be considered a use of force under this Order when the canine inflicts injury to any person.

III.   Reports and Documentation

A.   When any force is used to control, arrest or prevent the escape of any suspect, all officers involved will submit a detailed report outlining the circumstances and the exact type and amount of force used.

---

*   [Revised 05-01-91]

**   [Section Inserted 05-01-91]

B.   The following procedures will be followed when any force is used:

1.   An Information Report will be completed.

2.   An Officer's Report [5600-2] will be made with a complete and detailed account of the exact force used.

3.   The reports will be reviewed by the officer's supervisor, who will make a written evaluation and forward the reports through the Chain of Command, to be reviewed at each level and submitted to the Office of the Chief of Police.

4.   The Division Commander will ensure that all provisions of this Order are observed and reports are submitted on a timely basis.

5.   Division Commanders will maintain all documents as directed in this Order.

*C.   Files regarding the use of force [including resisting arrest and canine bites] will be prepared as follows:

1.   All documentation shall be placed in a file folder and secured at the top with an ACCO two hole fastener.

2.   Any photographs or audio/video tapes will be placed in a manila envelop and attached to the inside front file cover.

3.   The initial evaluating supervisor shall be responsible for ensuring that necessary documentation is obtained and properly placed in the file before routing it through the Chain of Command.

4.   The file shall include:

a)   Lieutenant's evaluation [5600-2];

b)   Sergeants evaluation [5600-2];

c)   Information Report(s) [copies];

d)   Involved Officer's report [5600-2];

e)   Arrest Report [if any];

f)   Medical treatment information [if any];

g)   Computer printout of suspect's arrest record [if any]; and,

h)   If an injury has occurred to an involved employee, copies of the Worker's Compensation Forms shall be included.

*   [Section Inserted 05-01-91]

IV.   **Deadly Force**

    A.   Statement of Philosophy

        1.   The Little Rock Police Department, in establishing a philosophy for the use of Deadly Force, places the ultimate value on human life, while considering the legal, moral and ethical implications of its application.

        2.   The citizens of Little Rock have vested their police officers with the responsibility to protect life and property and apprehend criminal offenders. The apprehension of criminal offenders and protection of property must at all times be secondary to the protection of life. Therefore, the use of Deadly Force is not allowed to protect property interests.

        3.   Police Officers are confronted daily with situations where control must be exercised to effect arrests and to protect the public safety. The officers may achieve control of situations by the use of verbal warnings or the use of reasonable physical force. The use of any reasonable physical force must be based on reasonable alternatives that have been considered and would be ineffective. The use of Deadly Force shall be the last alternative, and the officer's responsibility to protect human life must include his own.

    B.   Purpose

        1.   This Order states the Department's policy regarding a police officer's use of Deadly Force; and,

        2.   Establishes policies under which the use of Deadly Force by police officers is permissible.

    C.   Definition - Deadly Force

        1.   "Deadly Force" as used in this policy is defined as that force which creates some specified degree of risk that a reasonable and prudent person would consider likely to cause death or serious physical injury.

    D.   Avoiding the Use of Deadly Force

        1.   Regardless of the nature of crime or the justification for directing Deadly Force at a suspect, officers must remember that their basic responsibility is to protect life. Officers shall not fire their weapons under conditions that would unnecessarily subject bystanders or hostages to death or possible injury, except to preserve life or to prevent serious physical injury. Deadly Force is an act of last resort and will be used only when other reasonable alternatives are impractical or have failed.

        2.   Officers will plan ahead and consider alternatives which will reduce the possibility of needing to use Deadly Force.

E.   The Authorization To Use Deadly Force

　　　1.   Officers may use Deadly Force to protect themselves or others from
　　　　　　what they reasonably believe to be an immediate threat of death
　　　　　　or serious physical injury.

F.   Discharging Firearms at Moving Vehicles

　　　1.   Discharging firearms at a moving or fleeing vehicle is prohibited
　　　　　　unless it is necessary to prevent imminent death or serious
　　　　　　physical injury to the officer or another person.

　　　2.   Officers will not voluntarily place themselves in a position in front of
　　　　　　an oncoming vehicle where Deadly Force is the probable
　　　　　　outcome. When confronted by an oncoming vehicle, officers
　　　　　　will move out of its path, if possible, rather than fire at the
　　　　　　vehicle.

G.   Drawing, Displaying Weapons and Warning Shots

　　　1.   Officers will not fire warning shots.

　　　2.   Officers may draw or display firearms when there is a threat or
　　　　　　reasonable belief that there is a threat to life or when they have
　　　　　　a reasonable fear for their own safety and/or the safety of others.

　　　　　*a)   The use of a firearm itself to strike a suspect is prohibited
　　　　　　　　unless it is necessary to prevent imminent death or
　　　　　　　　serious physical injury to the officer or another person.

　　　3.   Officers will not fire into a building or through doors unless the officer
　　　　　　or someone else is drawing fire and the suspect can be
　　　　　　identified and is clearly visible.

V.   Deadly Force Investigation and Review

A.   Investigation Requirements

　　　1.   Whenever a Little Rock Police Officer becomes involved in an
　　　　　　incident in which either the officer or another person is
　　　　　　seriously injured or killed as a result of police action and/or the
　　　　　　use of Deadly Force, or whenever an officer intentionally
　　　　　　employs Deadly Force but no injury or death results, two (2)
　　　　　　separate investigations shall be initiated - a criminal
　　　　　　investigation and an administrative investigation. [This shall not
　　　　　　be applicable to those instances where the death or injury is the
　　　　　　result of a motor vehicle accident.]

*   [Inserted 05-01-91]

2. The Detective Division will conduct the criminal investigation to facilitate successful prosecution, if deemed appropriate by the Prosecuting Attorney's Office.

   *a) The Crime Scene Search Unit will be summoned to the scene of all officer-involved shootings and will process the scene for evidence in compliance with standard investigative procedures.

3. The Internal Affairs Unit will conduct a separate administrative investigation to ensure compliance with Little Rock Police Department Rules and Regulations and the General Orders. [Internal Affairs will be immediately notified of all intentional uses of Deadly Force and will respond to the scene to conduct the administrative investigation.]

4. Unintentional weapons discharges not resulting in physical injury will be investigated by the involved officer's Chain of Command.

B. On Scene Investigation and Responsibilities

1. The first supervisor on the scene of an officer involved shooting or other incidents established above shall take charge and limit unnecessary access to the scene.

   a) The field supervisor in charge at the scene will be responsible for the integrity of the crime scene until it is released to the Detective Division supervisor.

   b) The ranking supervisor from the Detective Division will be in command of the overall initial investigation and will notify the Pulaski County Prosecuting Attorney's Office.

2. Once the situation has been stabilized, the officer involved will relate a brief account of the incident to the field supervisor, prior to the arrival of Detective personnel, so the supervisor may brief ranking officers requiring administrative information.

3. The Shift or Section Commander and/or Division Commander may relate basic facts to the news media or have the Public Information Officer make the initial release.

4. If the officer involved is not injured, he should retire some distance from the scene to await the arrival of the officer-in-charge of the investigation. This should be done in the company of some companion such as another supervisor or an officer of equal rank [who was not involved in the incident] chosen by the involved officer. The purpose of the companion is to serve the involved officer in a supportive role.

* [Inserted 05-01091]

5.   When the Detective supervisor arrives at the scene he will be briefed by the field supervisor and , if he deems it necessary, the involved officer will report back to the scene and respond to the needs of the investigation.

      a)   When the Detective Division supervisor determines that the involved officer is no longer needed at the scene, the "companion" will transport him to the Detective Division.

6.   The field supervisor at the scene shall have someone not involved in the incident prepare the initial Information Report and other necessary reports and have copies delivered to the Detective Division after supervisory review.

7.   The involved officer shall be afforded an early opportunity to communicate with family members. The person designated as "companion" may assist in making this notification. The Detective supervisor shall ensure that this is accomplished.

C.   Detective Division Investigation

1.   Officers who actually employ Deadly Force shall be requested to make a written and/or oral statement.

2.   Statements from officers involved in the incident shall be taken by Detective Division supervisors.

3.   It shall be the responsibility of the Detective Division supervisor to update the officer, his supervisors, the Office of the Chief of Police, and the Pulaski County Prosecuting Attorney's Office as to the status of the investigation.

4.   The Detective Division will prepare a briefing sheet for the Shift and Section Commanders, who will brief their personnel as soon as practical.

5.   Upon completion of the Detective Division's investigation, a copy of the investigative file will be forwarded to the Chief of Police for review.

D.   Employee Assistance Referral

1.   Officers who have employed Deadly Force which has resulted in injury or death to any person will be referred to the Employee Assistance Program as soon as practical after the incident.

2.   Officers will attend the confidential counseling which will be provided by the Employee Assistance Program.

E.   Internal Affairs Investigation

1.   The Internal Affairs investigation will be conducted upon the completion of the Detective Division's investigation.

2.   The Internal Affairs Investigator shall advise the involved officer(s) of their rights as to the administrative investigation process. Those rights are:

   a)   The right of the Department to conduct an administrative investigation into the specific Deadly Force incident;

   b)   The right to know if he is suspected of misconduct which, if sustained, could be grounds for administrative disciplinary action to include dismissal;

   c)   The right to refuse to answer any questions, but such refusal shall be grounds for disciplinary action including dismissal;

   d)   That the results of the Internal Affairs investigative interview will not be used against the officer(s) in any subsequent criminal proceeding [Garrity v. New Jersey 385 U.S. 493 (1967)];

   e)   The interviewed officer will, upon request, be provided a copy of any of his own statements made during the course of the administrative investigation.

3.   The Internal Affairs investigator shall prepare a report on adherence to policy and submit the Internal Affairs file to the involved officer's Chain of Command for review and recommendations, to be forwarded to the Chief of Police .

F.   Deadly Force Review

1.   The Deadly Force Review Board is established for the purpose of reviewing and evaluating incidents of firearms discharge, both intentional and accidental, resulting in injury or death by sworn members while in the performance of their duties as a police officer and those incidents where an officer or another person is killed by any other means except motor vehicle accidents.

   a)   All incidents as noted above will be reviewed within ten (10) days after the Internal Affairs Unit has completed its investigation.

2.   The Chief of Police, at his discretion, may have the Deadly Force Review Board review any other firearms discharge or intentional use of Deadly Force not resulting in injury or death.

3.   The objective of the Deadly Force Review Board is to make recommendations to the Chief of Police concerning firearms discharges and other incidents described herein based on:

   a)   Avoidability of similar incidents in the future;

   b)   Adequacy of training;

   c)   Adherence to training;

        d)   Adequacy of supervision;

        e)   Adequacy of investigation; and,

        f)   Policy compliance.

4.   The Assistant Chief of Police — Police Operations Bureau shall appoint the Deadly Force Review Board for each incident, comprised of the following:

        a)   Chairman, Captain, not in the officer's Chain of Command.

        b)   Member, Lieutenant, not in the officer's Chain of Command.

        c)   Member, Lieutenant, not in the officer's Chain of Command.

        d)   Member, Sergeant, not in the officer's Chain of Command.

        e)   Member, Training Division representative (Sergeant or above).

5.   The Chairman will convene the Deadly Force Review Board for the purpose of reviewing the Detective Division investigation and the Internal Affairs investigation of each incident.

6.   After conducting the review, the Review Board shall develop its findings and recommendations. The Chairman will submit a written report specifically covering the issues identified in Section F.3.a. through f. and any recommendations to the officer's Division Commander within five (5) days.

7.   The Division Commander will review the Deadly Force Review Board's report and will forward his report to the Office of the Chief of Police.

8.   All investigations, Review Board actions and Chain of Command reviews shall be completed within thirty (30) days from the date of the incident.

VI.   Accidental Discharge of Firearm By Police Officer [No injuries involved]

A.   Purpose

1.   This procedure will be followed any time a member of the Department, on or off duty, accidentally discharges a firearm [and where no injury or death occurs].

B.   Procedure

1.   Any officer who accidentally discharges a firearm will contact an on duty police supervisor, who will initiate an investigation.

2.   The supervisor will complete an Information Report and ensure that the officer(s) involved submit a detailed Officer's Report [5600-2] on the incident.

3. The supervisor will evaluate the officer's performance and submit in writing his findings to be reviewed at each level in the Chain of Command.

C. Monitoring

1. The involved officer's Division Commander will review and maintain the files on all accidental weapons discharges.

VII. Handling Firearms

A. The following rules will govern the safe handling of weapons:

1. Officers will not clean, repair or load firearms in police buildings, except the range, unless ordered to do so by a supervisor.

2. Handguns will not be carried cocked in the holster.

3. Handguns will not be cocked while pursuing, subduing, arresting or searching a suspect or at any other time when the use of Deadly Force is not imminent.

4. Shotguns will not be carried inside a police building with the breach closed.

5. Only Departmentally issued shotguns and ammunition will be carried while on duty.

6. Shotguns shall be carried in shotgun racks in patrol vehicles with the breach closed, chamber empty, magazine full and the safety on.

7. Under no circumstances shall a shotgun be placed in the rack with a round in the chamber or with the safety off.

*8. Officers shall at all times adhere to standard firearms safety instructions provided by Departmental training processes.

VIII. Firearms and Ammunition

A. The only authorized on or off duty firearms are those issued by the Department or those authorized weapons inspected and approved by the Training Division, based on established Departmental criteria approved by the Chief of Police.

B. Only Departmentally issued or approved ammunition will be carried.

C. Officers on duty in plain clothes shall wear their weapon in a holster and in a manner that it will not attract attention or be open to the view of the public outside Departmental offices. [Undercover officers may wear

---

*   [Inserted 05-01-91]

their weapon concealed, without the use of a holster.]

D.   Officers will qualify with authorized weapons on at least an annual basis.

IX.   **Off Duty Weapons Guidelines**

A.   Officers may carry an approved weapon off duty, but will exercise discretion as to when and where it is worn. All sworn personnel will qualify at least annually with their approved off-duty weapon.

1.   Any display or use of an off duty weapon will be governed by the same regulations that apply to on duty officers.

2.   Off duty weapons carried while not in uniform must be kept concealed.

3.   Prior to carrying any non-issue weapon during off duty hours, officers shall have such weapons approved through the Chain of Command and the Office of the Chief of Police.

a)   Off duty weapons shall be submitted to the Training Division for inspection prior to qualification.

b)   Following inspection of the off duty weapon, officers shall be required to maintain an annual range qualification with the weapon until such time as the officer requests that the weapon be no longer considered authorized for off duty use. [Qualification will be accomplished on the requesting officer's off duty time and at his own expense for ammunition.]

c)   Officers who are authorized to carry an automatic pistol on duty shall be limited to an automatic pistol as an off duty alternative; officers authorized to carry a revolver on duty shall be limited to a revolver off duty.

4.   Officers are authorized to carry their on duty weapon while off duty, but as an alternative, they may be authorized for one (1) other Departmentally approved off duty weapon. Approved off duty weapons will not be carried while on duty.

a)   The Training Division shall maintain a current list of weapons which are approved for off duty use. Requests to carry off duty weapons which do not appear on the approved list must be evaluated by the officer's Chain of Command and the Training Division, with final approval from the Chief of Police.

b)   The Training Division will maintain all other records pertaining to the selection of, qualification with, and authorization to carry off duty weapons.

5.   Officers shall not make any modifications to off duty weapons after approval. Any repairs will require that the weapon be resubmitted to the Training Division for inspection.

6.   This Order should not be construed to restrict the legitimate possession and use of sporting or recreational firearms.

X.   Weapon Repairs and Maintenance Guidelines

A.   Only certified police armorers assigned to the Training Division will repair, modify or otherwise work on Departmentally owned weapons.

B.   Officers will be responsible for maintaining issued and personally owned weapons in a clean and serviceable condition.

C.   Officers may install Pachmayr type grips at their own expense.

D.   Officers may purchase and use speed loaders after they have demonstrated proficiency in their use to a Range Officer.

1.   Speedloaders will be carried in a black leather basket weave style carrier.

XI.   Optional 9 MM Pistol Program

A.   Mandatory Requirements

1.   Officers will be allowed to carry an optional 9 mm semiautomatic pistol in lieu of the primary weapon only under the following conditions:

a)   Officers who wish to participate in the Semiautomatic Pistol Program must purchase an approved weapon and all required leather gear at their own expense. [NOTE: Probationary Police Officers are not eligible to participate in this program.]

b)   The Department will provide all ammunition for training and on duty use for all approved 9 mm service weapons. [Ammunition will not be modified.]

c)   Participants must attend and successfully complete a minimum of twenty-four (24) hours of semiautomatic pistol training. [The training course may be extended beyond 24 hours according to the officer's ability to qualify and to handle the weapon to the satisfaction of the Training Division.]

d)   Officers who successfully complete the prescribed training program will be allowed to carry only the authorized 9 mm semiautomatic pistol while on duty. [Upon receipt of 9 mm authorization, officers shall return the issued service revolver to the Training Division.]

B.   Authorized Weapons & Registration Requirements

1.   Optional semiautomatic weapons must be caliber 9mm parabellum only, and will be limited to the following models exclusively:

          a)   Beretta, Model 92SB

          b)   Beretta, Model 92F

          c)   Ruger, Model P-85

          d)   Sig Sauer, Model P225

          e)   Sig Sauer, Model lP226

          f)   Glock, Model 17

          g)   Glock, Model 19

    2.   Weapons must be standard factory production with no modifications.

    3.   Grips must be black high-impact plastic or wood, designed to be used with either hand.

    4.   All weapons declared for use in this program must be inspected and registered with the Department armorer prior to training.

  C.   Leather Gear

    1.   All leather gear is limited to those pieces which conform to the specifications established by the Training Division.

    2.   All leather gear will be purchased by the officer requesting the optional weapon and must be a basketweave design and black in color.

    3.   It shall be the responsibility of each officer desiring to participate in the 9mm program to contact the Training Division to obtain the list of approved leather gear.

  D.   Requests

    1.   Officers who wish to participate in the 9 mm training program must submit their name through the Chain of Command.

    2.   The Division Commander will forward the list of interested personnel to the Training Division for scheduling.

*XII.   Secondary Firearms

  A.   Officers may carry one approved secondary firearm in conjunction with and as a back-up to the officer's primary Departmentally issued or approved firearm.

---

*   **[Section Added 01-08-91]**

B.   The secondary firearm is to be viewed **only** as a weapon of last resort and the use of a secondary firearm will be limited to those instances where an officer's use of Deadly Force is authorized under this General Order **and** the officer's primary firearm has been:

      1.   Lost, stolen, or rendered inoperable during the course of the specific incident authorizing the use of Deadly Force; or,

      2.   Exhausted of ammunition under circumstances which clearly limit the officer's ability to immediately reload.

C.   Secondary firearms are not limited by system [i.e., revolver, semiautomatic, or derringer type] and may be of any standard caliber not to exceed the authorized caliber by firearms type of primary firearms [9mm for semiautomatics, .38 caliber for all others].

D.   Ammunition for secondary firearms will be of a conventional lead or semi-jacketed hollow point variety. Armor piercing, Glazer Rounds, or other types of exotic ammunition, modified ammunition or reloads will not be used.

E.   Secondary firearms will be carried on an officer's person in a concealed, secure, yet accessible manner.

F.   Officers electing to carry a secondary firearm shall comply with the following procedure prior to actually bearing the firearm:

      1.   The secondary firearm and the ammunition for the firearm will be submitted to the Training and Crime Prevention Division for inspection. [**NOTE:** This inspection may include test-firing of the weapon at the applying officer's expense.]

            a)   Training and Crime Prevention Division personnel shall establish that the firearm is safe, functional and in good repair, and that the firearm and ammunition is in compliance with this Order.

            b)   Training and Crime Prevention Division personnel will, upon approval of the firearm and ammunition, complete a Secondary Weapon Authorization Card [L.R.P.D. Form 91-1] and will return the firearm, remaining ammunition, and authorization card to the officer. The authorization card shall record the firearm description, serial number, ammunition type and confirmation that an N.C.I.C. check has been made on the firearm.

            c)   Officers will not be required to qualify with the firearm.

          *d)   Weapons equipped with a "firing pin block" [semiautomatics] or a "hammer block" [revolvers] are preferred; however, some weapons equipped with other external or internal safeties will be authorized providing the officer carried the weapon without a round in the chamber. Safety will be the primary concern of the firearm inspection/authorization process.

    2.   The officer will then submit the secondary firearm, ammunition, and authorization card to his Section/Shift or Watch Commander [Lieutenant]. The Section/Shift or Watch Commander shall satisfy himself that the officer fully understands the limitations on the use of the secondary firearm, that the officer has prepared a suitable manner for carrying the secondary firearm, and that the authorization card is in order. The Section/Shift or Watch Commander will sign the authorization card and forward it to the Training and Crime Prevention Division.

    3.   The Training and Crime Prevention Division shall maintain the Secondary Firearm Authorization Cards in a secure file.

    4.   Training and Crime Prevention Division personnel and/or the Section/Shift or Watch Commander may disallow any firearm or ammunition which they determine does not comply with this General Order.

    5.   Only **one** secondary firearm will be authorized for an officer at any given time. In the event that an officer who is authorized to carry a secondary firearm wishes to carry a different secondary firearm, the new weapon will be submitted to the inspection process described in this Section and, upon approval, the previously authorized weapon will be removed from service. **An officer will carry only the one currently authorized secondary weapon.**

G.   Once an officer has been authorized to carry a particular secondary firearm, he shall carry that secondary firearm only in the prescribed manner whenever he is on duty. While secondary firearms are optional, they will be subject to inspection at any time by any police supervisor.

H.   The authorized secondary firearm may be carried in the prescribed manner whenever the officer is off duty or working in an off-duty capacity and is armed with a Departmentally approved or issued firearm.

I.   In the event that an officer discharges a secondary firearm, accidentally or intentionally, all investigative and reporting procedures established by the General Orders shall apply.

J.   Officers who wish to carry a secondary firearm must provide the weapon, carrying mechanism, and all required ammunition at their own expense.

Research on Deadly Force Policy

Research focusing on shooting policies has addressed the effect of policy restrictiveness and policy enforcement on police shooting behavior. Additionally, some interesting studies have assessed officers' knowledge of departmental policy and state law. These areas are reviewed below.

Policy Restrictiveness and Shooting Rates

Uelmen (1973) conducted one of the earliest studies on deadly force policy. He collected information from 50 police agencies in Los Angeles County to assess policy content, effectiveness, and enforcement. He found great diversity across jurisdictions in terms of policy regarding the use of deadly force against fleeing felons, and lamented that (pp. 59-60):

> A fleeing burglar is neither more nor less dangerous because he happens to be in Azusa rather than Downey. Whether a fleeing juvenile felony suspect should be shot or allowed to escape should not depend upon whether he is in El Monte or El Segundo.

This diversity of content across jurisdictions, which Uelmen found in the early seventies, has been lessened due to the move toward more restrictive policies culminating with the *Garner* decision.

Uelmen also found, as one would expect, that shooting rates correlated with policy restrictiveness. He commented that (1973:44),

> If police policy regarding the use of deadly force does act as a restraining influence upon police officers, then those departments with the most restrictive policies should have relatively fewer incidents in which firearms are discharged than those departments with less restrictive policies.

To test this proposition, he divided the 50 departments into five categories based on restrictiveness of policy and compared the groups with regard to the rate of shooting incidents per 1,000 felony arrests. He found that the departments in the most restrictive policy category had approximately one-half the shooting rates of departments with the least restrictive policies. The shooting of fleeing felons accounted for a large part of the differences in rates, which corresponds with the differences in policies. However, Uelman found that departments with more restrictive policies had fewer defense of life shootings as well.

Fyfe (1979) documented the effects of a new shooting policy and new shooting review procedures in New York City. The New York City Police Department adopted a more restrictive policy in 1972, which delimited further a Forcible Felony statute and provided for a Firearms Discharge Review Board to investigate and evaluate all discharges by department police. Fyfe studied all police discharges in that city between January 1, 1971 and December 31, 1975 to assess the effect of this more restrictive shooting policy and the more comprehensive follow-up procedures on the "frequency, nature, and consequences of police shooting in New York City" (p. 312). He found a "considerable reduction" in police firearms discharges following the policy modifications. The greatest reduction was in the "most controversial shootings," that is, those involving fleeing felons or the prevention or termination of a crime. Similarly, Meyer (1980) found a reduction in police shootings following the implementation of a more restrictive policy in Los Angeles, and Sherman (1983) reported reductions in police gun use in Atlanta, Georgia and Kansas City, Missouri following policy changes. Most of the studies which documented decreases in shooting rates following implementation of more restrictive policies also found no increase in risk of harm to officers (Fyfe, 1979; Sherman, 1983).

There is no better example of the effects of a change in a deadly force policy than what took place in May, 1980 in Miami, Florida. A riot broke out in the streets and looters were observed taking goods from stores which had been set on fire or had their doors or windows broken. According to the 1980 Florida state statutes and departmental policy, these looters, or fleeing felons, could be shot. In fact, during the first day of the riot, several were shot. However, on May 18, 1980, the deadly force policy was changed in the midst of the riot and officers were not permitted to shoot at fleeing felons to effect an arrest. It has been reported that many looters were not shot but could have been shot under the old policy and state law (Porter and Dunn, 1980).

Policy Enforcement and Shooting Behavior

Persons researching deadly force policy have emphasized that the *content* of the guidelines is not the only departmental factor related to shooting rates. Sherman (1983), for instance, maintained that findings of reduced shootings following policy adoption in the cities he studied (123):

> . . . do not suggest that these results can be achieved by the mere invocation of a written policy. The policy changes in each of these cities were all accompanied by intense public criticism of the police and an increasingly severe administrative and disciplinary posture toward shooting. The public criticism eventually died down without the gun use rate returning to earlier levels, but the criticism might have been a necessary condition for unfreezing the patterns of organizational behavior. When the administrative climate changed in Kansas City, however, due to the departure of the chief who implemented the new policy, gun use went back up to its prepolicy change levels.

Other researchers, too, have documented the effects of "administrative posture regarding compliance" (Waegel, 1984:137) and, relatedly, enforcement modes. Fyfe noted the importance, not only of the new, more restrictive policy in New York City but also the establishment of the Firearms Discharge Review Board for policy enforcement. Waegel (1984) examined police shootings in Philadelphia between 1970 and 1978 to assess departmental compliance with a statutory change in deadly force law which occurred in 1973. The change was from a common law any-fleeing-felon law to a forcible felony statute. Waegel found "substantial noncompliance" with the new law. He reported that 20 percent of the shooting incidents after the statute change were unlawful, suggesting that "statutory change alone may not be sufficient to bring about desired changes in police behavior" (p. 136). Instead, he argued that without a strong administrative stance the changes in behavior called for by a statutory revision will not occur.

Fyfe (1988) criticized the methodology of Waegel but agreed with the conclusion. Fyfe looked closely at the Philadelphia experience in terms of the role played by Frank Rizzo, who served first as police commissioner and then as Mayor during the period 1970 and 1979. Fyfe reported (1988:182): "From [1973] until Rizzo left office, PPD adopted an operating style in which police were effectively free to do anything with their guns, as long as they did not use them to resolve their own personal disputes." The rate of homicides by police per 1,000 officers was 2.09 during the time Rizzo was police commissioner and was 2.29 when he was mayor. After he left office, the rate dropped to 1.05.

Officer Knowledge of Policy

In addition to assessing the effects of policy restrictiveness and enforcement on police shootings, research has addressed officer knowledge of policy. Uelmen (1973) included this focus in his study of Los Angeles County departments. He found a great deal of disparity in the interpretations of individual policies within departments, in large part because "(m)any of the written policy statements encountered in Los Angeles County appear to be models of ambiguity, rather than clarity" (p. 26). Though it can be argued that policies have, over the years, been stated in clearer terms, Binder, et al. (1982) found an alarming rate of officer ignorance regarding departmental policy and state law. For the four-city study described above, surveys were developed which assessed officers' knowledge of the parameters for use of deadly force in their jurisdictions. Binder, et al. found, for instance, that 22 percent of the officers surveyed in Oakland incorrectly believed they could shoot any fleeing felony suspect. In Birmingham, 23 percent of the officers believed it was lawful to shoot a fleeing misdemeanant!

Training Methods

Advances in policy restrictiveness and enforcement have been accompanied by advances in deadly force training. In their 1981 publication, Geller and Karales referred to four components of deadly force training. These are the teaching of departmental policy, human relations, tactics, and weapons proficiency. These components have not changed, but the improvement of police training in firearms use has resulted in a blurring of the distinctions among these areas. That is, the components have become more integrated with each other, and training methods have become more comprehensive and more realistic. Training has advanced from the use of a simple bull's eye course emphasizing marksmanship to much more sophisticated programs which provide training in decision-making and defusing potentially violent confrontations. The direction of training reflects the broader conceptualization of police-citizen violent encounters discussed in previous chapters.

Bull's Eye and Practical Pistol Courses

Not too many years ago, training in deadly force consisted of teaching departmental policy in a classroom setting and developing firearms expertise using a bull's-eye course. On the bull's-eye course, a trainee in a standing position would shoot an already-unholstered weapon at a static paper target (maybe 60 feet away) on command from the training officer during daylight hours. "Enhanced" training of this type might include "double action" firing (hammer is not cocked manually prior to pulling the trigger) or target practice with a shotgun. Scharf and Binder (1983:202) described some of the drawbacks of the bull's-eye course:

> Critics point out that such range shooting does not prepare officers for real-life armed confrontations. For one thing, realistic levels of stress are certainly absent from such training exercises. Observations of officers who had achieved high scores in static training revealed that accuracy scores tended to plummet dramatically when the men were harassed by range officers or after they ran 100 yards. Furthermore, officers will often practice shooting while firing from an arm rest in a static position. As one officer who had been involved in several shootings sarcastically commented, "It's completely unrealistic, a police Disneyland. You have time to set up; no one is trying to kill you and you aren't completely stressed out from six other insane assignments. Also you're not moving and the target's not moving. Otherwise the training is fantastic here."

A more advanced training technique, the Practical Pistol Course, addressed some of these problems. Officers training with this type of course shoot from various (and more realistic) distances, from various positions (e.g., standing, crouching, and kneeling), in the open or from behind barricades, under various lighting conditions, and under time constraints. The course might employ multiple (pop-up or rotating) targets so that the officer had to distinguish quickly between the "good guy" and the "bad guy" and shoot the latter. "Stress courses" incorporated physical exertion (such as running a quarter of a mile before shooting) in an attempt to enhance the reality of training.

Shoot/Don't Shoot

Though the practical pistol and stress courses are improvements over the bull's eye course, they are still a far cry from simulating the reality of a deadly force situation. One important aspect of this lack of reality is that the above techniques lack adequate training on decision-making. That is, they focus on how to shoot (and possibly *whom* to shoot), not *when* to shoot. As important as having proficiency in the use of firearms is having the skills to make the appropriate decision to shoot or not to shoot in a particular situation, and having the skills to minimize the possibility of a shooting. This emphasis for deadly force training was advocated by the Dade County, Florida Grand Jury following an investigation precipitated by a "number of police shootings which . . . occurred in a short period of time" (Dade County Grand Jury, 1983). Specifically, the Grand Jury recommended, "a new emphasis in police work which recognizes that training in restraint and patience is at least as important as training in the use of deadly weapons" (p. 2).

This move from exclusive emphasis on firearms proficiency to deadly force decision-making marks a major advancement in deadly force training. One of the first applications of this philosophy is the "shoot/don't shoot" program in which an officer is placed in a room in which a film portraying an encounter with a citizen (or citizens) is projected on the front wall. The officer is instructed to act as he would if he were involved in this situation on the job; all of the scenarios require a decision regarding whether to use deadly force. The better programs have the officers make use of cover and tactical skills when responding to the stimuli on the screen.

Edholm (1978) described one of the scenarios which an officer might face in a shoot/don't shoot training session. In this situation, an officer patrolling the downtown alone hears the dispatcher's voice:

> "Any unit in the vicinity, we have a report of a major 415 at the Beverly Hills Tavern, located at 900 SSM. Irate customers who were ejected from the bar have returned and are now assaulting employees and customers and breaking up furniture."
>
> . . . Arriving on the scene, [the officer] pulls into the rear alley. As he exits the vehicle, additional information comes over the radio.
>
> "Three suspects are reported still at the location. All are white male adults, 6 feet and 200 lbs. One is armed with a crowbar, another with a butcher knife, and the third with an unknown type weapon. Nearest backup unit has an ETA of three minutes."
>
> Alone, Smith moves cautiously toward the rear of the location. Suddenly four persons come running out of the rear door of the tavern. At first in the dimly-lit alley Smith cannot distinguish any of the suspects, but as they move toward him he can tell that three are male and one is female. All appear to be carrying objects and are rapidly closing in on his position.

In this, as in other "shoot/don't shoot" scenarios, the officer must decide whether to shoot and whom to shoot.

There are several variations on the "shoot/don't shoot" training. One variation is the use of live persons in setting up the police-citizen encounter. For instance, Geller and Karales (1981) describe a tactical training course in a simulated apartment which uses both live persons and mannequins to provide "shoot/don't shoot" stimuli to officers. Another variation in the "shoot/don't shoot" method incorporates technology which provides detailed information regarding the officer's decision to shoot, specifically, whether he shot in time and hit his target. Doerner and Ho (n.d.:10) described the Firearms Training Systems (FATS) which provides this type of feedback:

> Besides deciding if the use of lethal force is warranted, the officer must select which target poses the greatest hazard if there are multiple suspects. When the officer discharges the weapon, the system marks bullet "holes" instantly and sequentially on the screen with different colors.
>
> . . . FATS displays three scores (decision, reaction time, and accuracy) at the end of the scenario. Decision refers to whether the judgment to shoot or to refrain from shooting was sound under the circumstances. The computer calculates reaction time in seconds from the point of confrontation to when a bullet strikes the target. Marks of "too slow reaction" or "late hit" appear when the officer discharges too late or is shot first. Accuracy is a tally of the number of hits and misses.

Defusing or Avoiding Violent Encounters

The "shoot/don't shoot" training method has been criticized for promoting the idea that police are in constant danger, thus creating "undue anxiety on the part of the officers" (Blumberg, 1989:460) and because the focus of the training is on the "final frame" of the encounter. Addressing this latter deficit, the training of "tactics" has broadened considerably to involve educating officers in ways to "reduce the risk of armed confrontation" (Scharf and Binder, 1983:206). This latter focus reflects the Binder/Scharf phase conceptualization of potentially violent encounters, described in Chapter 4. Recall that these researchers argued that decisions made by police early in encounters with citizens may increase or decrease the likelihood of a violent outcome. Thus, the new tactical training "attempts to influence officer decision making well before the actual decision to shoot" (Scharf and Binder, 1983:207). Major emphases of this training include gaining tactical advantage and appropriate use of cover, as well as de-escalating volatile or potentially volatile situations.

"Survival City," of the Metro-Dade Police Firearm Range uses role-playing of police/citizen encounters to "enhance patrol officers' skills in defusing the potentially violent situations (PV) they encounter every day" (Fyfe, 1988:1). Officers in groups are assigned various roles, such as that of a perpetrator, bystander, or officer. Those in non-officer roles have a fair amount of discretion in playing their roles, but are told to "exploit officers' mistakes to the maximum and to illustrate their consequences as forcefully as possible" (Fyfe, 1987a:52). Fyfe (1987a:52) who, with The Police Foundation, evaluated the training regimen, described one of the potentially violent scenarios and the consequences of police mistakes:

One PV scenario, for example, involved a "high-risk vehicle" officers knew only to be the subject of a vague "be on the lookout" bulletin, but which was, in fact, occupied by heavily armed robbers and a victim they had taken hostage. Officers who approached it nonchalantly, or without first calling for assistance, were almost invariably shot to death; officers who allowed the vehicle's occupants to exit in a group (rather than one-by-one) or without first taking measures to assure that they had no weapons in their hands almost invariably found themselves in stand-offs with kidnappers armed with a machine gun, a sawed-off shotgun, and a revolver, and protected by the hostage they used as a shield.

The designers of the training emphasized the importance, not just of safety tactics, but of officer sensitivity and politeness when dealing with citizens in order to avoid escalation to violence. In this vein, Scharf and Binder (1983) described the relevance of teaching officers interpersonal skills and crisis intervention skills which may help to defuse confrontations with agitated citizens. Geller (1982) also noted the importance of multi-cultural awareness on the part of officers. He explained (1982:172) that we need to "sensitize officers to . . . cultural differences among racial and ethnic groups that might lead officers to misread the dangerousness of a situation on the street."

Conclusion

Police policies on both firearms use and pursuits attempt to balance the need to apprehend suspects with the value of human life. The research that has been conducted in both of these areas has been helpful in discerning effective policy parameters. The move for both firearms use and pursuits has been toward policies which further restrict police power.

Concurrent with these changes in policy content has been the adoption of more effective policy enforcement mechanisms. An increasing number of departments, for instance, require that officers submit a report for each firearms discharge and each pursuit. These reports are reviewed by various persons or panels within the departments, and, in many communities, the more serious incidents are reviewed by entities outside the department (e.g., the Prosecutor's Office and/or a board of citizens).

Training of officers has also improved greatly over the years. There clearly is a corollary between the advances in researchers' conceptualizations of deadly force and the methodologies used to train officers in this area. Deadly force is no longer conceived of as a "split second decision" to shoot a firearm, but rather as an event characterized by a series of decisions which may culminate in a choice to use deadly force or to exercise restraint. Reflecting this conceptualization, training has advanced from the 60-foot shoot at concentric circles on the chest of a silhouette to some very advanced methods emphasizing the avoidance of violent encounters with "smart" early decisions and appropriate decisions not to use deadly force.

The Minnesota Board of Peace Officer Standards and Training (POST) has
taken a major step by sponsoring legislation requiring all departments in the state
to have a written policy, training to the policy and a mandatory reporting system.
Similar to what POST has done for pursuit driving (See Chapter 6), this new
law (Minnesota Statutes 1990, § 626.553) requires that all intentional firearm
discharges shall be documented and a written report shall be submitted to POST.
In turn, this information will be analyzed and submitted to the legislature (see
Minnesota Board of Peace Officer Standards and Training, 1991). This requirement represents significant progress in the compilation and analysis of shooting
statistics.

There have been many advances in the area of police use of firearms during
the past three decades. The material in the previous chapters has described these
methodological advancements and research findings which have increased our
knowledge. This information has led to changes in policy and advances in training
which were also reviewed above.

In the two chapters that follow, the corresponding topics in police pursuit driving
are addressed. The research, research methodologies, and the policies and training
programs for pursuit, however, have not reached the level of sophistication
attained for firearms. This is due to the differential attention the two areas have
received from the public and, consequently, practitioners and researchers. We
will return to the discussion of the public responses to the use of deadly force
with firearms and with vehicles in the final chapter.

Research on Police Pursuits

6

Compared to research on police use of firearms, research on pursuit is conspicuously deficient. Therefore, and unfortunately, this chapter summarizing the research on pursuit is relatively simple and brief! It was not until the 1960s that police pursuit was considered a problem for either the police or the public, or as a topic for research. During that decade, several influential civic groups began to notice and to comment publicly that pursuit driving resulted in disastrous and expensive outcomes. Others, mainly members of the law enforcement community, contradicted these claims by stating that the nature and extent of these negative outcomes were being grossly exaggerated and that pursuit was a necessary tactic for law enforcement. Opinions from both sides were being reflected in media reports and editorial comments. Although only anecdotal information was available, it was being stated as fact. Just as quickly as one side would issue a statement, there would be a counter-proposal or statement issued by the other side. This battle was fought with rhetoric by both schools of thought for many years without a real winner or loser (see Fennessy et al., 1970). However, the controversy surrounding pursuit driving continued to escalate. The positive result from this debate was the discovery that empirical research would help answer many of the questions.

During the 1960s, the self-appointed and unofficial representatives publicizing the negative aspects of pursuit were The Physicians for Automotive Safety. Members from the law enforcement community soon banded together to counter the attack (see Fennessy et al., 1970). The Physicians for Automotive Safety released a report in 1968 citing the dangers of high-speed pursuit which shocked the American public. The figures, which are still cited in the 1990s, included the following:

1. one out of five pursuits ends in death;
2. five out of ten pursuits end in serious injuries;
3. seven out of ten pursuits end in accidents;
4. one out of 25 killed is a law enforcement officer;
5. four out of five pursuits are for minor offenses; and
6. pursuits cause more than 500 deaths each year.

99

The conclusions of the report were stated unequivocally:

> Our study casts grave doubt on the payoff in rapid pursuit. The costs in deaths
> and injuries hardly sustain the risks involved, especially for the police and
> innocent bystanders. The whole paramount concern is public health, we have
> no conflict in judging the value of human life before all other considerations
> (quoted in Fennessy et al., 1970:9).

The report and its conclusions created a commotion within law enforcement
circles. Beyond the obvious threat to the police machismo, pursuit was considered
a necessary tactic to maintain credibility and to deter criminals from fleeing. The
police community justified its position by stating that "more and not less crashes
would result if their apprehension credibility were threatened. Further, they
contend that a majority of pursuits are successfully terminated without accident"
(see Fennessy et al., 1970:10).

The Fennessy Report

These claims and their counter-claims formed the basis for the two schools of
thought evaluated by the courts and discussed in our chapter on legal issues
(Chapter 2). Although there had been attempts to assess police emergency driving
and particularly pursuit driving during the 1960s, the first complete study on pursuits was sponsored by the U.S. Department of Transportation and published by
Fennessy et al., (1970 and see Fennessy and Joscelyn, 1972). This important study
summarized previous work on pursuits and characterized it as being "distinguished
primarily by the absence of any work of quantitative substance" (1970:151). The
researchers reached the following conclusions based upon a combination of their
limited quantitative data and their thorough review of other available information
(1970: 150, 153):

> Hot pursuit is a highly controversial topic, bound up in the broader issue
> of what constitutes effective law enforcement. From a sizable and influential
> police viewpoint, their freedom to pursue law violators is a vital measure
> of their deterrent capability not only in terms of their traffic supervision
> mission, but also in relation to their broader crime control responsibilities.
> The basic argument advanced by this group is that if police were forbidden
> to engage in hot pursuit or unduly restricted then chaos on the highways
> would be the result.
>
> By way of contrast, an equally influential group from the traffic safety
> 'community,' particularly physicians, believes that high-speed hot pursuits
> result in an unacceptable number of casualties. They further believe that
> human life is much too valuable to be jeopardized in the maintenance of
> what they regard as an unproved police assertion.
>
> The basic reason for this divergence of opinion is the almost total lack of
> reliable data on the nature of the hot pursuit situation. It would not be
> meaningful or scientifically defensible, to compute ratios of the relationships
> of pursuits to crashes because of the conceptual uncertainties present in and
> the wide variability of the data.

In an effort to determine the public's response to pursuit driving, a small public opinion survey was conducted which measured the support for police pursuit driving. According to Fennessy et al. (1970:11), a random sample of the driving population of Fairfax County, Virginia was questioned about pursuit driving and penalties for fleeing from the police. Each subject was given a short scenario in which a motorist did not respond to a police officer's emergency signals and began to flee. Sixty-four percent of the subjects agreed that the police should chase the suspect, 33% responded that they should not chase the suspect and 3% did not reply. In addition, members of the driving public were asked to indicate whether a fleeing motorist should be sent to prison, lose his license, receive a heavy fine or receive a light fine. Almost 11% responded that the fleeing motorist should be sent to prison and almost 63% reported that he should lose his license. Twenty-six percent wanted the law violator fined heavily and no one reported a light fine as an appropriate punishment. There is no doubt from the data reported in this survey that the public in the late 1960s was less than unanimous in its support for pursuit driving and regarded fleeing from a police officer as a serious law violation and supported relatively heavy sanctions.

After reviewing the available information, Fennessy and his associates recognized that no solution should be considered which would impair the ability of the police to fulfill their responsibilities. Unfortunately, Fennessy et al., did not define or analyze these responsibilities and did not determine the risk of pursuit. However, they identified the most appropriate outcomes by which future research should evaluate pursuit driving. They suggested that the reduction of crashes, injuries and deaths are the main goals of any policy or practice. Although many individual police agencies and professional associations responded to their call for investigation and improvements in police pursuit policies and practices, it was not until the 1980s that any additional empirical research was reported.

The California Highway Patrol Study

The second generation of research on police pursuits was initiated in the early 1980s. The California Highway Patrol (CHP), responding to the pleas from the decade before, conducted an exploratory study on police pursuit. Although limited to a six-month period, and substantially limited to freeways, the study follows many of the suggestions made by Fennessy et al. (1970) and provides an excellent base of information. The CHP study reports findings from an analysis of almost 700 pursuits. The data from this study demonstrated that:

1. 683 pursuits were conducted;
2. 198 pursuits (29%) resulted in accidents;
3. 99 pursuits (11%) resulted in injuries;
4. 7 pursuits (1%) resulted in deaths;

5. 27 pursuits (4%) were voluntarily terminated by the officer.

6. 429 (63%) of the pursuits were initiated for traffic offenses;

7. 179 (26%) of the pursuits were initiated for DUI;

8. 75 (11%) of the pursuits were initiated for serious criminal activity; and

9. 243. (36%) pursuits, were voluntarily terminated by the driver who surrendered.

Two of the most important findings reported by the California Highway Patrol are that:

1) 77 percent of the suspects were apprehended; and

2) 70 percent of the pursuits ended without an accident.

These data were the first to refute the claims of The Physicians for Automotive Safety. The earlier report improperly estimated the rate of accidents, injury and death. These data elements have become the cornerstones of research and are used by law enforcement agencies which conduct research on pursuit.

One aspect of the CHP study which has not been replicated in subsequent research is the suspect's reason for avoiding arrest (1983:72). Although these data were based on the judgment of the arresting officer, they provide an interesting and important supposition. The four most prevalent reasons are:

1. To avoid a DUI-drug arrest. 130 (19%);

2. To avoid a citation. 93 (14%);

3. Suspect was fleeing in a stolen vehicle. 84 (12%);

4. To avoid a penal code related arrest. 74 (11%).

Other answers included that the suspect was afraid of the police, disliked the police, enjoyed the excitement of the chase and one officer reported that the suspect ran because he was unclothed (1983: 72).

The California study, in spite of being mostly limited to freeways, moves far beyond earlier work and provides findings and conclusions for other researchers to test. The data reported by the Highway Patrol adds empirical support to the conclusions suggested by the Fennessy report. The CHP concluded that pursuits do not typically end in injury or death as the various media and information presented in police textbooks often imply. There is little doubt that research conducted subsequent to the CHP study will continue to improve on the methods used and to test the generalizability of some of the findings.

The 1970 Fennessey study recommended the *outcome* of the pursuit as the best measure of its risk. Decisions about pursuits that must be made and reduced to policies and rules depend, in part, on these risks. While measures other than outcome are important, it is the outcome of a pursuit which most concerns the parties involved. The general opinion of the California Highway Patrol, based upon its data, is that pursuits are worth the inherent risks; the CHP report concluded:

Attempted apprehension of motorists in violation of what appear to be minor traffic infractions is necessary for the preservation of order on the highways of California. If approximately 700 people will attempt to flee from the officers who participated in this six-month study, knowing full well that the officers would give chase, one can imagine what would happen if the police suddenly banned pursuits. Undoubtedly, innocent people may be injured or killed because an officer chooses to pursue a suspect, but this risk is necessary to avoid the even greater loss that would occur if law enforcement agencies were not allowed to aggressively pursue violators (1983: 21).

Not all police administrators, policy makers or politicians will agree with the conclusions drawn by the California Highway Patrol study. Certainly, citizens reading about the damage, injuries and deaths which result from police pursuits will be concerned. Politicians reading about the spectacular pursuits which often end in death or injury may encourage or insist that law-enforcement agencies reduce or eliminate pursuits. One excellent justification for this concern is a recommendation made in the Report of The California Highway Patrol. "[A] very effective technique in apprehending pursued violators may be simply to follow the violator until he voluntarily stops or crashes" (1983:17). Pressure brought on police administrators may influence them to restrict pursuits in one or more ways in order to avoid or reduce accidents and to meet local expectations. Departmental regulations may vary between vague policies which leave discretion to the officers and very specific rules which remove discretion from the officers. These regulations may discourage police from pursuing offenders, or they may say nothing about who should and should not be pursued and under what conditions. Although departmental policies determine the actions which should be taken by the officers, the expanding area of law which was discussed earlier must be considered by legal advisors and policy-makers responsible for policy development, training and supervision of pursuit driving.

Beyond The Highway Patrol Study

Since the publicity of the California Highway Patrol Study, several agencies and researchers have initiated their own empirical research. These efforts range from simplistic and flawed to complex and important. Professor Erik Beckman has reported findings from his research (1986, 1987) and has concluded that offenders are most often captured (77%) but escape from almost one-fourth of the pursuits (22%). He reports that 1% of the pursuits result in a category labeled "other." Beckman concludes (1986:34) that "no pursuit speed, distance or duration in time is particularly safe." Professor Beckman's study is noted as information only, as its methodology restricts its contribution. Beckman bases his results on data sent to him from 40 police departments and 35 sheriff's departments in Alabama, Arizona, California, Florida, Georgia, Hawaii, Louisiana, South Carolina, Tennessee as well as Guam and the Virgin Islands between April 1, and September 30, 1984. In other words, he reports data from 424 pursuits from 75 law enforcement agencies in nine states and two territories over a six-month period. This averages to less than six pursuits from each department, and there is no indication whether the data represent all pursuits or a convenient sample sent to professor Beckman. Unfortunately, the lack of control and questionable quality of the data diminish the value of his analyses.

Among the most comprehensive studies which contribute to our empirical knowledge of pursuit are those of The Solicitor General's Office in Ontario, Canada (1985), Alpert and Dunham (1989, 1990) and The Minnesota Board of Police Officer Standards and Training (1989). As these are the most comprehensive, they deserve further attention. Any interpretation of the data from The Solicitor General's Office Report must recognize the cultural and social differences between Canada and the United States. Perhaps the best example demonstrating those differences is the comparative study on homicide in Seattle and in Vancouver, British Columbia. In that study, the authors reported the need to understand the cultural differences and the differential respect for law and order between the citizens of the two countries (Sloan et al., 1988). The data from studies conducted in this country also require an understanding of the context in which they were collected. Unfortunately, the lack of uniform data elements or collection instruments limits the comparisons that can be made among the studies.

The Solicitor General's Office in Ontario, Canada

The Solicitor General's Special Committee on Police Pursuit (1985) reported several important observations and findings for the four year period, 1981-1984:

1. 6,757 pursuits were conducted;
2. 1,578 pursuits (23%) resulted in accidents;
3. 642 pursuits (10%) resulted in injuries;
4. 32 pursuits (.5%) resulted in deaths;
5. 1,219 pursuits (18%) were voluntarily terminated by the officer;
6. 57% of the pursuits were initiated for simple traffic offenses;
7. 27% of the pursuits were initiated for dangerous driving or impaired driving;
8. 2% of the pursuits were initiated for suspended driver's licenses;
9. 9% of the pursuits were initiated for auto theft; and
10. 5% of the pursuits were initiated for serious criminal activity.

Unfortunately, no data were reported concerning apprehensions or escapes. However, after studying the problem of pursuit driving in Ontario, the Report concluded that (1985:1):

In comparison to the hazards created by vehicle pursuit, the offences usually responsible for pursuit are minor and the reason a motorist chooses to flee is rarely related to a grave or violent crime This generally disproportionate relationship between the hazards of and causes of pursuit, and the fact that only rarely are grave offenders, whose violations warrant their immediate arrest, apprehended by means of vehicle pursuit, indicate that many vehicle pursuits permitted under present policy in Ontario should not occur.

The Alpert and Dunham Studies

These studies are based on aggregated pursuit data which were collected from the two major police departments in Dade County, Florida (MDPD, the Metro-Dade Police Department and MPD, the City of Miami Police Department) during the years 1985, 1986 and 1987 (see Alpert, 1987, Alpert and Dunham, 1988b, 1990). There are nine hundred and fifty-two pursuits included in this analysis. The major findings consistent with the data reported in the other studies are:

1. 952 pursuits were conducted;
2. 364 pursuits (38%) resulted in accidents;
3. 160 pursuits (17%) resulted in injuries;
4. 7 pursuits (.7%) resulted in deaths;
5. 40 pursuits (4%) were voluntarily terminated by the officer;
6. 512 (54%) of the pursuits were initiated for traffic offenses;
7. 19 (2%) of the pursuits were initiated for reckless driving or impaired driving;
8. 312 (33%) of the pursuits were initiated for serious criminal activity; and
9. 107 (11%) of the pursuits were initiated for a BOLO.

As more detailed information has been recorded from these pursuits than in any of the other studies, a more complex analysis will be presented. The descriptive statistics, including the number and duration of pursuits, the reason for beginning the pursuits (BOLO refers to be on the look-out for . . .), and the outcomes of the pursuits (i.e. arrests, deaths, escapes, accidents, injuries and property damage) are presented in Table 6.1.

As indicated by the data in Table 6.1, 952 pursuits were analyzed in this study. Sixty-three percent of the pursuits involved only one police vehicle, and 329 of the pursuits (68% on which data were available) lasted 5 minutes or less. Six hundred and forty-six offenders (68%) were arrested, while 298 (31%) escaped, and 7 (1%) died. Five hundred and twelve pursuits were initiated for traffic violations (54%), and 305 pursuits (49% of those arrested) resulted in pursuit-related arrests. An additional 314 pursuits (50%) resulted in felony arrests. Three hundred and ten pursuits ended in an accident—33% of all pursuits or 47% of the 653 pursuits ending in an arrest or death. Seven hundred and eighty-two of

---

Table 6.1
Overview of Police Pursuits

Number of Pursuits:			952	

Duration of Pursuits (minutes):	< 3	3 – 5	6 – 9	10 +
	217	329	141	114

Reason for Pursuit:

Traffic	BOLO	Felony Stops/ Suspected Felons	Reckless/ DUI
512	107	312	19

Pursuits Ending in Arrests	646
Pursuits Ending in Death	7
Pursuits Ending in Escape	298
Total Accidents	310
Personal Injuries	160
Property Damage	364
Voluntarily Terminated By Officer or Supervisor	40*

---

* This figure does not include the police being outrun.

---

the pursuits ended with no personal injuries (83% of all pursuits), while 102 pursuits ended with injuries to the suspect or his passenger. Seventeen pursuits resulted in injuries to police officers, and 9 pursuits ended with injuries to bystanders only. Nine pursuits ended with injuries to an officer and a defendant, and four pursuits resulted in an injury to both an officer and a bystander. In other words, 160 pursuits (17%) ended in personal injuries. There were 7 pursuit-related deaths during the periods under investigation.

Focusing on the outcome of the pursuit may not be the best method of determining a good pursuit, but it is an important criterion that can be measured, and the outcome of pursuit driving is the major concern of interested parties. Additionally, what has been written about pursuits directs attention to their dangerousness. Specifically, there has been concern over the dangerousness of the traffic-related pursuit in relation to the relatively minor traffic infractions often prompting the chase. These issues concerning the danger of pursuits are addressed in the data presented in Table 6.2: an inspection of the bi-variate relationship between reasons for pursuing and the outcome of the pursuit.

The data presented in Table 6.2 reveal the relationship between two important pursuit variables: why they are initiated, and how they end. There were 952 pursuits, the majority of which were initiated for traffic offenses (54%). Police initiated 11% of the pursuits for memoranda and calls instructing them to "Be

Table 6.2

Outcome of Pursuit by Reason for Pursuit

Reason	Traffic	BOLO	Felony Stop/ Suspected Felon	Reckless/ DUI	Total
Outcome*					
Defendant Arrested	332 (65%)**	81 (76%)	218 (70%)	13 (68%)	644
Defendant Escaped	144 (28%)	25 (23%)	85 (27%)	4 (21%)	258
Death	4 (1%)	____	3 (1%)	____	7
Accident	150 (29%)	41 (38%)	112 (36%)	5 (26%)	308
Voluntary Termination	31 (6%)	1 (2%)	6 (2%)	2 (11%)	40

*In some cases there is more than one outcome per pursuit (i.e., an accident and an arrest). As a result, this Table is based upon 1257 outcomes rather than the 952 pursuits. It is for this reason that column percentages total to more than 100% and that the figures in this Table may not correspond to figures in Table 6.1.

**Percentages are based upon the reason for pursuit categories in Table 6.1 (i.e., in this case, 65% of all traffic-initiated pursuits resulted in an arrest).

Column percentages total to more than 100% because some cases fit into more than one category of outcome (i.e. accident and arrest).

On The Look-Out For" (BOLO) a specific offender. Thirty-two percent of the pursuits were initiated for felony stops and suspected felony stops. Two percent of the pursuits were initiated because the officers suspected reckless driving or driving under-the-influence.

There are five categories of pursuit outcome: arrest, escape, death, pursuit ending in an accident or voluntary termination on the part of the police. Obviously, more than one of these outcomes may happen in a single pursuit. For example, a pursuit may end in an accident and the defendant may be arrested. Therefore, these columns total to more than one hundred percent. In sixty-eight percent of the pursuits, the defendant was arrested. Thirty-one percent of pursuits resulted in the defendant's escape and one percent resulted in a death. Thirty-two percent ended in an accident and four percent were voluntarily terminated by the police.

Pursuits initiated by BOLO calls were the most likely to end in an arrest (76%), while pursuits initiated for traffic-related incidents resulted in the smallest proportion of arrests (65%). Defendants were most likely to escape in traffic-initiated pursuits (28%) and felony stops (27%); they were least likely to escape in reckless driving or DUI-initiated pursuits (21%). Traffic-related pursuits and felony stops were the most likely to result in a death. Accidents were most likely in BOLO and felony stops (38% and 36%, respectively). The pursuits least likely to end in an accident were pursuits initiated because of reckless driving and DUIs (26%) and traffic stops (29%). Voluntary terminations by the police were most likely in those pursuits initiated for suspected driving under the influence of alcohol or drugs and reckless driving (11%) and least likely in BOLO and felony stops (1% and 2%, respectively).

These findings can not be generalized to other departments or agencies which do not have similar safeguards. They must be understood in light of the strict policies, training, supervision and officer accountability maintained through mandatory report writing required of the MPD and MDPD officers during the research (see Alpert and Dunham, 1989 and 1990).

Minnesota Board of Peace Officer Standards and Training

In 1988, the Minnesota Board of Peace Officer Standards and Training (POST) promulgated pursuit policy guidelines for statewide adoption. Further, it required all law-enforcement agencies to collect and submit for analysis a minimum of eleven data elements concerning pursuits and their outcomes. All the police departments in Minnesota were reporting their pursuits by October, 1989. Although the first year's summary statistics probably have some minor errors due to the nature and extent of information received, it represents the only state-wide reporting effort available. The data provided by Minnesota POST reflect information reported during the calendar year, 1989. However, it is unclear when departments began submitting reports. As this system matures and the analysts are able to cross-tabulate reasons for pursuits and outcomes for departments affected by numerous variables such as different size and jurisdiction (rural v. urban v. suburban), the data will become more meaningful. The data reported for 1989 reveal the following:

1. 823 pursuits were conducted;
2. 358 pursuits (44%) resulted in accidents;
3. 194 pursuits (24%) resulted in injuries;
4. 2 pursuits (.2%) resulted in deaths;
5. 38 pursuits (21%) were voluntarily terminated by the officer;
6. 420 (51%) of the violators stopped;
7. 627 (76%) of the pursuits were initiated for traffic offenses;
8. 46 (6%) of the pursuits were initiated for DWI;
9. 133 (16%) of the pursuits were initiated for felony vehicle; and
10. 6 (.7%) of the pursuits were initiated for warrant service.

It is encouraging that many other individual departments are improving their pursuit policies and collecting information on their pursuit driving practices. Different departments are approaching the task from different directions and without sufficient guidance from the research community, but at least there is some attempt to assess what is happening in these various departments. Police departments including Phoenix, Tucson, Dallas, Baltimore County, Chicago and many others have kept reasonable and useful statistics on their pursuits.

To single out and report only a few examples from those many departments which are improving their record keeping may be unfair, but the data are instructive. In Phoenix, a new policy was implemented in April, 1986 and during the first 12 months, 128 pursuits were initiated (Nugent et al., 1989). During 1989, the following statistics were reported:

1. 144 pursuits were conducted;
2. 26 pursuits (18%) resulted in accidents;
3. 7 pursuits (5%) resulted in injuries;
4. 1 pursuit (.7%) resulted in a death;
5. 60 pursuits (42%) were voluntarily terminated by the officer or supervisor;
6. 46 (32%) of the violators stopped; and
7. 40 (28%) of the offenders escaped.

The Chicago Police Department reported 403 pursuits in 1985 (Patinkin and Bingham, 1986: 61) and 1007 pursuits in 1989. Their accidents have gone from 59 (15%) in 1985 to 279 (28%) in 1989, injuries increased from 12 (3%) in 1985 to 74 (7%) in 1989 and the number of supervisory terminations has increased from 40 (10%) in 1985 to 199 (20%) in 1989. Before judging the department's efficiency or effectiveness, however, it would be necessary to review the 1985 and 1989 policies, number of vehicles in the fleet, miles driven, jurisdiction, arrests made and many other factors which have only been reported in the Miami study (Alpert and Dunham, 1990).

Baltimore County police department has published a pursuit study analyzing its pursuits and their outcomes. They conclude that there is a ". . . limited amount of other pursuit studies available (but) [O]verall, our study data seems to concur with data from other studies except for one area, rate of apprehension, which was significantly lower in this study than in other studies" (Baltimore County Police Department, 1988:ii). Hopefully, other departments are following this lead, collecting and analyzing their own data and learning from their mistakes and reducing their costs. When the recording and reporting of pursuit activities becomes mandatory and uniform it will be a valuable exercise to compare and contrast different departmental records over time and across jurisdictions. Certainly, the departments with the most restrictive policies, solid training, strong supervision and workable accountability systems such as the Metro-Dade County (Florida) Police and the Phoenix Police Department, are likely to experience the fewest problems.

A Comparative Analysis

Attempts have been made to compare police shootings across different cities and departments. Although there have been significant improvements in the data collection and analyses, barriers to comparative analyses exist. As long as the definitions, data elements, reporting methods and categories among different agencies vary, comparing data or studies from different jurisdictions will remain problematic. Additionally, when making comparisons across cities, organizational and environmental issues must be controlled. Our Chapter 3 details the progress that has been made and reviews the research findings and why they can or cannot be generalized to other departments. Unfortunately, the current research on pursuit suffers from many of the shortcomings of the research on firearms. In other words, even the most elementary data elements must be analyzed with due attention to the circumstances surrounding the event.

While some studies rely on incidents as the base line, others utilize raw numbers of persons. This difference can create improper analyses and faulty conclusions. For example, pursuits resulting in death may be reported and analyzed by incidents or total numbers (of deaths). The incident driven analysis may ignore multiple deaths in one accident and the analysis relying on total numbers may distort the interpretation of fatal crashes. In any case, there is a need to improve data collection and reporting. In one study (Alpert and Dunham, 1989), many reported injuries occurred after the pursuit driving had ended but during the process of arrest. While these injuries were computed in the final analysis as pursuit related, it could be argued that this is inappropriate and inflates the danger of pursuit driving.

Further, the outcome of pursuit must be understood and evaluated in the light of the size and location of the jurisdiction, crime statistics, political environment, state laws, number of vehicles in the fleet, miles driven, arrests made, departmental policy, training, supervision and accountability system, among other factors. Similar to reporting research on the use of firearms, research on pursuit should provide the identification, description, explanation and possible control variables.

Although a comparison of the number or rate of pursuit related accidents or injuries among jurisdictions without more information may be misleading, it is instructive to provide examples. During 1990, seminars on risk assessment and pursuit driving were sponsored by the Southwestern Law Enforcement Institute and delivered in multiple sites throughout the country. Each participating agency was requested to submit pursuit data for the preceding year. A significant majority of representatives from the agencies which participated in the seminars returned the form. Unfortunately, almost one-third of the agencies reported that they did not maintain the information (but were going to begin keeping records). The agencies that returned completed data forms were grouped into several categories:

1. Rural (1-25 patrol officers);
2. Small Agencies (26-100 patrol officers);

3. Mid-Sized Agencies (101-250 patrol officers);

4. Large Agencies (251-500 patrol officers); and

5. Very Large Agencies (501+ patrol officers).

The data from these cities were merged with other comparable data which were sent to the senior author from other jurisdictions. The data from 151 agencies serve as the basis for Table 6.3. The data from the California Highway Patrol Study are presented for the reader's convenience. These data must be interpreted with extreme caution. These data do not represent any sample other than one of convenience. The data can only be used as an empirical base for theory building. The similarities among the categories suggest that problems exist in all jurisdictions and their differences suggest the opportunities to lower the number and rate of negative outcomes in departments by size and type.

The data presented in Table 6.3 represent the average number of pursuits in which officers from the cities were involved. All other data are presented as percentages which were reported by the departments.

Obviously, with such small cells, data from one or two agencies can skew the results. Specifically, the average number of pursuits for large agencies has been lowered by the inclusion of several departments which have restrictive policies and extensive training. Briefly, the highest percentage of accidents is reported in small agencies while the lowest is reported in very large ones. The percentage of injuries ranges from 8 in the very large agency to 15 in large agencies. The percentage for initiating the pursuit for a traffic offense ranges from 40 to 74. Again, this difference may indicate differential policies and training. Perhaps the most important figure to evaluate is the percentage of pursuits terminated by the

Table 6.3
Comparative Percentages Concerning Pursuit in Multiple Jurisdictions

	Rural Agencies	Small Agencies	Mid-Sized Agencies	Large Agencies	Very Large Agencies	CHP
Number of Agencies	52	43	22	7	1	27
Number of Pursuits (Average)	23	41	82	425	683 (6-Mos)	12
Accidents	42	35	39	23	29	30
Injuries	14	9	12	15	8	11
Deaths	1	1	1	1	1	1
Initiated for Traffic Offenses (Not DUI)	74	40	62	57	51	63
Escaped	14	19	24	34	36	23
Terminated by Officer/ Supervisor	2	3	6	16	18	4

officer and the supervisor. Here, we loose some data by the combined measure which ranges from 2 to 18. While these percentages can be interpreted differently, they can be tracked over time to demonstrate the departmental commitment to having officers terminate the chase when the risks become too great. Again, this figure is difficult to evaluate as terminations in departments that primarily pursue traffic offenders may have a different meaning than terminations in departments that do not mainly pursue traffic violators. In any case, due attention must be given to methods by which the data were collected, the meaning of the data, and its quality prior to any accurate interpretation.

Beyond the Data

Beyond the departments which have reported their statistics, however meaningful, numerous commentators have written about their personal observations concerning pursuit driving. Almost every publication with a law-enforcement audience, including *Police Chief, FBI Law Enforcement Bulletin, Police Magazine, Law and Order*, has published a critique on some aspect of pursuit driving (for examples, Penrod, 1985; Misner, 1990; O'Keefe, 1989; and Auten, 1990). These appraisals are moving away from the defensive driving aspects of pursuit driving and are focusing on the mental aspects and risk. Two of the better essays include Abbott (1988: 9), who observes that "poor driver attitude contributes to more accidents than does lack of skill." He reports that overconfidence, pride, a false sense of proficiency, and impatience on the part of the officer all contribute to negative outcomes in pursuit driving. Abbott warns that it "is easy to become personally caught up in the heat of the chase when the adrenalin starts flowing" (1988: 11). Following this lead, Nowicki (1989) details the influences of attitude and mental training concerning pursuit driving and notes his concern that pursuit driving can become a personal vendetta. In addition to these publications, several state organizations, including The Michigan Association of Chiefs of Police (1986), The Minnesota Board of Peace Officer Standards and Training, the Ohio Governor's Office Law Enforcement Committee (1986) and the New Jersey Attorney General's Office (1986) are becoming involved in reform movements.

The Ohio Governor's Office published written pursuit guidelines in 1986. The document noted that in lieu of specific legislation, departmental guidelines should be written to balance the need for immediate apprehension of a law violator and the risk created by the pursuit. Specifically, it noted:

> Given the obvious hazards of conducting high speed pursuits, certain basic philosophical positions must be considered: first, human life has immeasurable worth and must be foremost in considering the pursuit circumstances and second, society's interest in capturing a serious offender may be so great that at times a certain amount of risk may be required to protect the welfare of others (1986: 21).

Also in 1986, the Attorney General of New Jersey promulgated statewide guide-lines regarding police pursuit driving. These guidelines follow many of the general patterns set forth by the Ohio Governor's Office but introduce specific regulatory language. The guidelines provide in part (1986:4), "that non-hazardous violations such as motor vehicle equipment defects, inspection and registration violations, do not warrant high speed or prolonged pursuit. Also, completed violations where the danger has passed such as failure to obey a stop sign or a traffic signal, improper passing, etc., seldom warrant a prolonged pursuit at excessive speeds. In these instances, the risk exceeds the necessity for immediate apprehension."

One researcher looking at future trends and impact of pursuit driving paints a gloomy picture. Grimmond (1991) writing for the California Peace Officer Standards and Training (POST), calls for significant changes in policy, training supervision, accountability and technological systems to reduce the need for pursuit. His observations are consistent with those of others but he warns that without significant reform, civil litigation may result in the banning of pursuits by municipal governments and the bankruptcy of those which permit their police agencies to pursue.

Although the above referenced works are included as examples only, they point to a trend in the increased awareness and concern of police pursuit and its role in the police mission. As the chief mission of the police is to protect lives, it is difficult to encourage any policy or practice which has death as a probable or highly possible outcome without analyzing the potential benefits which can be derived from the activity. In order to realize or accomplish the police mission in the most effective and efficient manner, restrictive policies, solid training, strong supervision and workable accountability systems must be implemented. The next chapter will focus on those issues.

A Call for National Pursuit Statistics

It is unfortunate and disturbing that similar to the use of firearms, no national statistics on pursuit are collected. In fact, only a few states legislate the need to have policies. This oversight has enabled a number of departments to operate without the benefit of policy. Two efforts to determine the extent of this void in state and local agencies reveal frightening results.

The Bureau of Justice Statistics administers the Law Enforcement Management and Administrative Statistics Survey (LEMAS). Several reports were published from the data collected in 1987 (Bureau of Justice Statistics, 1989) but the results from the question concerning the existence of policies on pursuit have not been reported. This question was asked of only those agencies which had 135 or more officers. The survey revealed that 11% of the nation's sheriffs' departments, 2% of the local police and 4% of the state police agencies were operating with *no* pursuit policy. It must be emphasized that these data only reflect the existence of a policy and not its quality. Further, the data are limited to large departments.

The only data available on small departments were limited to South Carolina (Office of Agency Research and Service, 1990). Unfortunately, the results from that study are biased as the non-response for the smallest agencies was extremely high. In fact, approximately 50% of the agencies with one to nine officers did not respond and approximately 25% of the agencies with ten to twenty-four officers did not respond. The reported data reveal that only 62% of the agencies with one to nine officers were operating with a pursuit policy. Similarly, 76% of the agencies with ten to twenty-four officers were operating with a pursuit policy, 88% of the agencies with twenty-five to forty-nine officers were operating with a pursuit policy, 71% of the agencies with fifty to ninety-nine officers were operating with a pursuit policy and 85% of the agencies with one hundred or more officers were operating with a pursuit policy (Office of Agency Research and Service, 1990: 50). Unfortunately, there was no comparative analysis of the responding agencies and the non-responding agencies, and it would be inappropriate to speculate the percentages of agencies with or without policies which did not respond.

Minnesota deserves to be singled out as taking a giant leap forward in the collection of pursuit statistics. To insure that research on pursuit driving does not follow the same circuitous path as research on the use of firearms, some operational definitions and standardized data collection instruments must be designed and utilized based upon the Minnesota model (see Alpert and Dunham, 1990). Further public concern must be documented and expressed to the law enforcement officials and politicians. One specific challenge is to determine the public's tolerance of pursuit initiated for traffic violations that involve high risk. Whether or not public opinion concerning those who flee has changed since the 1960s remains unanswered.

Policy Issues for Pursuit Driving

7

Just as research on the use of firearms increased our knowledge and provided information to improve policies, training and practices, research on pursuit is beginning to educate administrators, policy makers and trainers in a similar fashion. This chapter will incorporate the knowledge gained from legal precedents and research to develop a conceptual view of pursuit as a police tactic. Additionally, the materials presented will review the current standards and models for the creation of pursuit policies and training. Basically, it is important to train officers in the mechanics of driving and to educate them on the thinking process and assessment of risk. Training must focus officers' minds on the nuts and bolts of defensive and emergency driving, and education is necessary to broaden the officers' understanding of the risks and the decision making necessary to control a pursuit. Just as there are legitimate reasons and situations when police must use their firearms, situations exist when police must engage in pursuit driving. Both of these tactics must be understood and applied as part of the police mission: to protect life.

Policies on pursuit driving can be reduced to a simple concept: When the risk created by the driving outweighs the need for immediate apprehension of the suspect, such risky driving must be terminated. It is not only acceptable to terminate pursuits in which the potential benefit is minimal, but it is wise, safe and in good judgment to terminate pursuits which incorporate high risks! This chapter will review and analyze the elements necessary for creating an appropriate pursuit driving policy. After a critique of the types of policies available, specific policy elements, including in-chase tactics, accountability, terminating the chase and interjurisdictional considerations will be analyzed. Examples of pursuit situations will be provided along with an exemplary policy.

The Background

As we have noted, most states have adopted regulations from the Uniform Vehicle Code language which provides traffic law exemptions for the driver of an emergency vehicle. It states that a driver of an emergency vehicle is not relieved "from the duty to drive with due regard for the safety of

115

all persons using the highway, nor protect him from the consequences of an arbitrary exercise of the privileges granted under the exemption." In other words, even when an officer is exempt from the laws regulating traffic flow (stop signs and traffic lights) and is authorized to drive faster than the speed limit, he or she must drive with *due regard* for the safety of all persons using the roads. This regulation arguably places a special responsibility on the driver of an emergency vehicle who chooses to exercise this privilege. The driver of the emergency vehicle may be held to a higher standard than a citizen, as he is a professional, assumed to have the proper training and experience to warrant the special exemption. The due regard criterion is not always limited to situations where police are directly involved in accidents; it may extend to the totality of the situation and the driving of the offender as well as the officer. In other words, physical force used by the officer who crashes into another vehicle is likely to violate the "due regard" criterion. In addition, psychological force, or pressure placed on a suspect to flee may be considered as a violation of "due regard" for the safety of the motoring public. It is an officer's driving and its impact which will be judged by the reasonable man who is faced with the question, should this pursuit have taken place the way it did, with the risks it created and for the potential results it could have yielded?

While this is another way of balancing the need to apprehend the suspect immediately and the risk created by the pursuit, it reduces to plain language the two elements of apprehension and risk. First, was the pursuit driving and its inherent or predictable risk necessary? Second, what positive results or benefits could the pursuit have yielded based on what was known about the suspect? If the pursuit is terminated, is the issue merely another traffic violation for which no one was apprehended or an unsolved crime? Perhaps the real issue in framing a pursuit policy and training is how an officer should determine the risk factors and the potential value of the pursuit. There have been numerous responses, but unfortunately, the most frequent one has reflected a lack of a concern or a denial of a problem. The most progressive approach has been one based on the firearm analogy. All states require specialized firearm training and certification, and that trend for pursuit driving is becoming popular.

The requirement of specialized training *and certification* before an officer is "licensed" or permitted to participate in a pursuit is not materially different than firearms training and certification which is required by all law enforcement officers. In 1989, the British Association of Police Chief Officers (APCO) suggested that a unified system of driver classification be established and that only those police officers properly trained and certified in pursuit driving should take part in vehicle pursuits.

In this country, a trend is developing that follows the APCO model. For example, the College Station, Texas policy states that *"No officer will get involved in a pursuit until he or she has completed an approved training course."* While most police in this country have not adopted this clear or strong a system of control, there is little doubt that there is a move in that direction.

The firearm analogy provides an interesting conceptual way to understand pursuit. Consider a patrol officer sent to a convenience store for a silent alarm. As the officer, with the advantage of cover, approaches the store, he observes several people at the cash register and sees the suspect shoot the clerk. With gun in hand, the suspect turns toward the officer. Is it reasonable for the officer to shoot the suspect? The elements of this scenario used to evaluate justifiable deadly force include:

1. laws and policies;
2. what is known about the suspect;
3. what is known about the law violation;
4. likelihood of injuring an innocent bystander; and
5. probability of later apprehension.

What if the suspect had not shot the clerk and had only committed an armed robbery? What if the suspect had shot the clerk but was alone in the store? How should the officer define risk and how much should he or she take? Similarly, what are the benefits of shooting at a suspect?

If the suspect were to escape from the store and were in his vehicle when the officer arrives, what action should the officer take? Certainly, the officer should be concerned about an injured victim and the arrest of the criminal. Should an officer initiate a felony stop without back-up, should he continue to chase a suspect who shows no sign of slowing or who may be driving recklessly because of the officer's presence? The five points listed above must be analyzed both independently and together to determine the appropriate action. The use of firearms and pursuit driving have a great deal in common.

Toward a Policy of Pursuit Driving

To gain a proper perspective, pursuit driving must be looked at with the understanding that police serve the state and the state's interest, not the individual citizen. Law enforcement agencies must have rules, regulations, training and supervision to guide and control the discretion of their officers. Written and enforced policies are necessary for the proper management of all law enforcement functions. These policies must cover all operations and must anticipate potential activities. Policies and procedures must cover general duties and obligations as well as specific methods to achieve them. In other words, law enforcement agencies must have rules, training, supervision and must hold officers accountable for their actions. Departments must have a plan for their officers, including decision points and risk assessment. Too many officers and administrators are unable to answer the question, "what were you going to do with the offender when you caught up to him?" With no plan, the chase will likely take on characteristics of a drag race. The mission of law enforcement is to protect lives; nothing an officer does should compromise that mission.

As with any activity in which the police may engage, there is a need for a written policy to provide members of the organization with the expectations of the command staff and the community. (See McDonald, 1989). As James Auten (1988: 1-2) has noted:

> To do otherwise is to simply leave employees "in the dark" in the expectation that they will intuitively divine the proper and expected course of action in the performance of their duties . . . Discretion must be reasonably exercised within the parameters of the expectations of the community, the courts, the legislature and the organization, itself.

A policy consists of principles and values which guide the performance of the pursuit. It is formulated by analyzing the objectives and declaring those principles or ideas which will best guide the officer in achieving his or her objectives.

In the case of pursuit driving, all agencies must have some policy informing its officers what will be tolerated and what will not be tolerated. Anything less may fall into the abyss that the United States Supreme Court in *City of Canton, Ohio v. Harris* called, "Deliberate Indifference." Policies, while designed to consist only of principles and values which guide performance, must be tightened and made comprehensive. They usually fall into one of three models (see Fennessy, 1970 and Alpert, 1987):

1) Judgmental: allowing officers to make all major decisions relating to initiation, tactics and termination;

2) Restrictive: placing certain restrictions on officers judgments and decisions; and

3) Discouragement: severely cautioning or discouraging any pursuit, except in the most extreme situations.

Police departments operating under regulations which emphasize judgmental decision making provide only guidelines for their officers. Usually, these warnings require officers to weigh various factors before initiating a pursuit, to consider their safety and the safety of others during a pursuit, and to terminate a chase when it becomes too risky.

Departments which operate under restrictive regulations or specific rules limit individual officer's discretion. For example, these orders can restrict officers from initiating pursuits when the law violators are juveniles, traffic offenders, or property offenders. Similarly, in-pursuit driving behavior may be regulated. Specific speed, distance, or time limitations may be ordered. Additionally, a rule may restrict some types of driving such as going the wrong way on a one-way street, driving over curbs, or driving on private property.

For example, the 1990 Florida Highway Patrol Policy concerning pursuit includes some very specific rules for their troopers when chasing traffic offenders. Florida Highway Patrol Troopers must terminate a pursuit for a traffic offense when the offender leaves the freeway or if the pursuit has continued for a distance of three miles.

Discouragement policies only allow pursuit driving under specific conditions. Examples include chasing a known murder suspect or a suspect who has been observed committing a violent crime by the officer. These policies are very specific and leave little room for discretion.

In other words, there exists a policy continuum, ranging from detailed and controlled to general and vague. The latter emphasizes officer discretion, and the former has reduced the discretionary decisions made on the street and provides the officers with more structure. Discretion, whether controlled by the command staff through policies and procedures or left up to the line officer, must be reasonably exercised within the rule of law and expectations of the community. As a general proposition, an agency's policy should include the following principles:

1. be workable in real-world situations;
2. be adaptable to training;
3. be written in a positive manner;
4. reflect the values of the command staff and community;
5. refer to or incorporate relevant laws;
6. include input from officers at all levels;
7. be pre-tested to assure that all officers understand the specific intent and consequences of non-compliance;
8. include in-service training, as a matter of record, for all officers and supervisors; and
9. provide examples of behavior.

Determining the appropriate policies and procedures which balance deterrence and citizen safety is the key element in obtaining the desired police reaction to motorists who refuse to respond to emergency signals. In any case, it is always anticipated that a law enforcement officer can attempt a traffic or felony stop. The officer initiates the stop, *but it is the law violator who initiates the pursuit.*

There is a strong relationship between a policy and the training necessary to support it. The vagueness of the judgmental type of policy permits officers to make most of the decisions about risk and therefore requires the most training, supervision and control, as well as requires a specific plan to take the suspect into custody. There are agencies, such as Baltimore City Police, which do not allow pursuit driving. Their policies state that pursuit driving is too dangerous and will not be tolerated. In either case, the issue has been considered and officers have been informed about how to carry out their ultimate obligation to protect lives.

The strategy of chasing an alleged offender until he is caught must be weighed against the reasonable and foreseeable costs. It is inappropriate to hope that an offender will stop voluntarily, get into an accident, or run out of gas. There must be some plan to take the person into custody, or the foreseeability of an accident increases as the chase becomes a race. Jim Fyfe has identified some of the underlying reasons that pursuit driving has become a controversial tactic in need of strong control (1989:118-119). "Police officers, accustomed to dealing with citizens who accede to their wishes and directives, often take motorists' flight as the ultimate sign of disrespect, and are likely to react out of anger and sudden rushes of adrenalin, rather than on the basis of logic and professional responsibility." When police officers react to the "crime" of Contempt of Cop in such a risky and dangerous manner, they must be controlled and supervised to reduce potential damage or injury.

Supervision

Perhaps the most important person to insure that policies are being followed and that risk is balanced appropriately is the *supervisor*. Since pursuits are all potentially dangerous, they often disorient and drastically increase the adrenalin of the participants. It is necessary to have a detached supervisor who can take charge of a pursuit by radio contact, manage it, and—when necessary—terminate it. This aspect of policy must be well-known to the officers. Supervisors are always in charge and must take extraordinary precautions to assess risk during pursuits. When the supervisor is monitoring the chase and does not curtail it, it is reasonable to believe that he, the officer in charge, approved the escalation of the pursuit (see *Kibbe v. City of Springfield*, 1985). While the driver of the primary unit has initial responsibility, it is the supervisor who must compensate for the officer's excitement, possibly impaired decision making, or other elements not known to the officer. Both the officer and the supervisor must pay attention to the risks created by the driving actions of the offender.

In sum, both the officer and the supervisor must compensate for the driving of the offender, as it is his aggressive driving which is most likely to be the direct cause of an accident. After the fact, it may be discovered that the officer, through psychological force, caused the offender to be even more fearful, careless and reckless. There may be an accusation that the officer was the moving force behind the negative outcome, or that the officer created the situation in which a suspect fled and initiated a pursuit. Supervision is necessary to manage and to control pursuit driving in any law enforcement agency. Administrative controls will be related directly to the specific details of the incident.

Accountability

It is necessary to hold any officer who has been involved in a pursuit accountable. Writing an analytical critique is the first step. This accountability serves several purposes: **first**, the information contained in a critique can help determine if the pursuit was necessary and conducted within the departmental policy; **second**, critiques will help determine if specific training is needed; **third**, critiques will help determine if a change in policy is needed; and **fourth**, an analysis of the data generated in these reports will reveal trends and demonstrate specific risk factors.

A critique of a pursuit must include an analysis of items specific to the incident as well as variables concerning the individual and the organization. Specifically, information contained in the policy and taught in training should be scrutinized in a critique. Knowledge of why the offender is wanted, the area and conditions, the likelihood of successful apprehension (the identification of the offender, probability of apprehending offender at a later time, and the extent to which offender will go to avoid capture), and the extent to which the officer's driving has influenced the offender must be considered during the pursuit and analyzed in the critique. These are the same data that must be communicated to dispatch and analyzed by a supervisor during a pursuit. For example, pursuing one who has demonstrated that he has no intention of stopping, will create a greater danger than terminating the pursuit and searching for the person at a later date. How much danger is created by not apprehending a traffic offender?

General Principles and Specific Rules

The purpose of a policy is to reduce officer discretion; it can include specific requirements and prohibitions as well as general guidelines. The restriction of specific actions such as limiting the maximum speed and the duration of a pursuit can be controlled independently by specific rules, which will be discussed below under Termination of Pursuit. Similarly, these actions can be considered within the context of other variables, depending upon the type of policy which is desired and the type of training provided. The variables to be considered include:

1. **Officers' background and preparation**.
   a. tactical preparation (training, experience and familiarity with area including escape routes);
   b. type of vehicle (condition, equipment, etc.).
2. **Nature and characteristics of incident, area and conditions**.
   a. traffic conditions (density, speed, etc.);
   b. pedestrian traffic;
   c. road conditions (width, lanes, fitness, surface);
   d. geographic area (hills, sidewalks, curb breaks, etc.;
   e. weather and visibility;
   f. location of pursuit (residential, commercial, freeway, school zones, etc.);
   g. time of day; and
   h. speed of each vehicle.
3. **Information pertaining to Offender**.
   a. the offense committed by the offender;

b. likelihood of successful apprehension (identification of offender, type of vehicle, probability of apprehending offender at a later time, and extent to which offender will go to avoid capture);

c. age or maturity of offender; and

d. effect of officer's driving on offender's driving (i.e., is the officer's action the moving force of the offender's recklessness?).

The policy can help create tactical knowledge and advanced preparation, which involves knowing as much as possible about a situation before taking or continuing action to resolve it. The pursuing officer may be familiar with the area and may even be familiar with the density of pedestrian or vehicular traffic, but does not make the decision regarding the exact route to be taken or the spontaneous driving maneuvers taken by the law violator. A strong policy and training, however, can control the overall risk, the most critical factor of a police pursuit. There are specific ways to decrease and to control the omnipresent risk. Improving knowledge and preparation can achieve this goal, and the following elements are necessary:

1. A clear and understandable *policy* delineating departmental requirements within the context of state laws and the police mission;

2. Specific *training* to the policy, using examples of risk assessment;

3. A detached supervisor, trained in risk assessment, who takes *control* over the pursuit, who assumes its *supervision* and who will terminate it when it becomes too risky; and

4. *Accountability*, by requiring officers to complete pursuit critiques and having the forms reviewed individually to determine if the pursuit driving was within policy and collectively to provide information to trainers and policy makers. Additionally, officers must receive feedback on the appropriateness of their pursuit driving.

Any analysis is incomplete without the consideration of the actions of at least three actors in a pursuit scenario: The police officer(s), the law violator and the innocent third party, who happens to be at the wrong place at the wrong time. This complexity creates uncertain events and unpredictable contingencies. If police officers are regulated by a strong policy, follow that policy, and are controlled by their supervisors, they will rarely become involved in accidents. If problems occur, their behavior can be observed, reported and modified. The driving behavior of the law violator appears to be the most significant factor involved in the outcome of the pursuit. Once a person decides not to stop for a police vehicle which is displaying its emergency lights and siren, it is difficult to predict how that person will drive, the degree of recklessness he will display, and whether or not he will show concern for his welfare or that of others. *There are no rules for the law violator*. However, if the law violator recklessly has evaded the police in congested traffic for even a short period of time, it is safe to predict that he will continue to do so. The few offenders who voluntarily terminate their pursuit do so after a relatively small amount of risk has been taken and most often within a minute or so (Alpert and Dunham, 1990). It is the driving actions of the pursued law violator which the police can not control; consequently, it is the law violator who ends up in accidents more often than any one else. It is a natural urge for an officer to respond in a reflexive manner to this driving, but a reflexive action must be replaced by knowledge and preparation to reduce risk and officers' blame.

Blaming the Police Officer!

One of the most intriguing issues relates to the claim by law violators that they base their degree of recklessness on the driving of the police. In other words, it is the officer's and department's fault that the law violator became so reckless that a serious injury occurred: Has psychological force been used? Furthermore, was it foreseeable that an accident was likely to occur and that the proximate cause of the accident was the police officer's driving (which pushed the offender or was the moving force behind the offender's actions)?

At present we have theories and opinions, but only weak data. The courts, however, have convicted several officers of criminal charges and are awarding large sums of money to those injured as the result of accidents caused by pursuit driving (see Chapter 2). This certainly is an area which requires further inquiry.

One fundamental relationship requiring study is that between the pursuing officer and the pursued driver. It is worthwhile to compare the driving of the suspect when first observed with his driving during the pursuit. Also, the environmental conditions and risks deserve analysis. For example, if the driver were reckless while running a stop sign and an officer attempts a traffic stop and the law violator continues his recklessness at the same level, has the officer influenced the offender's driving? If the suspect's driving and the conditions did not change during the pursuit, it can be argued that the officer did not raise the risks and, in fact, the risks were not increased by the pursuit. However, if traffic became heavier, intersections were congested, the law violator became more reckless, there were near accidents, speed was increased or other environmental conditions changed, the pursuing officer could be blamed for knowingly increasing the risks. In other words, was the first violation an isolated situation, or did the offender's driving, based on the officer's intervention or a change in the environment, become more evasive, reckless or dangerous and increase the likelihood of an accident? Unfortunately, such an analysis disregards the law violator's continued recklessness which may be due to a passive police presence. Further, it disregards the likelihood of alternatives, including the offender's voluntary termination or an inevitable accident. The best indicator that a suspect will not voluntarily terminate his escape is his recklessness and unreasonableness.

One universal aspect of pursuit driving and training which has been stressed is the balance between the need for immediate apprehension of the law violator against the risk created by the driving. Since all good pursuits do not end with the apprehension of the bad guy and no damage and not all bad pursuits result in accidents or injuries, it is difficult to propose a specific formula to determine the amount of risk involved in a pursuit. Fortunately, there are some factors which can be identified.

Pursuit Policy

Specific elements, based on the information discussed above, are necessary to create a pursuit policy. In other words a pursuit policy must incorporate ideas and principles derived from several sources. A policy's *first* principle is that an officers' primary responsibility is to protect lives. Because pursuits are all so "potentially" dangerous and because officers are likely to react to the heat of the moment, an overall **mission statement** must be included as a first element and as a reminder. *Second*, as the mission is to protect lives, a statement concerning the **rationale** or reason for pursuit driving should follow. This must include "the need to immediately apprehend a suspect balanced against the danger created by the pursuit."

Third, a **definition** of pursuit should follow—and a standard one is that "the driver of a vehicle is aware that an officer driving a police vehicle with emergency lights and siren is attempting to apprehend him or her and the driver of this vehicle attempts to **avoid apprehension by increasing speed or taking other evasive actions or refuses to stop**."

Fourth, there should be some statement concerning the number of vehicles permitted to be involved in a pursuit—and their roles in the pursuit. There are, however, some important considerations that must be made. First, if there is only one police vehicle available, the officer must consider an attempted felony stop a very dangerous procedure. Further, more than two vehicles actively pursuing an offender will likely create more danger and risk to the officers and the motoring public than it will help to bring the pursuit to a successful conclusion. In other words, the number accepted today is two—a lead and a support vehicle. These two can operate in an emergency mode, with lights and siren. A limited number of back-up vehicles can position themselves at strategic locations with the purpose of warning the public. The number of vehicles and their specific function must be determined by policy and each vehicle must be assigned and monitored by a supervisor.

Pursuit Tactics: Initiation, Communication, Operation

It is important that officers recognize what it is that they are focusing on during a pursuit situation and that they are not engaged merely in a contest to win. Officers must continually evaluate the situation to determine the need to apprehend a suspect immediately balanced against the danger created by the pursuit. For example, if a chase becomes similar to a drag race, and there is no real way to apprehend or capture the suspect, there must be a compelling justification for risk. Also, as officers may be caught up in the moment, it is important that a *detached supervisor* take control of the pursuit. But this other individual, must rely upon the information provided by the lead officer in order to make proper decisions. This requires that sufficient information is provided to dispatch by the pursuing officer.

Communication at a minimum includes:

1. what is known about the suspect and his actions;
2. what he is wanted for;
3. his location and direction;
4. the environment in which the pursuit is taking place, including vehicular or pedestrian traffic — likelihood of traffic increasing (3 pm on a school day);
5. speed of both vehicles;
6. driving behavior of the pursued; and
7. any description of vehicle and passengers.

If this information is not provided voluntarily by the officer, it must be requested and/or demanded by the supervisor.

It is essential to stress that *officers can **not** assume that an individual observed for a traffic violation **must** be involved in something more serious because he is fleeing.* Although officers are likely to assume, they must rely on what they know, not what they think or sense. Maintaining or increasing risk during a pursuit can only be justified by what is known.

As the purpose of pursuit is to apprehend a suspect, this goal or purpose must be kept in mind at all times, and all tactics or activities undertaken must be with apprehension in mind. For example, the police officer who is an expert driver must take into consideration the driving of the pursued and the possibility of bystanders getting involved. Further, he or she must be trained to evaluate risks and to determine whether the facts justify the chase. It must always be remembered that the purpose of a pursuit is a successful apprehension. Two and sometimes 6 or 10 cars racing down the road is more like a drag race than anything else.

Would a reasonable person understand why a pursuit occurred if it resulted in an accident or injury? Why it was continued or why it was necessary? These questions posed in a similar fashion may ultimately be asked and it is appropriate to have such a concern presented in the policy.

The *strategy* suggested here is to have a statement in the policy and to stress it in training — that it is necessary to balance the need for immediate apprehension and created risk. *One way to help an officer balance his decision is to have him apply the same standards in weighing alternatives to fire his weapon in a situation where innocent bystanders may be endangered.* As in our earlier example, whenever the officer fires his weapon he is concerned that the bullet may accidentally hit an unintended target. By comparison, the officer in a pursuit has not only his vehicle to worry about but he must also consider the pursued vehicle creating dangerous situations and other vehicles creating danger by attempting to get out of the way. An officer would probably want to take some of these risks if he were chasing the individual who just robbed the convenience store and killed the clerk. He may even choose to use a roadblock, shoot at the car or take some other drastic action which will be considered use of deadly force.

For either a traffic violator or a suspected property offender, reasonable risks must be determined and articulated. Further, a policy should include the warning that the officers' behavior will likely be reviewed and analyzed by a "common man" mentality, i.e., will the officer be able to convince a group of non-police that his behavior—the risks he took—were reasonable under the conditions?

Termination of Pursuit

When the dangers or risks of a pursuit, or the likelihood of an accident, outweighs the need to immediately apprehend a law violator, the lead officer or his supervisor must terminate it. This is usually dictated by the nature of the offense for which the law violator is wanted and the risk created by the recklessness of his driving. Other considerations are also important. These include an analysis of whether speed dangerously exceeds the normal flow of traffic, the likelihood and extent of pedestrians or vehicular traffic, the danger of erratic maneuvering by the violator such as driving the wrong way on a one way street, driving without lights, or driving over curbs or through private property. Although these elements represent guidelines or factors which must be included in policy and analyzed to establish the degree of risk and when to terminate a pursuit, specific rules must also be stressed.

First, do not duplicate impetuous maneuvers made by the offender. Second, all officers and supervisors must balance the natural and emotional urge to catch the law violator with the need to preserve the safety of the public by conducting and controlling the pursuit with due regard for the safety of all persons using the roads. Third, when an officer makes the decision to terminate a pursuit, he must slow to a safe speed and turn off all emergency equipment. This sends the message that a pursuit no longer exists. There are many other questions which must be addressed by policy including the use of offensive tactics, passing, spacing of vehicles, and use of firearms, among others.

Interjurisdictional Pursuit

The possibilities of an interjurisdictional pursuit must be considered and addressed. Possible issues include: who is in charge into and out of a jurisdiction? What are the responsibilities of the dispatcher? What type of assistance will a department provide? Answers to all these questions are necessary.

Interjurisdictional pursuits have created some real and unnecessary disasters. Two examples will be provided. The first shows how easily problems can be avoided by policy and training. The second, although more complex, dramatic and tragic, provides a similar lesson.

The strange case of Mr. and Mrs. Parson (*Parson v. City of Claremore et al.*, 1989) began in the early hours of July 3, 1988. A report concerning a pursuit and a request to establish a roadblock was heard by the dispatcher and numerous Claremore City police officers who were in their patrol vehicles. The ranking Claremore officer, in response to the radio request, established a roadblock and assigned an officer to stand in the road prior to the roadblock to wave at and attempt to stop the fleeing vehicle. The officer observed the chased vehicle and began to wave but retreated to his patrol car as the fleeing vehicle did not stop or slow down. As other officers were concerned that the chased vehicle would collide with motorists on the road and they believed a serious accident could occur, several officers began firing their weapons at the vehicle. This was done in accordance with the policy (and custom) of the Claremore Police Department, which stated that use of firearms was only to disable a vehicle. In other words, the officers were not firing at the occupants of the vehicle. After several shots entered the fleeing vehicle, the driver stopped and was arrested without accident or injury.

As the saying goes, things are not always as they appear. The facts of this chase are fairly straightforward, but not as they appear! Early in the morning of July 3, Mrs. Parson, a young, pregnant Native American woman entered labor and her husband was driving her, at excessive speed, to the Claremore Indian Hospital. A Tulsa City police officer observed the speeding couple and engaged his lights and siren in an effort to make a traffic stop. Mr. Parson stopped his vehicle and explained to the officer the situation. The Tulsa officer, after observing the woman, told Mr. Parson that he would lead him to the hospital. He instructed Mr. Parson to wait while he radioed his dispatcher. The impatient father-to-be became anxious and thinking that the officer stated that he would follow him to the hospital, took off. The Tulsa officer, after requesting that Claremore department be advised of the situation took off to catch and escort the Parsons. The officer claimed he was unable to catch and pass the Parson vehicle. A few miles down the road, a Rogers County officer observed the "chase" and radioed that he and a Tulsa City officer were chasing a vehicle on Highway 66 heading toward Claremore and that a roadblock should be established.

As the "pursued" vehicle continued on its route, Mrs. Parson observed several police vehicles and asked her husband what was happening. Parsons advised his wife that the officers were there to help block traffic and to help them get to the hospital. In fact, the couple stated that they waved to the police in appreciation. As they entered Claremore, Mrs. Parsons was pleased to see more police vehicles. As they passed these cars, they heard noises like firecrackers and suddenly the back window was shattered. Realizing that they were being shot at, Mr. Parson stopped the car at the roadblock. As it turned out, the Tulsa Police dispatcher teletyped a message to the Claremore Police Department which was received a few minutes late and a few dollars short.

The second case occurred in Duval County, Florida and demonstrates the need to develop and require standards for pursuit driving (Jacksonville Police Department, CCR #89365 Incident Report). While this fact situation was selected for its conscious-shocking activities, there exist far too many other examples which could have been chosen.

At approximately 2:00 AM on February 12, 1989, a Sergeant from the Fernandina Police department observed a vehicle spinning its wheels near several youths in a Buccaneer Park parking lot. Rather than stop and question those involved in the dispute at the parking lot, the Sergeant attempted to stop the vehicle. The suspect fled through back streets of Fernandina Beach until he reached the main highway (A1A) and turned onto it heading west. During this time, the Sergeant informed dispatch that he was involved in a pursuit. The only illegal activities known were traffic violations. As the pursuit continued south on A1A, a Naussau County Deputy with a civilian in his vehicle and a second Naussau County Deputy were dispatched to assist the Fernandina Sergeant. They attempted a rolling roadblock near Harry Greene Road, east of Yulee, in an effort to stop the pursued vehicle. Rather than stop, the pursued vehicle, at a high rate of speed, drove across the grass median strip and headed west, the wrong way in the eastbound lanes on A1A. As they were driving the wrong way on A1A, the suspect vehicle ran other vehicles off the road. The officers continued west in the appropriate lanes while the suspect drove the wrong way on A1A.

At the intersection of A1A and U.S. 17, the suspect vehicle, wanted only for traffic violations, lost control and slid into a concrete median or pillar. One of the deputies drove beside the car and was hit in the side by the suspect vehicle as the driver attempted to continue his escape. This Deputy fired two shots from his service weapon at the fleeing vehicle. The pursued vehicle continued in a westerly direction in the westbound lanes pursued by several police vehicles. During this segment of the pursuit, another Sergeant fired at the suspect vehicle. As the suspect vehicle approached Interstate 95, another officer had set up a roadblock just past the offramp, hoping the pursued vehicle would stop. Rather, the vehicle took its escape route, up the freeway ramp, the wrong way. At this time, the law enforcement officers were all in pursuit. A Sergeant followed the suspect vehicle for approximately 1/2 mile the wrong way on I-95 until the suspect vehicle cut across the median of Interstate 95 and travelled southbound in the south lanes. The pursuit continued on I-95 into Duval County, and the suspect vehicle exited east on Heckscher Drive and travelled to North Main Street. By this time Jacksonville County officers had also joined the chase. During this segment of the chase, a Naussau County Deputy attempted to pull next to the suspect vehicle, and the suspect attempted to ram the Deputy's vehicle. Approaching 50th and Main Street, a Deputy instructed his civilian passenger to shoot his personal shotgun at the suspect vehicle's tires. The pursuit continued south on Main. At approximately 42nd Street, the left rear tire started to separate.

The suspect vehicle turned east onto East 5th Street and continued with officers following to Walnut Street. The vehicle turned North on Walnut and east on East 8th Street. While on East 8th Street, one of the Sergeants shot at the tires in an attempt to disable the vehicle completely. The Sergeant attempted to pass the suspect vehicle at Sylvan Court and the suspect vehicle hit the Sheriff's vehicle at Sylvan Court and Florida Avenue and came to rest. The Sergeant, in primary pursuit, exited his car, took control of the scene and ordered the occupants out of the pursued vehicle. A Deputy and his civilian observer along with several other law enforcement officers arrived at the scene. Although the suspect vehicle was virtually blocked in by trees, vehicles and buildings, the Deputy (or his civilian observer) reacted to the revving of the suspect vehicle's motor and sparks from the spinning rim and fired at the only remaining tire, missing the tire and killing a passenger in the back seat.

Preventing Disaster

Progress is being made by law enforcement, yet pursuits such as the ones presented above continue to take place. Obviously, the most serious crime committed by either Mr. Parson or the driver of the car in Duval County was "contempt of cop." A good policy, training, supervision/control and accountability would eliminate these obvious disasters. For example, in Oklahoma, proper communication among the various jurisdictions would have provided sufficient information to help the Parsons rather than to create the nightmare that occurred. In the Florida example, the Sergeant only had to ask the people at Buccanneer park what was going on and who was involved, as the driver and passengers were known to them. In fact, the original incident began at a high school basketball game earlier that evening and all the participants knew each other.

A Look at an Exemplary Policy

One of the most progressive pursuit policies available is that of the Little Rock Police Department and is highlighted with permission of Chief Caudell.

LITTLE ROCK POLICE DEPARTMENT
GENERAL ORDER

TITLE:

OPERATION OF DEPARTMENTAL VEHICLES

DATE:	DISTRIBUTION:	REPLACES:	NUMBER:
12/01/90	DEPARTMENTAL	EXISTING	G. O. 14

I.   **Emergency Driving - General [Non-Pursuit Situations]**

   A.   The Police Department's primary concern in emergency driving situations is the protection of the lives and safety of all citizens and officers. During emergency driving situations, officers will operate their vehicles with extreme caution and in compliance with Ark. Code Ann. 27-37-202 (1987), which requires that the emergency light bar **and** siren be activated on authorized emergency vehicles. Driving under emergency conditions does not relieve the officer from the duty to drive with due regard for the safety of all persons, nor will these provisions protect the driver from the consequences of his disregard for the safety of others.

   B.   Definition of Emergency Driving [Non-Pursuit Situations]

      1.   Emergency driving is defined as the operation of an authorized emergency vehicle (emergency lights and siren in operation) by a police officer in response to a life threatening situation or a violent crime in progress, using due regard for the safety of others.

   C.   The decision to drive under emergency conditions will be discretionary with each individual officer, based on the following considerations:

      1.   When deciding to initiate or continue driving under emergency conditions, officers will consider such factors as traffic volume, time of day, and potential hazard or liability to themselves and the public.

      2.   Emergency responses shall be made only when the call involves a life threatening situation or a violent crime in progress.

      3.   Officers will have sufficient information to justify the decision to drive under emergency conditions.

      4.   Officers responding to an "officer needs assistance" type call must bear in mind that even though a rapid response is important, they must arrive at the scene safely in order to be of assistance.

         [NOTE: Officers who are operating in emergency status should not operate the emergency flashers, as that will make the turn signals inoperative.]

D.   Officers , upon deciding to make an emergency response to any situation, will immediately notify Communications of their decision.

1.   All officers, when making an emergency response, will notify Communications of such by using the term "Code Three." This will indicate that the officer will be employing emergency equipment [emergency blue lights and siren].

2.   Field Sergeants will override the officer's decision to make an emergency [Code Three] response if, in their judgement, it is not warranted or cannot be done safely. The Sergeant of the officer making an emergency response will normally be responsible to make this determination.

E.   No officer will operate a police vehicle in emergency [Code Three] status if it is occupied by any passengers other than another police officer or a person who has signed a release or waiver of liability.

F.   Police vehicles without emergency lights and sirens will not make emergency [Code Three] responses.

II.   Pursuit Driving - General

A.   The Police Department's primary concern in pursuit situations is the protection of the lives and safety of all citizens and officers. The operation of emergency vehicles is governed by Ark. Code Ann. 27-51-202 (1987), which authorizes emergency vehicles (activated blue light and siren) to exceed the posted speed limit, but does not relieve the driver of an authorized emergency vehicle from the duty to drive with due regard for the safety of all persons. It also does not relieve the driver of any emergency vehicle from the consequence of a reckless disregard of the safety of others.

B.   Definition - Pursuit Driving

1.   A motor vehicle pursuit is an active attempt by a law enforcement officer operating an emergency vehicle and utilizing simultaneously all emergency equipment (blue lights and siren) to apprehend one or more occupants of another moving vehicle, when the driver of a fleeing vehicle is aware of that attempt and is resisting apprehension by maintaining or increasing his speed, disobeying traffic laws, ignoring the officer or attempting to elude the officer.

C.   The following policies will govern vehicular pursuits:

1.   Police vehicles not equipped with emergency lights and sirens are prohibited from becoming involved in any vehicular pursuit.

2.   No more than two (2) marked emergency vehicles will be involved in the immediate pursuit. Other police vehicles will be support units and will not become actively involved in the pursuit or operate in an emergency mode.

3.   The first unit to become involved in a vehicular pursuit will be

designated the primary vehicle and will have the following responsibilities:

a) The officer **will** activate the police vehicle's emergency lights and siren and notify Communications of the following information:

   (1) The unit identifier;

   (2) The location and direction of the suspect vehicle;

   (3) The charges involved; and,

   (4) The license number, vehicle description and number of occupants.

4. In a pursuit, the second marked police unit will become the backup. Upon joining the pursuit, the backup officer will activate the vehicle's emergency lights and siren and advise Communications.

   a) Only one backup unit is to be used unless authorization for additional backup units is obtained from a police supervisor.

   b) The backup vehicle will follow the primary vehicle at a safe distance.

   c) Additional police units will not assume emergency status and follow the primary and backup units.

5. Additional units will be support vehicles and **will not** become actively involved in the pursuit or violate traffic laws, or operate in emergency status.

   a) Support units will cover escape routes.

   b) Marked support units will be available to assume a backup or primary role should one of those units be unable to continue the pursuit.

   c) If a support vehicle inadvertently intercepts the suspect vehicle, **the support vehicle will not attempt to intervene.** The support vehicle will attempt to obtain additional vehicle description.

6. Officers **will not** operate their vehicles as primary or secondary units when their vehicles are occupied by any passengers other than another police officer or a person who has signed a release or waiver of liability.

7. Police motorcycle units may become involved in a pursuit as primary units only when they initiate the pursuit. The motorcycle unit will, however, turn the pursuit over to a marked police car as soon as possible and discontinue emergency operation.

8.   Police vehicles **will not** be used for the following purposes:

a)   Ramming of suspect vehicles;

b)   Boxing in or surrounding a suspect vehicle;

[NOTE: Marked and unmarked units may be used to box in an unaware suspect in order to avoid a pursuit.]

c)   Overtaking, driving next to, or forcing suspect vehicles off the roadway;

d)   Creating roadblocks.

9.   Pursuits **will** be immediately terminated under the following conditions:

a)   When **any** police supervisor orders the pursuit terminated.

b)   The officer knows the suspect's identity and knows that the suspect is wanted only for a traffic violation, misdemeanor or nonviolent felony.

c)   The distance between the officer and suspect is such that, in order to continue the pursuit, it would place the officer or the public in unreasonable danger.

d)   The primary officer loses visual contact with the suspect for an extended period of time (approximately 15-20 seconds). This is not to imply that the officers must cease looking for the suspect, but they must slow the pursuit after loss of contact.

e)   When there is a clear and unreasonable danger to the officer, fleeing suspect and/or any other persons. This may be due to excessive speed, reckless driving techniques, or the erratic driving by the suspect which exceeds the performance capabilities of the vehicles or the drivers.

f)   When the danger created by the pursuit outweighs the necessity for immediate apprehension.

10.   The following factors shall be considered by officers and supervisors in making the decision to continue or terminate a police pursuit:

a)   Environmental factors such as rain, fog, ice, snow or darkness that would substantially increase the danger of the pursuit.

b)   The officer's familiarity with the area and his ability to accurately notify Communications of his location and the direction in which the pursuit is proceeding.

c) Road conditions are congested by traffic or pedestrians. This would be especially important during rush hours or in the area of any school.

d) The pursued vehicle proceeds the wrong way on any freeway, divided highway, or one-way street. **AT NO TIME** will officers pursue violators the wrong way on a freeway.

e) The pursuing officer knows or has reason to believe that the fleeing vehicle is being operated by a juvenile who has committed a traffic violation, misdemeanor or nonviolent felony, and who is driving in such an unsafe manner that it is obvious he does not have the maturity to deal with the danger involved.

11. Pursuits - Other Agencies or Jurisdictions

a) When other agencies pursue vehicles into the city limits the following shall govern Little Rock Police Department involvement:

(1) Little Rock Police Department officers will not assist in active pursuit, unless requested by the pursuing agency **and** such assistance is approved by an L.R.P.D. police supervisor.

(2) At no time will L.R.P.D. units become actively engaged in a pursuit if two police vehicles from another agency are already in active pursuit.

(3) If the pursuing agency is joined by L.R.P.D. units, and the agency's backup unit arrives to assist, L.R.P.D. units will terminate active pursuit and cease emergency operations.

b) When L.R.P.D. pursuits leave the city limits and enter other jurisdictions the following will apply:

(1) The primary officer will advise Communications that the pursuit is leaving the city.

(2) The supervisor handling the pursuit will evaluate the entire incident and make the decision to let the pursuit continue or terminate.

(3) If the agency with jurisdictional authority joins in active pursuit, the L.R.P.D. backup unit will discontinue pursuit and cease emergency operations. If two units from the other agency join the pursuit, all L.R.P.D. units will safely terminate their pursuit and discontinue emergency operations. **[At no time will L.R.P.D. units be involved in pursuits when two police units from another agency are already involved.]**

c)   When other agencies become involved in L.R.P.D. pursuits, within the city limits of Little Rock, the following shall apply:

    (1)   If another agency becomes involved in the immediate pursuit, the L.R.P.D. backup unit will terminate emergency operations.

    (2)   The primary unit will, if possible, advise Communications of the identity of the other agencies involved so that Communications can make contact and begin communications with the involved agency.

    (3)   Due to limited radio communications with other agencies, the assigned supervisor shall re-evaluate the pursuit and terminate if necessary.

    (4)   At no time will L.R.P.D. units be involved in multi-vehicle pursuits with other agencies. For the purpose of this policy, a maximum of two units are authorized in pursuit situations.

12.   Supervisor's Responsibilities

a)   A patrol field sergeant will immediately, upon hearing of a police pursuit, take command of the situation.

    (1)   He will be accountable for compliance with this policy until the pursuit is terminated. [The supervisor of the officer who initiates the pursuit should normally be the supervisor assuming command.]

b)   In the event that a sergeant does not take command immediately, the shift lieutenant will assume command and/or assign a sergeant.

c)   Any police supervisor may order a pursuit terminated, if in his best judgement, the necessity of apprehension is outweighed by the level of danger.

13.   Supervisory Reviews

a)   A formal review of **all** pursuits will be conducted by the officer's Chain of Command.

b)   The purpose of the review is to determine if:

    (1)   The pursuit was necessary and within Departmental policy;

    (2)   There are training needs to be considered; and,

        (3)   Any policy changes need to be considered.

14.   Reports

    a)   All officers who are involved in a pursuit will complete an Information Report and an Officer's Report [5600-2], detailing the facts of the pursuit.

    b)   The officer's supervisor will review the Information report and officer's report for accuracy and policy compliance.

    c)   The supervisor will submit a detailed written evaluation of the pursuit incident and make his recommendations.

    d)   Supervisors will obtain a copy of the Communications tape of all radio traffic pertaining to the pursuit for inclusion in the file.

    e)   The file will be forwarded through the Chain of Command for evaluation and review at each level.

*15.   File Format

    a)   All documentation will be placed in a file folder and secured at the top with an ACCO two hole fastener.

    b)   Any photographs or audio/video tapes will be placed in a manila envelop attached to the inside front cover of the file.

    c)   The initial evaluating supervisor shall be responsible for ensuring that all necessary documentation is obtained and properly placed in the file before routing it through the Chain of Command.

    d)   The file will be constructed as follows:

        (1)   Lieutenant's evaluation;

        (2)   Sergeant's evaluation;

        (3)   Information Report;

        (4)   Involved Officer(s) reports;

        (5)   Arrest Report [if any];

        (6)   Medical treatment information [if any];

*   [Section Inserted 05-01-91]

(7)   Computer printout of suspect's arrest record; and,

(8)   If an injury has occurred to an involved employee, copies of the Worker's Compensation Forms.

III.   Non-Emergency Operation of Departmental Vehicles

A.   Police employees will comply with all city ordinances and state laws when operating vehicles owned, rented, leased or seized by the city.

B.   Officers will use seat belts at all times when operating any city vehicle.

C.   Officers will insure that their assigned vehicles have sufficient gas and oil for their assigned shift and that tires are properly inflated.

D.   All vehicles shall be pre-tripped in accordance with driver's training instruction.

E.   All officers will inspect their assigned vehicles prior to their shift for any damage, missing equipment, and inspect the rear seat area for contraband or evidence. [Officers shall inspect the rear seat area after transporting every prisoner.]

F.   All vehicle damage or missing equipment will be reported to a supervisor prior to the vehicle being placed in service. The supervisor will initiate an investigation to determine the cause and document his findings. The reports will be forwarded through the Chain of Command to the Division Commander for resolution.

G.   Officers will insure that their police vehicles are kept clean and free of trash.

H.   Officers will, at all times, insure that the spare tire is in its proper location and secured to avoid damage to radio equipment. When a police vehicle has a flat tire at any time, the assigned officer will complete a work order and forward it to the Automotive/Equipment Coordinator to initiate repairs.

I.   Careless, abusive, negligent or reckless handling of any vehicle will result in disciplinary action.

IV.   Accidents and Damage to City Vehicles

A.   Any officer who damages a city vehicle or becomes involved in a motor vehicle accident with a city owned, rented, leased or seized vehicle, will immediately notify a police supervisor.

B.   A police supervisor will personally complete an Arkansas Motor Vehicle Traffic Accident Report. In instances where a fatality, serious injury or extensive property damage occurs, the supervisor may request the assistance of a supervisor or officer trained in accident reconstruction to assist in the investigation.

1.   The investigating supervisor is responsible for completing the State SR-1 form, the city's "Supervisor's Investigation Report - Motor Vehicle" Form, and logging the damage with O.E.S. communications.

2.   A repair order will be made detailing the damage and a copy of the accident report attached for submission to Fleet Services.

C.   The file containing all forms and a written evaluation from each officer in the Chain of Command will be submitted to the Division Commander.

*D.   The file will be assembled as follows:

1.   All documentation will be places in a file folder and secured at the top with an ACCO two hole fastener.

2.   Any photographs or audio/video tapes will be placed in a manila envelop attached to the inside front cover of the file.

3.   The evaluating supervisor shall be responsible for ensuring that all necessary documentation has been properly placed in the file before routing it through the Chain of Command.

4.   The file shall include:

a)   Lieutenant's evaluation;

b)   Sergeant's evaluation;

c)   Accident Report [copy];

d)   Involved Officer's report [5600-2];

e)   Arrest Report/Traffic Summons [copy, if any].

f)   Supervisor's Investigation Report [copy];

g)   SR-1 Form [copy];

h)   Copy of vehicle damage book notation;

i)   Copy of Repair Slip; and,

j)   If an injury has occurred to an employee, copies of the Worker's Compensation Forms.

5.   The original SR-1 Form, Supervisor's Investigation Report, and a copy of the Accident Report shall be attached by paper clip to the inside front cover of the file.

V.   **Monthly Vehicle Inspection**

A.   Division Commanders shall be responsible for insuring that all vehicles assigned to their respective Divisions are inspected monthly, with all

*   [Section Inserted 05-01-91]

documentation completed by the 1st of the month.

B.   Division Commanders shall review and then maintain monthly vehicle inspection forms.

VI.   **Off Duty Police Officers - Private Vehicle Accidents**

A.   When a sworn police officer is involved in a motor vehicle accident in a private vehicle, a police supervisor will be responsible for investigating the accident and completing an accident report.

B.   Police officers will investigate accidents involving cadets and civilian employees when they are driving a private vehicle.

It is obvious that this policy has been written with concern for the officers and the motoring public. Two other issues which should be considered include the requirement of specialized training to "license" officers to continue a pursuit and the public accountability issue requiring the officers to consider how each would justify a continued pursuit to the "common man." Perhaps the best example of this language comes from the Oakdale, Minnesota Police Department's pursuit policy:

> The (original) decision to continue a pursuit shall lie with the individual officer, after considering the restrictions imposed by this procedure, as well as the wide variety of mitigating factors. These factors shall include, but are not limited to, the seriousness of the original offense and its relationship to community safety, time, day, and location of the pursuit; weather and roadway conditions, vehicular and pedestrian traffic/presence; familiarity with roadway design; capability and quality of police equipment, including communications; pursuit speeds and evasive tactics, etc.

Summary

It is important to stress statutory requirements and that a driver of an emergency vehicle is not relieved **from the duty to drive with due regard for the safety of all persons using the highway.** When officers are exempt from the laws regulating traffic flow (stop signs and traffic lights) and are authorized to drive faster than the speed limit, they must continue to drive with *due regard* for the safety of all persons using the roads, which places a special responsibility on the driver of an emergency vehicle who chooses to invoke this privilege.

As illustrated in the present and previous chapters, a great deal of progress has been made in the research, policy development and training associated with pursuit driving. Although the information available concerning pursuit lags a decade or two behind what we know about the use of firearms, the major advances in the use of firearms has expedited the corresponding movement in pursuit. In the next chapter the forces of change for police practices are discussed. The focus is on the comparison between firearms and pursuit conceptualization, policy and practice.

The Forces
of Reform

8

A great deal of effort has been expended to determine whether or not the disproportionate representation of black subjects of police shootings is the result of police bias. However, for purposes of analyzing the forces of change in the area of deadly force with firearms, the precise answer to that question is less important than public perception. Regardless of whether or not the police have "one trigger finger for blacks and one for whites," this perception has been reality for a large segment of the minority community. Indeed, the consequences of these perceptions have been critical, not just for police use of deadly force policies and practices, but for policing in general. This chapter includes a discussion of the forces that generated the social movement of reform in the area of police shootings and coverage of the resulting changes in policy, changes in the nature and extent of police use of deadly force, and increase in empirical research. Finally, this change process is contrasted with the much slower pace of reform in the area of police pursuit driving, focusing on the factors associated with a social movement discussed in the first chapter.

The Minority Community's Perception of the Excessive Use of Deadly Force by Police

The concern of the ethnic minority community regarding police use of excessive force was discussed by Gilbert G. Pompa, Director of the Federal Department of Justice Community Relations Service (CRS), at a convention in 1980. He reported (1980:1):

> During recent years, charges of police use of excessive force have grown to replace school desegregation as the issue that most dominates the caseload of the CRS.

> Not even the Ku Klux Klan promotes more community resentment or minority/white hostilities, or has more potential for sparking open community violence than allegations that police use force excessively against minorities.

Speaking specifically of police use of deadly force, he stated elsewhere, "Of the many impediments to harmonious relationships between police and minority communities, one of the most serious, and clearly the most inflammatory is use of deadly force by police" (Pompa, n.d.).

141

A considerable amount of research has been conducted to assess community attitudes toward the police in general (e.g., Bayley and Mendelsohn, 1969; Smith and Hawkins, 1973; Hindelang, 1975; Alpert and Dunham, 1988c), and this research consistently indicates that blacks view police less favorably than do whites (Biderman, et al., 1967; Ennis, 1967; Hahn, 1971; Smith and Hawkins, 1973; Hadar and Snortum, 1975). One survey (Fridell, 1983) looked specifically at community attitudes toward police shootings of citizens with a particular focus on racial differences. This telephone survey of 455 residents of Los Angeles indicated that significantly more blacks than Hispanics or non-Hispanic whites (referred to below as "Anglos") believed Los Angeles police shot when it was avoidable. Overall, 38.1 percent of the survey respondents maintained that L.A. police overused deadly force, with this figure accounting for a full 55 percent of the black respondents, 31.4 percent of the Hispanic sample and 27.9 percent of the Anglos. Further, more than one-third of the blacks claimed police "often" (as opposed to "sometimes" or "almost never") shot and killed people when this could have been avoided, compared to only 12.6 percent of the Hispanics and 8.5 percent of the Anglos. Additionally, over one-half of the blacks who believed that one ethnic group was disproportionately involved in police-citizen shootings maintained that this was due to racial prejudice and/or police fear of minority groups.

A 1986 survey conducted as part of the New York State Commission (1977) inquiry into the use of force (not limited to deadly force) by police found similar racial differences. A larger proportion of black and Hispanic respondents than white respondents reported that misuse of force by police was directed disproportionately at specific kinds of persons—most notably, minority citizens. Proportionately more blacks and Hispanics than whites viewed police misuse of force as a very serious and important problem. Interestingly, when asked to identify types of "misuse of force" in which police are involved, more blacks (19%) than either Hispanics (8%) or whites (2%) mentioned deadly force (New York State Commission, Volume III, 1987).

The Civil Rights Movement and Police Use of Deadly Force

Both of these surveys, which were conducted in the 1980s, indicate a deep concern of minorities regarding police misuse of force, especially deadly force. Miami during the 1980s experienced a series of civil disturbances which were caused by police use of deadly force against members of the minority community (see Alpert, 1989b). Also in recent years, police shooting incidents have led to violence in cities including Los Angeles, St. Louis, Brooklyn, Birmingham and San Francisco. However, the concern was most intense during the 1960s and 1970s. The civil rights movement reflected ethnic minority group anger at what was perceived as the repressiveness and inequality of society. Walker (1980:222-223) explained the focus of these alienated persons on police practices during the civil rights era:

As black Americans demanded full equality, their tolerance for long-standing abuses dropped accordingly. The police became the symbol of an unjust society . . . Ironically, the conduct of police officers had improved substantially since the days of the Wickersham Commission report on police brutality. But in the intervening 30 years, black expectations had far outpaced police improvements. By the mid-sixties the ghettos were a tinderbox.

Walker reported that a police encounter with a minority citizen was the precipitating event for many of the urban riots during this period. Specific incidents where the minority community perceived excessive force, including excessive deadly force, by police was the basis of at least 84 of the 136 major riots in the 1960s (Law Enforcement Assistance Administration, 1980; Graham and Gurr, 1969). As Walker and Fridell (1989:10) explained:

There can be little doubt that conflict between the police and racial minorities has been one of the most important aspects of American policing since the early 1960s and that complaints about discriminatory patterns in police shootings has been a major point of controversy.

The two-day Harlem riot of 1964 was precipitated by the shooting of a black teenager by a New York City police officer. Riots erupted in Philadelphia, Jersey City, and other cities that same year and the following summer brought the riots in the Watts ghetto of Los Angeles, Chicago, and San Diego. The next two years saw disturbances in 43 cities (Walker, 1980).

Aspects of Change

The civil rights movement made an enormous contribution to the development of First Amendment law (Kalven, 1965), the law of equal protection (Kluger, 1978), and the law of due process (Cover, 1982). Also, Walker (1977, 1980) noted that the social forces resulting from the civil rights movement were major stimuli for closer scrutiny of police practices, the police-community relations movement, and the further advancement of police professionalism. Similarly, Williams and Murphy (1990) attributed major changes in policing to the civil rights movement:

It was that movement, led primarily by black Americans, and that political empowerment that finally began to produce the putative benefits of professional policing: a fairer distribution of police services, less use of deadly force, greater respect for individual rights, and equal opportunity for minorities within the nation's police departments.

The changes that took place within law enforcement specifically regarding police use of firearms included the delimiting of the police power to use deadly force, a resulting decrease in the use of deadly force by police, and greater interest in and financial support for research addressing this topic. As Blumberg (1989:442) explained:

Despite the harm that results from [deadly force] incidents, it was only in recent years that any meaningful attempt to examine or control the use of deadly force by police officers was undertaken. Prior to the 1970s, police officers had tremendous discretion regarding the use of firearms; police departments often had poorly defined or nonexistent policies . . . and no meaningful attempt to measure the incidence of police killings on a national basis had been undertaken.

Policy Content

The delimiting of police power to shoot citizens over the years can be demonstrated by comparing deadly force policies recommended by the International Association of Chiefs of Police in 1940, 1966, and 1980. The statement issued in 1940 was insistent that restrictions on the use of deadly force *exist* and that an officer only shoot a person who had committed a "very serious crime" (presumably, consistent with common law, at least a felony). The policy read:

> The use of firearms must of necessity be restricted in our cities; otherwise, there will be fatal shootings. The fact that a suspected person is running away from the police and fails to halt when called upon to do so does not justify the police officer in shooting him. There must be some reliable evidence that the fleeing person is guilty of some very serious crime before a police officer is justified in firing at him. Far better to let him escape for the time being than to run the risk of killing him or, worse still, killing some innocent person.

Though the 1966 policy recommended by the IACP increased in length and specificity, it still allowed for the use of firearms against any person "whom the (officer) has reasonable cause [to believe] has committed a felony," except a felonious motor vehicle violation. The standard adopted in 1980 had again increased in length and specificity and provided for considerably more restrictive standards for police use of deadly force compared to the 1966 policy. As noted in chapter 5, this directive allows for use of deadly force only when the officer reasonably believes that there is an immediate threat of death or serious bodily harm to the officer or another. In evaluating whether this level of threat is posed by a fleeing felon the officer may consider whether the fleeing person "previously demonstrated threat to or wanton disregard for human life" (IACP, 1980).

The major changes in the parameters on police use of deadly force nationwide were not a result of activity in the state legislatures or the courts, but rather came from within the police departments themselves. These policy changes came, in many cases, as a direct result of the urban unrest following specific incidents of police use of deadly force. Sherman, et al., reported (1986:11): "Massive protests in many black communities after killings of unarmed youths posed a political problem for many mayors, and provided a continuing source of pressure for restraint in shootings at blacks." As described below, two specific shooting incidents in Los Angeles (the second one being the shooting of Eulia Love) resulted in changes in deadly force policy for that city, demanded by the black and Hispanic communities. In New York City, a firearms policy change had been under consideration when an 11-year-old black male was shot by police in 1972. As Sherman (1983:101) explained: "The community uproar over the shooting . . . created what the police commissioner later called an opportunity for implementing and deflecting criticism of the new policy . . ."

Sherman also described the adoption of a new policy in Kansas City, Missouri, in 1973, following the shooting of an unarmed 15-year-old black male. Sherman noted that it was not just the shooting, but multiple factors (not the least of which was a new police chief with a reform agenda) which led to the policy change. Though acknowledging the existence and importance of "reform-oriented" chiefs during the change years, Walker and Fridell (1989:9) reported that:

> Few if any observers of the subject of police use of deadly force . . . seriously believe that police executives in the pre-Garner years adopted restrictive shooting policies wholly on their own initiative. Rather, it would appear that they were prompted in large part because of the continuing protests about police shootings by civil rights and community groups . . .

Walker and Fridell (1989) pointed out that this nationwide modification of police policy at the local level was unusual for law enforcement. Specifically, the modification of deadly force policy differs from other areas of police change in that the police departments initiated the changes *before* the U.S. Supreme Court mandated restrictive policies. (In fact, the U.S. Supreme Court, in *Tennessee v. Garner*, made note of the adoptions of restrictive policies by departments in justifying its decision.) This contrasts with policies regarding other controversial police practices (e.g., search and seizure) where the U.S. Supreme Court "was in the advance guard of change—enunciating new standards of Constitutional law and forcing the police to conform to them" (Walker and Fridell, 1989:7).

Reduced Use of Force

It is not surprising that a nationwide reduction in the use of deadly force by police followed the policy changes implemented within many of the major cities in the U.S. Certainly, a major factor in this reduction is the tightened standards regarding the shooting of fleeing felons. However, an interesting study revealed another aspect of this decline. Research conducted by the Urban League (Mendez, 1983) looked at race in justifiable homicides by police for the years 1970 through 1979 and found that the decrease in the number of citizens killed was due in very large part to a decrease in shootings of black citizens, rather than whites. In 1971, seven black citizens were killed by police for every one white citizen. By 1979, this ratio had dropped to 2.8 black citizens killed for every one white citizen. It is important also to note, as the author did, that the black arrests did *not* decrease during this time period.

Research

The reform associated with the police use of deadly force included increased attention to empirical work. The legal aspects of police use of firearms was addressed in law journals as early as the 1920s (e.g., Bohlen and Shulman, 1927; Note, 1929), but, as noted above, Robin's 1963 study was the first empirical work to receive widespread attention and was the only major study from the 1960s. Fyfe (1988:166) lamented:

> Criminology and criminal justice scholars apparently did not notice that police officers in most states were authorized by law and by their departments to kill people whom they suspected of bicycle theft; with . . . slight exceptions . . . they left us no clues as to how often or in what circumstances the police shot suspected bicycle thieves or anybody else.

The 1970s and 1980s saw a proliferation of empirical and theoretical work of increasing sophistication (e.g., Knoohuizen, et al., 1972; Kobler, 1975; Milton, et al., 1977; Fyfe, 1978; Geller and Karales, 1981; Binder, et al., 1982) which was described in Chapter 3. Many of these studies were made possible by government funding for research, which increased precipitously in the area of criminal justice in general, and policing in particular, following the unrest of the 1960s (Walker, 1980).

The Case of Los Angeles

The story of police shooting reform in Los Angeles parallels in many ways the reforms in other cities across the United States during the same time period. Uchida (1982) documented the history of the social movement within this city led by the angry black and Hispanic communities which effected major revisions in policy content and in procedures for ensuring policy compliance.

Uchida described how (1982:13), "In the late 1950s and early 1960s the civil rights movement engulfed Chief Parker and the LAPD." This was not the first period during which persons in the minority communities voiced concern about the police, but this time the outcry was louder and the actions violent. A gun battle between police and black militants who had been demanding reforms took place in April, 1962, resulting in one black death and nine persons wounded, including three police officers. The Watts riot occurred in August of 1965, following the police arrest of a young black youth. Walker (1980) reported that in the 30 months preceding this major disturbance, Los Angeles police had shot and killed 60 persons! The accumulated anger of the citizens over perceived police abuse erupted into violence in Watts that took 34 lives, led to 1,000 injuries, and destroyed $20-$40 million in property.

A report of the commission, appointed by the governor to investigate the Los Angeles riots, led to few changes in LAPD practices. Uchida (1982:20) reported, however, that during the next 15 years:

the public response to police violence intensified and changes began to take place in the department . . . (W)ith the onslaught of the urban troubles of the 1960s, the public began to ask questions about the policies of police departments. Slowly a movement developed that concentrated on making the police more responsive to the community they served.

In Los Angeles, the black and Hispanic communities focused primarily on the issue of deadly force. Several specific incidents of police use of deadly force kept the issue at the forefront: the death of an Hispanic reporter during a riot, the erroneous shooting of a black male in his apartment, and the shootout with the Symbionese Liberation Army (Uchida, 1982).

The shootings of Ronald Burkholder and Eulia Love in 1977 and 1979, respectively, led to LAPD policy changes. Though Burkholder was not an ethnic minority, the questionable circumstances of his death created a "major controversy among the white and minority communities" (Uchida, 1982:28). One month after his death, the any-fleeing-felon policy of the Los Angeles Police Department was changed to a Model Penal Code standard.

The community was pleased with the policy change and police-community relations were relatively uneventful for 16 months. Then, in January 1979, Eulia Love was killed by Officers O'Callaghan and Hopson. The minority communities were outraged, first by the shooting itself, and then by the news that the officers would not be disciplined. Uchida observed that compliance with and enforcement of policy, not just revised content, were essential to meeting the community's demands (1982:37):

> Part of the problem emanated from the low probability of a resolution occurring within the criminal justice system. The police and the criminal justice system had not developed solutions for the problem of questionable police shootings of civilians to adequately satisfy the citizenry.

The pressure from the minority communities led to hearings and investigations including a thorough investigation and four-part report by the Police Commission. The Commission determined that the relatively new deadly force policy content was satisfactory, but the implementation of it was inadequate. Specifically, the commission members called for changes in the investigation and adjudication procedures following police-involved shootings to promote policy enforcement.

One recommendation was that the shooting investigations include an assessment of the decisions made by officers prior to the "final frame." Corresponding with this, the Commission called for enhanced training of officers which focused on deadly force decision-making and avoiding police-citizen violent encounters (e.g., training in crisis intervention, psychological techniques for resolving family disputes, and police-minority relations).

The story of change in Los Angeles represents just one component of the social movement during the late 1960s and 1970s which led to major changes in deadly force policies and practices. Significant actors in Los Angeles were the black mayor elected in 1973, the city council, and the media. However, the primary agents of change were the minority communities. These communities had unity and organization which facilitated their challenge of police practices when they perceived that these practices were being misused to their collective detriment.

The Challenge to Police Pursuit Driving

In his book, *Police Revitalization*, Caiden (1977:3) stated:

> Reform movements do not appear by magic. They are caused by dissatisfaction with the status quo and optimism about the efficacy of remedial action. The dissatisfaction must carry people over their threshold of tolerance and inertia to the point where they demand action and support promising prescriptions.

Caiden's description fits the history of reform in the area of deadly force and reflects what we have seen with regard to the public's reaction to the criminal justice system's responses to drunk driving (Jacobs, 1989) and domestic violence (Binder and Meeker, 1991). Caiden's quote also reflects what we see currently in the area of police pursuit driving. This monograph began with a discussion of the differences between the public's responses to the two uses of deadly force: firearms and pursuit driving. The major (and related) differences between the two responses is 25 years of concern and the nature of the groups demanding change. The limited and unorganized public outcry concerning the use and abuse of pursuit driving is not yet focused or threatening, but it has recently begun to unite. Because pursuit driving is color blind, the most active voices are not those of minority group members but include relatives of victims and other concerned citizens. These persons perceive that police pursuit driving practices do not reflect an appropriate balance between effective law enforcement and officer and public safety. Rather, they believe these practices give too little regard to safety, and thus their protest has begun.

These victims and other concerned citizens do not have the pre-existing unity and organization that the minority communities drew upon. Until recently they did not have a leader to provide that organization and unity. In 1990 G.W. LaCrosse initiated the Deseré Foundation which is challenging the laws, policies, and practices related to police pursuit driving. The impetus for his involvement is described best by Mr. LaCrosse.

THE DESERÉ FOUNDATION
Center for the Study of Alternatives to Pursuit
(1-800-441-1786)

On May 3, 1988 John Basaman was driving home from a day trip to Philadelphia along with his wife and two children. As he entered a controlled intersection in Evesham Township, N.J.,

---

his car was struck by a man being chased by the police [for a minor traffic offense]. His wife and infant son were killed and his two year old son was critically injured. The Basaman family lived not more than a mile from us.

Just three days later, on May 6, 1988, Erin Walsh, a neighbor and a schoolmate of my daughter's, was coming home from her job at a handicapped facility. A man being chased by the police [again, for a minor traffic offense] crossed into her lane and collided head-on with her car. Tragically, not only was Erin killed, but her mother, who was travelling in the car directly behind her daughter's, witnessed the entire scene. Understandably the community was outraged that three totally innocent people had been killed, three others had suffered injuries and that two families had been devastated within a few days.

I was one of those who was outraged that someone would have so little respect for the law that they would risk the lives of innocent people just to avoid a traffic ticket. During a conversation with my state assemblyman I learned that eluding the police was a disorderly persons offense and was seldom if ever prosecuted. So, as a councilman in Beachwood, I called upon our state legislature to introduce a bill which would increase the penalty for those convicted of eluding. Assembly Bill A-1825 was introduced, debated, passed and signed into law by Governor Kean in May, 1989.

Early on November 16, 1988 a young lady was coming home from visiting with friends when she was struck by a man being chased by the police [for a broken head light]. After nine hours in a trauma center, her magnificent heart could no longer wage the battle for life and she left this world and her family behind. The young lady's name was Deseré, she was nineteen years old and she was my daughter.

Mr. LaCrosse, with the help of the media, has raised the national consciousness and garnered additional support for the challenge to police pursuit practices. His grass roots amassing of support is similar to the events which transpired early in the movement against drunk driving, when Candy Lightner founded MADD. A reporter from NBC Nightly News, whose friend had recently been killed as a result of a police pursuit, interviewed Mr. LaCrosse for a special report on police pursuit driving. This interview led to guest appearances on the Larry King Live Show, Inside Edition, the Geraldo Rivera Show, Joan Rivers and Donahue.

(Several of these were joint appearances with the senior author of this monograph.) After each show, Mr. LaCrosse received more phone calls from concerned persons around the country and was able to garner the support of organizations such as consumer advocate Ralph Nader's Center for the Study of Responsive Law and the National Association of Professional Law Enforcement Emergency Vehicle Response Trainers.

The Deseré Foundation is "dedicated to finding viable alternatives to pursuits." The organization stresses the reduction of high risk pursuit driving through legal, educational, and technical means. Legislatively, the foundation advocates laws which make penalties against fleeing from police in automobiles harsh and allows for the confiscation of automobiles involved in pursuit. The purpose of these laws is to deter law violators from running from the police. Legislation might also contain a "rebuttable presumption" that the owner of the car is the person fleeing. This would allow the officer to call off a chase and to arrest the registered owner of the automobile later.

The Deseré Foundation emphasizes that education should target both drivers and law enforcement officers. With regard to the former group, this organization proposes that the dangers and penalties associated with eluding police be presented in every high school drivers' education course and in learner's permit or driver's license manuals. For the police, the organization advocates heightening the awareness of police as to the dangers associated with pursuit driving and improved training of policy.

The Deseré Foundation suggests increased use of existing technology and development of new technologies which might reduce the need for police pursuit driving. Photo-radar cameras, which clock and photograph speeders, might reduce speeding and allow for the citation of drivers without on-scene police interventions. Anti-theft and ignition interrupt systems might reduce automobile theft or, at least, reduce the need for police to engage in high speed pursuits to apprehend the suspect to recover the stolen automobile. These devices allow the police to locate the automobile and, when it is determined to be safe to do so, disable the ignition, making the car immobile.

The Deseré Foundation is the initial catalyst for those interested in reform of pursuit driving. The number of concerned citizens and public officials appears to be growing. Reform in pursuit driving may follow the trend established in the social movement against drunk driving and police use of firearms.

The Most Deadly Weapons: Some Concluding Thoughts

How successful the protest is against pursuit and what reforms will become institutionalized as a result of public input cannot be predicted. However, it appears likely that changes in law, policy, and practices are forthcoming and that the change process will be much less painful than that associated with the use of firearms. The lessons learned and the doors opened during the previous reform movement have paved the way for the reform in police pursuits and other areas.

First of all, the underlying policy issue of police pursuit is the same as that of the use of weapons; it involves a balancing of officer and citizen safety with the need to apprehend fleeing suspects. The policy debate in deadly force provides many of the answers to questions which are posed by the issue of police pursuit driving. In fact, during the past few years, there has been some governmental recognition of the dangers associated with pursuit and some reforms on the local and state levels have taken place in the absence of great public outcry.

Another parallel between the two reforms is that the broader conceptualization of deadly force with firearms has been incorporated into the thinking about police pursuit driving. Similar to the analysis of the use of a firearm, the current focus is not solely on the outcome of a pursuit but on the precipitating factors and phases of a pursuit, with an emphasis on developing ways to avoid unnecessary pursuits and terminate them when they create unnecessary risk.

Reform in the area of pursuit driving has been facilitated by the relationship which has been established between researchers and law enforcement policy makers. Researchers studying deadly force were among the first to conduct in-depth studies within law enforcement agencies and thus get partial credit for the mutual cooperation and respect between these two entities that has emerged in the last 20 years or so. Uchida (1989:27-8) described the effects of the 1960s unrest on research in policing:

> The events of the 1960s forced the police, politicians, and policymakers to reassess the state of law enforcement in the United States. For the first time, academicians rushed to study the police in an effort to explain their problems and crises. With federal funding from LEAA and private organizations, researchers began to study the police from a number of perspectives. Sociologists, political scientists, psychologists, and historians began to scrutinize different aspects of policing.

The relationship between police researchers and policy makers with the associated increased recognition of the value of research for policy making and policy implementation will further reform in law enforcement in the years to come.

The willingness of law enforcement agencies to listen to and work with researchers parallels an increased willingness to listen to and work with their constituents. There is disagreement about the extent to which the police-community relations movement that emanated from the civil rights era has been effective (see e.g., Walker, 1983 and Greene, 1989). Regardless of whether policing has achieved the goals set forth during those years of great police-community tension (see Task Force on the Police, 1967), it is apparent that citizens today are more involved in the formal and informal processes of establishing and regulating policies than in the past. The police are more interested in and sensitive to the concerns of the citizenry. Some cities (e.g., Omaha, Nebraska and Tampa, Florida) have formalized citizen involvement in policy making through the establishment of civilian policy advisory boards. This increased responsiveness to the community has ramifications for the reform movement in pursuit driving as well as other areas of police policy.

The history of the reform movement in deadly force by firearms is a painful reminder of the costs when police and community are at odds. The result of that movement, especially the establishment of more cooperative relations between the police and the public, provides promise for continued reform within law enforcement with the assistance, input, and support of concerned citizens.

Cases

Baker v. McCollan, 443 U.S. 137 (979).

Baratier v. State, 462 N.Y.S 2d (N.Y.C.C. 1983).

Bell v. Wolfish, 441 U.S. 520 (1979).

Brower v. County of Inyo, 489 U.S. 593 (1989).

Brown v. City of Pinnellas Park, 15 FLW D468 (February 23, 1990).

California v. Hodari D. _____ U.S. _____ (1991), 111 S.Ct. 1547 (1991).

Cameron v. City of Pontiac, 623 F. Supp. 1238 (D.C. Mich. 1985).

Cannon v. Taylor, 782 F. 2d 947 (11th. Cir. 1986).

Chambers v. Ideal Pure Milk Co. 245 S.W. 2d 589 (Ky. 1952).

City of Redlands v. Sorensen, 176 Cal. App. 3rd 202 (1985).

City of Canton v. Harris, 489 U.S. 378 (1989).

City of Miami v. Harris, 490 So. 2d 69 (Fla. App. 1986).

City of Oklahoma City v. Tuttle, 471 U.S. 808 (1985).

Daniels v. Williams, 474 U.S. 193 (1986).

Davidson v. Cannon, 474 U.S. 344 (1986).

Delaware v. Prouse, 440 U.S. 648 (1979).

Dent v. City of Dallas, 729 S.W. 2d 114 (Tex. App. 1986).

Fiser v. City of Ann Arbor, 339 N.W. 2d 413 (Mich. 1983).

Frohman v. City of Detroit, 450 N.W. 2d 59 (Mich App. 1989).

Gail v. Clark, 410 N.W. 2d 662 (Iowa, 1987).

Galas v. McGee, 801 F. 2d 200 (6th. Cir. 1986).

Gilmere v. City of Atlanta, 774 F.2d 1495 (11th. Cir. 1985), cert.denied, 476 U.S. 115 (1986).

Graham v. Connor, 490 U.S. 386 (1989).

Hubert v. Boelt, 620 P. 2d 156 (Cal 1980).

Jackson v. Olsen, 712 P. 2d. 128 (Or. App. 1985).

Johnson v. Glick, 481 F.2d 1028 (2d Cir.), cert. denied, 414 U.S. 1033 (1973).

Kennedy v. City of Spring City, 780 S.W. 2d 164 (1989).

Kibbe v. City of Springfield, 777 F. 2d 801 (1st Cir. 1985).

Kortum v. Alkire, 69 Cal App 3d 325, 138 Cal. Reporter 26, 1977.

Mattis v. Schnarr, 547 F.2d 1007, 1976.

Michigan v. Chesternut, 486 U.S. 567, 569 (1988).

Michigan State Police v. Sitz, 496 U.S. 444 (1990).

Mobell v. Denver, 671 P. 2d 433 (Colo. App. 1983).

Oberkramer v. City of Ellisville, 650 SW 2d 286 (Mo. App. 1983).

Parson v. City of Claremore, United States District Court for the Northern District of Oklahoma, Case No. 89-C-L87-B (1989).

Pincock v. Dupnik, 703 P. 2d 1240 (Ariz. App. 1985).

Reid v. Georgia, 448 U.S. 438 (1980).

Rhodes v. Lamar, 490 So. 2d 1061 (Fla. App. 1986).

Smith v. City of West Point, 475 So. 2d. 816 (Miss. 1985).

State v. Malone, 724 P.2d 364 (Wash. 1986).

Tagstrom v. Pottebaum, 668 F. Supp 1269 (N.D. Iowa 1987).

Tennessee v. Garner, 471 U.S. 1 (1985).

Tetro v. Town of Stratford, 458 A. 2d 5 (Conn. 1983).

Terry v. Ohio, 392 U.S. 1 (1968).

Thornton v. Shore, 666 P.2d 655 (Kan. 1983).

Tomcsik v. United States, 720 F. Supp 588 (E.D. Mich. 1989).

Travis v. City of Mesquite, In the Supreme Court of Texas. No. C-85-76 (Decided December 31, 1990).

United States v. Cortez, 449 U.S. 441 (1980).

Ybarra v. Illinois, 444 U.S. 85 (1979).

United States v. Place, 462 U.S. 696 (1983).

West Virginia v. Fidelity Gas & Casualty Co. of N.Y., 263 F. Supp 88 (D.W.Va. 1967).

West v. United States, 617 F. Supp. 1015 (D.C. Cal. 1985).

Wiley v. Memphis Police Department, 548 F.2d 1247 (1977).

Wright v. District of Columbia, Memorandum Opinion. No. 87-2157 (June 21, 1990).

References

Aadland, Rebecca L. 1981. "The Prediction of Use of Deadly Force by Police Officers in Simulated Field Situations." Unpublished Dissertation, California School of Professional Psychology, Los Angeles.

Abbott, Les. 1988. "Pursuit Driving." *FBI Law Enforcement Bulletin,* November: 7-11.

Alpert, Geoffrey P. 1987a. "Questioning Police Pursuit in Urban Areas." *Journal of Police Science and Administration,* 15: 298-306.

_____. 1987b. "Police Use of Deadly Force in the Miami Police Department, 1980-1986." Unpublished report.

_____. 1987c. "Review of Deadly Force Training and Policies of the Dallas Police Department." Unpublished Report.

_____. 1988. "Police Pursuit: Linking Data to Decisions." *Criminal Law Bulletin,* 24: 453-642.

_____. 1989a. *"City of Canton* and the Deliberate Indifference Standard." *Criminal Law Bulletin,* 25: 466-472.

_____. 1989b. "Police Use of Deadly Force: The Miami Experience." In *Critical Issues in Policing: Contemporary Readings,* edited by Roger G. Dunham and Geoffrey P. Alpert, pp. 480-495. Prospect Heights, IL: Waveland Press.

_____. 1989c. "Metro-Dade Police Department Discharge of Firearm Study, 1984-88." Unpublished Report.

_____. 1991. "Establishing Roadblocks to Control the Drunk Driver: *Michigan Department of State Police vs. Sitz."* *Criminal Law Bulletin,* 27: 51-58.

Alpert, Geoffrey P. and Roger G. Dunham. 1988a. "Research on Police Pursuits: Applications for Law Enforcement." *American Journal of Police,* 7: 123-131.

_____. 1988b. *Policing Multi-Ethnic Neighborhoods.* Westport, CT: Greenwood Press.

_____. 1989. "Policing Hot Pursuits: The Discovery of Aleatory Elements." *Journal of Criminal Law and Criminology,* 80: 521-539.

_____. 1990. *Police Pursuit Driving: Controlling Responses to Emergency Situations.* Westport, CT: Greenwood Press.

_____. 1992. *Policing Urban America,* Second Edition. Prospect Heights, IL: Waveland Press.

Alpert, Geoffrey P. and William Smith. 1991. "Beyond City Limits and into the Wood(s): A Brief Look at the Policy Implications of *City of Canton vs. Harris* and *Wood vs. Ostrander."* *American Journal of Police,* 10: 19-40.

Alpert, Geoffrey and Patrick Anderson. 1986. "The Most Deadly Force: Police Pursuits." *Justice Quarterly,* 3: 1-14.

Anderson, Patrick and Thomas Winfree, eds. 1987. *Expert Witnesses.* Albany: State University of New York Press.

Auten, James. 1990. "An Analysis of Police Pursuit Policy." *Law and Order*, 38: 53-54.

———. 1988. "Preparing Written Guidelines." *FBI Law Enforcement Bulletin*, May: 1-7.

Baltimore County Police Department. 1988. *Motor Vehicle Pursuit Study*. Baltimore County, Maryland.

Balkin, J.M. 1990. "The Rhetoric of Responsibility." *Virginia Law Review*, 76: 197-263.

Bayley, David H. and Harold Mendelsohn. 1969. *Minorities and the Police: Confrontation in America*. New York: Free Press.

Berk, Richard A. and Lawrence W. Sherman. 1988. "Police Responses to Family Violence Incidents." *Journal of the American Statistical Association*, 83: 70-76.

Biderman, Albert, L.A. Johnson, Jeanne McIntyre, and A.W. Weir. 1967. *Report on a Pilot Study in the District of Columbia on Victimization and Attitudes Toward Law Enforcement*. Washington, DC: United States Government Printing Office.

Binder, Arnold. 1983. "Book Review: *Split-Second Decisions: Shootings of and by Chicago Police* by William A. Geller and Kevin J. Karales." *Journal of Criminal Justice*, 11: 181-185.

Binder, Arnold and Lorie Fridell. 1984. "Lethal Force as a Police Response." *Criminal Justice Abstracts*, 16: 250-280.

Binder, Arnold and James Meeker. 1991. "The Use of Arrest to Control Misdemeanor Spousal Abuse." In *Domestic Violence: A Changing Criminal Justice Response*, edited by Eve Buzawa. Westport, CT: Greenwood Press.

Binder, Arnold and Peter Scharf. 1980. "The Violent Police-Citizen Encounter." *Annals of the American Academy of Political and Social Science*, 452:111-121.

Binder, Arnold, Peter Scharf, and Raymond Galvin. 1982. "Use of Deadly Force by Police Officers." Final report submitted to the National Institute of Justice, Grant No. 79-NI-AX-0134.

Blumberg, Mark. 1981. "Race and Police Shootings: Analysis in Two Cities." In *Contemporary Issues in Law Enforcement*, edited by James J. Fyfe, pp. 152-166. Beverly Hills, CA: Sage.

———. 1983. "The Use of Firearms by Police Officers: The Impact of Individuals, Communities and Race." Ph.D. Dissertation, State University of New York at Albany.

———. 1985a. "Research on Police Use of Deadly Force: The State of the Art." In *The Ambivalent Force: Perspectives on the Police, Third Edition*, edited by Abraham S. Blumberg and Elaine Niederhoffer, pp. 340-350. New York: Holt, Rinehart and Winston.

———. 1985b. "The Situational Characteristics of Police Shootings Across Eight Cities." Paper presented at the annual meeting of the Academy of Criminal Justice Sciences, Las Vegas, Nevada.

———. 1986. "Issues and Controversies with Respect to the Use of Deadly Force by Police." In *Police Deviance*, edited by Thomas Barker and David L. Carter, pp. 222-244. Cincinnati: Pilgrimage.

———. 1989. "Controlling Police Use of Deadly Force: Assessing Two Decades of Progress." In *Critical Issues in Policing: Contemporary Readings*, edited by Roger G. Dunham and Geoffrey P. Alpert, pp. 442-464. Prospect Heights, IL: Waveland Press.

Bohlen, Francis H. and Harry Shulman. 1927. "Arrest With and Without a Warrant." *University of Pennsylvania Law Review*, 75: 485-504.

Brown, Michael. 1981. *Working the Street.* New York: Russell Sage.

———. 1984. "Use of Deadly Force by Patrol Officers: Training Implications." *Journal of Police Science and Administration,* 12: 133-140.

Bureau of Justice Statistics. 1988. *Report to the Nation on Crime and Justice, Second Edition.* Washington, DC: United States Government Printing Office.

———. 1989. *Practice of State and Local Law Enforcement Agencies—1987.* Washington, DC: United States Government Printing Office.

Burger, Peter and Thomas Luckmann. 1967. *Social Construction of Reality.* New York: Doubleday.

Burnham, David. 1973. "Three of Five Slain by Police Here are Black, Same as Arrest Rate." *New York Times,* August 26: 56.

Caiden, Gerald E. 1977. *Police Revitalization.* Lexington, MA: Lexington Books.

California Highway Patrol. 1983. *Pursuit Study.* State of California.

Comment. 1986. "High-Speed Pursuits: Police Officers and Municipal Liability for Accidents Involving the Pursued and an Innocent Third Party." *Seton Hall Law Review,* 16:101-126.

Committee on Trauma Research. 1985. *Injury in America: A Continuing Health Problem.* Washington, DC: National Academy Press.

Cover, Robert. 1982. "The Origins of Judicial Activism in the Protection of Minorities." *Yale Law Review,* 91: 1287-1306.

Dade Association of Chiefs of Police. 1984. *Police Pursuit.* Dade County, Florida.

Dade County Grand Jury. 1983. *Final Report of the Grand Jury on Police Use of Deadly Force.* Eleventh Judicial Circuit of Florida.

del Carmen, Rolando. 1987. *Criminal Procedure for Law Enforcement Personnel.* Monterey, CA: Brooks/Cole Publishing.

Division of Criminal Justice. 1986. *Guidelines for High Speed Motor Vehicle Chases.* Newark, NJ: Office of the Attorney General.

Doerner, William G. and Tai-ping Ho. n.d. "Shoot, Don't Shoot: Police Use of Deadly Force Under Simulated Field Conditions." Unpublished paper.

Domm, John Wesley. 1981. "Police Performance in the Use of Deadly Force: An Analysis and a Program to Change Decision Premises in the Detroit Police Department." Unpublished Dissertation, Wayne State University, Detroit, Michigan.

Donahue, Michael Eugene. 1983. "Halt . . . Police! An Analysis of the Police Use of Deadly Force in a Large Midwestern City." Unpublished Dissertation, Michigan State University, East Lansing, Michigan.

Edholm, Paul. 1978. "Realism in Firearms Training." *Law and Order,* October: 30-32, 34-35, 45.

Ennis, Philip H. 1967. *Criminal Victimization in the U.S.: A Report of a National Survey.* A report prepared for the President's Commission on Law Enforcement and Administration of Justice. Field Survey II, Washington, D.C.: United States Government Printing Office.

Farber, William. 1985. Negligent Vehicular Police Chase, 41 Am. Jur. Proof of Facts, 2d. 79-132.

Fennessy, Edmund, Thomas Hamilton, Kent Joscelyn, and John Merritt. 1970. *A Study of the Problem of Hot Pursuit by the Police.* Washington, DC: United States Department of Transportation.

Fennessy, Edmund and Kent Joscelyn. 1972. "A National Study of Hot Pursuit." *Denver Law Review*, 48:389-403.

Ferdinand, Theodore H. and Elmer G. Luchterhand. 1970. "Inner-city Youth, the Police, the Juvenile Court and Justice." *Social Problems*, 17: 510-527.

Forslund, Morris A. 1972. "A Comparison of Negro and White Crime Rates." In *Race, Crime, and Society,* edited by Charles E. Reasons and Jack L. Kuykendall, pp. 96-102. Pacific Palisades, CA: Goodyear.

Fridell, Lorie. 1983. "Community Attitudes Toward Police Use of Deadly Force." Unpublished Thesis, University of California, Irvine.

_____. 1989. "Justifiable Use of Measures in Research on Deadly Force." *Journal of Criminal Justice,* 17: 157-165.

Fridell, Lorie and Arnold Binder. 1988. "Police Officer Decision-making in Potentially Violent Confrontations." Paper presented at the annual meeting of the American Society of Criminology, Chicago, Illinois.

_____. 1989. "Racial Aspects of Police Shootings Revisited." Paper presented at the annual meeting of the American Society of Criminology, Reno, Nevada.

Frisbie, Thomas. 1990. "Police Paradox." *Traffic Safety*, May/June:12-14.

Fyfe, James J. 1978. "Shots Fired: Examination of New York City Police Firearms Discharges." Unpublished Dissertation, State University of New York, Albany.

_____. 1980a. "Always Prepared: Police Off-Duty Guns." *Annals of the American Academy of Political and Social Science,* 452: 72-81.

_____. 1980b. "Geographic Correlates of Police Shooting: A Microanalysis." *Journal of Research in Crime and Delinquency,* 17: 101-113.

_____. 1981a. "Who Shoots? A Look at Officer Race and Police Shooting." *Journal of Police Science and Administration,* 9: 367-382.

_____. 1981b. "Race and Extreme Police-Citizen Violence." In *Race, Crime and Criminal Justice,* edited by R.L. McNeely and Carl E. Pope, pp. 89-108. Beverly Hills, CA: Sage Publishers.

_____. 1981c. "Observations on Police Use of Deadly Force." *Crime and Delinquency,* 27: 367-389.

_____. 1982. "Blind Justice: Police Shootings in Memphis." *Journal of Criminal Law and Criminology,* 83: 707-722.

_____. 1985. Personal communication, April 7.

_____. 1987a. "The Metro-Dade Police/Citizen Violence Reduction Project." An unpublished report submitted to the Metro-Dade Police Department by the Police Foundation.

_____. 1987b. "Police Expert Witnesses," In *Expert Witnesses,* edited by P. Anderson and T. Winfree, pp. 100-118. Albany, NY: State University of New York Press.

_____. 1988. "Police Use of Deadly Force: Research and Reform." *Justice Quarterly,* 5: 164-205.

Geller, William A. 1982. "Deadly Force: What we Know." *Journal of Police Science and Administration* 10:151-177.

_____. 1984. "Police and Deadly Force: A Look at the Empirical Literature." In *Moral Issues in Police Work,* edited by F. Elliston and M. Feldberg, pp. 197-223. Totowa, NJ: Littlefield, Adams.

Geller, William A. 1985. "Officer Restraint in the Use of Deadly Force: The Next Frontier in Police Shooting Research." *Journal of Police Science and Administration*, 13: 153-171.

Geller, William A. and Kevin J. Karales. 1981. *Split-Second Decisions: Shootings of and by Chicago Police*. Chicago, IL: Chicago Law Enforcement Study Group.

Geller, William A. and Michael Scott. 1991. *Deadly Force: What We Know—A Practitioner's Desk Reference on Police-Involved Shootings in the United States*. Washington, DC: Police Executive Research Forum.

Goldkamp, John. 1976. "Minorities as Victims of Police Shootings: Interpretations of Racial Disproportionality and Police Use of Deadly Force." *The Justice System: A Management Review*, 2: 169-183.

Goldman, Nathan. 1963. *The Differential Selection of Juvenile Offenders for Court Appearances*. New York: New York Council on Crime and Delinquency.

Goldstein, Herman. 1990. *Problem-Oriented Policing*. New York: McGraw-Hill.

Gottfredson, Michael and Don Gottfredson. 1988. *Decision Making in Criminal Justice*. New York: Plenum.

Governor's Office Law Enforcement Liason Committee. 1986. *High Speed Pursuit*. Columbus, OH: Office of the Governor.

Graham, H.D. and T.R. Gurr. 1969. *Violence in America: Historical and Comparative Perspectives*, Volume 2. Washington, DC: United States Government Printing Office.

Greene, Jack R. 1989. "Police and Community Relations: Where Have We Been and Where are We Going?" In *Critical Issues in Policing: Contemporary Readings*, edited by Roger G. Dunham and Geoffrey P. Alpert, pp. 349-368. Prospect Heights, IL: Waveland Press.

Grimmond, Timothy J. 1991. *The Role of Police Pursuits and their Impact on California Law Enforcement by the Year 2001*. Sacramento: Peace Officer Standards and Training.

Griswold, David B. 1985. "Controlling the Police Use of Deadly Force: Exploring the Alternatives." *American Journal of Police*, 4: 93-109.

Hadar, Ilana and John R. Snortum. 1975. "The Eye of the Beholder: Differential Perceptions of Police by the Police and the Public." *Criminal Justice and Behavior*, 2: 284-315.

Hahn, Harlan. 1971. "Ghetto Assessment of Police Protection and Authority." *Law and Society Review*, 6: 183-194.

Harding, R. W. 1970. *Police Killings in Australia*. Middlesex, England: Penguin Books, LTD.

Harding, Richard W. and Richard P. Fahey. 1973. "Killings by Chicago Police, 1966-1970: An Empirical Study." *Southern California Law Review*, 46: 284-315.

Hart, W.L. 1979. "Fatal Shootings by Police Officers." Unpublished report submitted to the Detroit Board of Police Commissioners, October 22.

Hayden, George A. 1981. "Police Discretion in the Use of Deadly Force: An Empirical Study of Information Usage in Deadly Force Decisionmaking." *Journal of Police Science and Administration*, 9: 102-107.

Hindelang, Michael J. 1975. *Public Opinion Regarding Crime: Criminal Justice Related Topics*. Washington, DC: United States Government Printing Office.

Hinds, Lennox A. 1979. "Police Use of Excessive and Deadly Force: Racial Implications." In *A Community Concern: Police Use of Deadly Force*, edited by R.H. Brenner and M. Kravits. Washington, DC: United States Government Printing Office.

Holzworth, R. James and Catherine B. Pipping. 1985. "Drawing a Weapon: An Analysis of Police Judgments." *Journal of Police Science and Administration*, 13: 185-194.

Horvath, Frank. 1987. "The Police Use of Deadly Force: A Description of Selected Characteristics of Intrastate Incidents." *Journal of Police Science and Administration*, 15: 226-238.

Ingraham, Barton. 1987. "The Ethics of Testimony: Conflicting Views on the Role of the Criminologist as Expert Witness." In *Expert Witness*, edited by P. Anderson and T. Winfree, pp. 178-208. Albany, NY: State University of New York Press.

Inn, Andres. 1976. "The Validity of Psychological and Background Characteristics in Predicting the Use of Firearms by Police." Proceedings, Midwest Conference of the American Institute for the Decision Sciences.

International Association of Chiefs of Police. 1980. Official resolution adopted by the membership pursuant to Article VII, Section 4 of the IACP Constitution. St. Louis, Missouri, September.

_____. 1986. "Limitations on the Police Use of Deadly Force." *Legal Points*, 1986:138.

International Association of Chiefs of Police and United States Department of Transportation. 1986. *A Manual of Police Traffic Services: Policies and Procedures*. IACP and United States Department of Transportation.

Jacobs, James. 1989. *Drunk Driving: An American Dilemma*. Chicago: The University of Chicago Press.

Jenkins, Betty and Adrienne Faison. 1974. *An Analysis of 248 Persons Killed by New York City Policemen, 1970-1973*. New York: Metropolitan Applied Research Center, Inc.

Kania, Richard R.E. and Wade C. Mackey. 1977. "Police Violence as a Function of Community Characteristics." *Criminology*, 15: 27-48.

Knoohuizen, Ralph, Richard P. Fahey, and Deborah H. Palmer. 1972. *Police and Their Use of Fatal Force in Chicago*. Chicago, IL: Chicago Law Enforcement Study Group.

Kobler, Arthur L. 1975. "Figures (and Perhaps some Facts) on Police Killing of Civilians in the United States, 1965-1969." *Journal of Social Issues*, 31: 185-191.

Koonz, Joseph and Patrick Regan. 1985. "Hot Pursuit: Proving Police Negligence." *Trial*, 21: 63, 65-69.

Kroeker, Mark and Candace McCoy. 1989. "Establishing and Implementing Department Policies." In *Police Practice in the 90s*, edited by James J. Fyfe, pp. 107-113. Washington DC: International City Management Association.

Langworthy, Robert H. 1986. "Police Shooting and Criminal Homicide: The Temporal Relationship." *Journal of Quantitative Criminology*, 2: 377-388.

Law Enforcement Assistance Administration. 1980. *Prevention and Control of Urban Disorders: Issues for the 1980s*. Washington, DC: University Research Corporation.

Law Enforcement News. 1990. Interview with Lawrence W. Sherman. *Law Enforcement News*, 26(311): 9-12.

Manning, Peter. 1988. *Symbolic Communication*. Cambridge, MA: MIT Press.

Margarita, Mona. 1980. "Killing the Police: Myths and Motives." *The Annals of the American Academy of Political and Social Science*, 452: 63-71.

Matulia, Kenneth. 1982. *A Balance of Forces*. Gaithersburg, MD: International Association of Chiefs of Police.

_____. 1985. *A Balance of Forces, Second Edition*. Gaithersburg, MD: International Association of Chiefs of Police.

McDonald, Phyllis. 1989. "A New Perspective on Law Enforcement Policy." In *Police Practice in the 90s*, edited by J. Fyfe, pp. 101-106. Washington, DC: International City Management Association.

Mendez, Garry A., Jr. 1983. *The Role of Race and Ethnicity in the Incidence of Police Use of Deadly Force*. New York: National Urban League.

Meyer, Marshall W. 1980. "Police Shootings at Minorities: The Case of Los Angeles." *Annals of the American Academy of Political and Social Sciences*, 452: 98-110.

Milton, Catherine H., Jeanne W. Halleck, James Lardner, and Gary L. Abrecht. 1977. *Police Use of Deadly Force*. Washington, DC: The Police Foundation.

Michigan Association of Chiefs of Police. 1986. *Michigan Pursuit Driving and Training Manual*. Okemos, MI: Michigan Association of Chiefs of Police.

Minnesota Board of Police Standards and Training. 1991. *A Study of Deadly Force by Police Officers*. St. Paul, MN: Post.

Minnesota Board of Police Standards and Training. Personal Correspondence with William R. Carter, III (January 24, 1989).

Moore, Robert. 1990. "Police Pursuits: High-Tech Ways to Reduce the Risks." *The Futurist*, 24: 26-28.

National Highway Traffic Safety Administration. 1989. *Fatal Accident Reporting System, 1988*. Washington, DC: United States Government Printing Office.

New York State Commission on Criminal Justice and the Use of Force. 1987. Report to the Governor, Volumes I to IV. New York: New York State.

Nielsen, Eric. 1983. "Policy on the Police Use of Deadly Force: A Cross-Sectional Analysis." *Journal of Police Science and Administration*, 11: 104-108.

Note. 1988. "Police Liability for Creating the Need to Use Deadly Force in Self-Defense." *Michigan Law Review*, 86: 1982-2009.

Note. 1929. "Legalized Murder of a Fleeing Felon." *Virginia Law Review*, 15: 582-586.

Note. 1981. "Police Liability for Negligent Failure to Prevent Crime." *Harvard Law Review*, 94: 821-840.

Nowicki, Ed. 1989. "The Heat of the Chase." *Police Magazine*, March: 24-26, 45-46.

Office of Agency Research and Servie. 1990. *South Carolina Law Enforcement Census 1988*. Columbia, SC: University of South Carolina.

Patinkin, H.P. and H. Bingham. 1986. "Police Motor Vehicle Pursuits: The Chicago Experience." *Police Chief*, 53: 61-62.

Petersilia, Joan. 1989. "The Influence of Research on Policing." In *Critical Issues in Policing: Contemporary Readings*, edited by Roger G. Dunham and Geoffrey P. Alpert, pp. 230-249. Prospect Heights, IL: Waveland Press.

Piliavin, Irving and Scott Briar. 1964. "Police Encounters with Juveniles." *American Journal of Sociology*, 70 (September): 206-214.

Police Executive Research Forum and The Police Foundation. 1981. *Survey of Police Operational and Administrative Practices, 1981*. Washington, DC: The Police Foundation.

Pompa, Gilbert G. 1980. "Police Use of Force: How Citizens Think it Should Be Dealt With." Paper presented at the 1980 National Convention of the League of United Latin American Citizens.

Pope, Carl E. 1979. "Race and Crime Revisited." *Crime and Delinquency*, 25 (July): 347-357.

Porter, Bruce and Marvin Dunn. 1984. *The Miami Riot of 1980*. Lexington, MA: Lexington Books.

President's Commission on Law Enforcement and Administration of Justice. 1967. Task Force Report: The Police. Washington, DC: United States Government Printing Office.

Project. 1990. Nineteenth Annual Review of Criminal Procedure. *Georgetown University Law Review*, 78: 699-1473.

Reiss, Albert J., Jr. 1980. "Controlling Police Use of Deadly Force." *Annals of the American Academy of Political and Social Science*, 452: 122-134.

Roberts, Ron and Robert Kloss. 1974. *Social Movements: Between the Balcony and the Barricade*. St. Louis: Mosby Co.

Robin, Gerald D. 1963. "Justifiable Homicide by Police Officers." *Journal of Criminal Law, Criminology and Police Science*, 54: 225-231.

Sasaki, Daniel. 1988. "Policy Trickery and Confessing." *Stanford Law Review*, 40: 1593-1616.

Scharf, Peter, Rod Linninger, Dave Marrero, Ron Baker, and Chris Rice. 1978. "Deadly Force: The Moral Reasoning and the Education of Police Officers Faced with the Option of Lethal Legal Violence." *Policy Studies Journal*, Special Issue: 451-454.

Scharf, Peter, and Arnold Binder. 1983. *The Badge and the Bullet: Police Use of Deadly Force*. New York: Praeger.

Schofield, Daniel L. 1988. "Legal Issues of Pursuit Driving." *F.B.I. Law Enforcement Bulletin*, 57: 23-30.

Sherman, Lawrence. 1983. "Reducing Police Gun Use: Critical Events, Administrative Policy and Organizational Change." In *The Management and Control of Police Organizations*, edited by Maurice Punch, pp. 98-125. Cambridge, MA: M.I.T. Press.

Sherman, Lawrence and Richard Berk. 1984. "The Specific Deterrent Effects of Arrest for Domestic Assaults." *American Sociological Review*, 49: 261-271.

Sherman, Lawrence W., Ellen G. Cohn, Patrick R. Gartin, Edwin E. Hamilton, and Dennis P. Rogan. 1986. *Citizens Killed by Big City Police, 1970-1984*. Washington, DC: Crime Control Institute.

Sherman, Lawrence W. and Robert Langworthy. 1979. "Measuring Homicide by Police Officers." *Journal of Criminal Law and Criminology*, 70: 546-560.

Short, James F. and Fred Strodbeck. 1965. *Group Process and Gang Delinquency*. Chicago: University of Chicago Press.

Silver, Isadore. 1986. *Police Civil Liability*. New York: Matthew Bender.

Small, Albion. 1897. "The Meaning of the Social Movement." *American Journal of Sociology*, 3: 340-354.

Smith, Joel E. 1986. "Liability of Governmental Unit or its Officers for Injury to Innocent Occupant of Moving Vehicle as a Result of Police Chase," 4 A.L.R. 4th. 865 and Supplement.

Smith, Paul E. and Richard O. Hawkins. 1973. "Victimization, Types of Citizen-Police Contacts, and Attitudes Toward the Police." *Law and Society Review*, 8: 135-152.

Solicitor General. 1985. *A Special Report from the Solicitor General's Special Committee on Police Pursuits*. Ontario, Canada: Solicitor General's Office.

Spiegel, Hans ed. 1974. *Citizen Participation in Urban Development: Concepts and Issues*. Fairfax, VA: Appleton-Century-Crofts.

Stone, Alfred and Stuart DeLuca. 1985. *Police Administration*. New York: Wiley.

Sutherland, Edwin H. and Donald R. Cressey. 1970. *Criminology, Eighth Edition*. Philadelphia, PA: Lippincott.

Takagi, Paul. 1974. "A Garrison State in a 'Democratic' Society." *Crime and Social Justice: A Journal of Radical Criminology*, 5: 27-33.

Territo, Leonard. 1982. "Citizen Safety: Key Elements in Police Pursuit Policy." *Trial*, August: 31-34.

The Traffic Institute. 1981. *Pursuit in Traffic Law Enforcement* (553). Evanston, IL: The Traffic Institute.

Thornberry, Terence P. 1973. "Race, Socioeconomic Status, and Sentencing in the Juvenile Justice System." *Journal of Criminal Law and Criminology*, 64: 90-98.

Uchida, Craig Denis. 1982. "Controlling Police Use of Deadly Force: Organizational Change in Los Angeles." Unpublished Dissertation, State University of New York, Albany.

_____. 1989. "The Development of American Police: An Historical Overview." In *Critical Issues in Policing: Contemporary Readings*, edited by Roger G. Dunham and Geoffrey P. Alpert, pp. 14-30. Prospect Heights, IL: Waveland Press.

Uelman, Gerald F. 1973. "Varieties of Public Policy: A Study of Policy Regarding the Use of Deadly Force in Los Angeles County." *University of Loyola at Los Angeles Law Review*, 6:1-65.

Urbonya, Kathryn. 1987. "Establishing a Deprivation of a Constitutional Right to Personal Safety under Section 1983: The Use of Unjustified Force by State Officials in Violation of the Fourth, Eighth and Fourteenth Amendments." *Albany Law Review*, 51:171-235.

_____. 1989. "Problematic Standards of Reasonableness: Qualified Immunity in Section 1983 Actions for a Police Officer's Use of Excessive Force." *Temple Law Review*, 62: 61-116.

_____. 1991. "The Constitutionality of High-Speed Pursuits Under the Fourth and Fourteenth Amendments." *St. Louis Law Journal*, 35: 205-288.

Van Maanen, John. 1974. "Working the Street: A Developmental View of Police Behavior." In *The Potential for Reform of Criminal Justice*, edited by Herbert Jacob, pp. 83-130. Beverly Hills, CA: Sage.

Waegel, William B. 1984. "The Use of Lethal Force by Police: The Effect of Statutory Change." *Crime and Delinquency*, 31: 121-140.

Webster, John A. 1970. "Police Task and Time Study." *Journal of Criminal Law, Criminology, and Police Science*, 61: 94-100.

Walker, Samuel. 1977. *A Critical History of Police Reform: The Emergence of Professionalism*. Lexington, MA: Lexington Books.

_____. 1980. *Popular Justice: A History of American Criminal Justice*. New York: Oxford University Press.

_____. 1983. *The Police in America: An Introduction*. New York: McGraw-Hill.

Walker, Samuel and Lorie Fridell. 1989. "The Impact of *Tennessee v. Garner* on Deadly Force Policy." Paper presented at the annual meeting of the American Society of Criminology, Reno, Nevada.

Weber-Brooks, Laure. 1989. "Police Discretionary Behavior: A Study of Style." In *Critical Issues in Policing: Contemporary Readings*, edited by Roger G. Dunham and Geoffrey P. Alpert, pp. 121-145. Prospect Heights, IL: Waveland Press.

White, Welsh. 1979. "Police Trickery in Inducing Confessions." *University of Pennsylvania Law Review*, 127: 581-627.

Williams, Hubert and Patrick V. Murphy. 1990. "The Evolving Strategy of Police: A Minority View." In *Perspectives on Policing 13*. Washington, DC: United States Department of Justice.

Zevitz, Richard. 1987. "Police Civil Liability and the Law of High Speed Pursuit." *Marquette Law Review*, 70: 237-284.

Index